NAMING COLONIALISM

AFRICA AND THE DIASPORA
History, Politics, Culture

SERIES EDITORS

Thomas Spear
David Henige
Michael Schatzberg

Spirit, Structure, and Flesh:
Gendered Experiences in African Instituted Churches among the Yoruba of Nigeria
Deidre Helen Crumbley

A Hill among a Thousand: Transformations and Ruptures in Rural Rwanda
Danielle de Lame

Power in Colonial Africa: Conflict and Discourse in Lesotho, 1870–1960
Elizabeth A. Eldredge

Nachituti's Gift: Economy, Society, and Environment in Central Africa
David M. Gordon

Intermediaries, Interpreters, and Clerks:
African Employees in the Making of Colonial Africa
Edited by Benjamin N. Lawrance, Emily Lynn Osborn, and
Richard L. Roberts

Naming Colonialism: History and Collective Memory in the Congo, 1870–1960
Osumaka Likaka

Antecedents to Modern Rwanda: The Nyiginya Kingdom
Jan Vansina

Naming Colonialism

HISTORY AND COLLECTIVE MEMORY IN THE CONGO, 1870–1960

Osumaka Likaka

THE UNIVERSITY OF WISCONSIN PRESS

This book was published with support from
the College of Liberal Arts and Science and the Department of History
at WAYNE STATE UNIVERSITY and from
the Anonymous Fund of the College of Letters and Science
at the UNIVERSITY OF WISCONSIN–MADISON.

The University of Wisconsin Press
1930 Monroe Street, 3rd Floor
Madison, Wisconsin 53711-2059
uwpress.wisc.edu

3 Henrietta Street
London WCE 8LU, England
eurospanbookstore.com

1   3   5   4   2

Printed in the United States of America

Library of Congress Cataloging-in-Publication Data
Likaka, Osumaka, 1953–
Naming colonialism: history and collective memory
in the Congo, 1870–1960 / Osumaka Likaka.
p.   cm. — (Africa and the diaspora: history, politics, culture)
Includes bibliographical references and index.
ISBN 978-0-299-23364-8 (pbk.: alk. paper)
ISBN 978-0-299-23363-1 (e-book)
1. Congo (Brazzaville) — Colonization.
2. Congo (Kinshasa) — Colonization.
3. Kongo language — Epithets.
4. Nicknames — Congo (Brazzaville) — History.
5. Nicknames — Congo (Kinshasa) — History.
I. Title.   II. Series: Africa and the diaspora.
DT546.265.L55   2009
967.51′02 — dc22   2009008138

For
FRANÇOISE
OSANDU
OFONA

CONTENTS

ILLUSTRATIONS

ACKNOWLEDGMENTS

Several institutions provided support at different stages of the research. The Humanities Center at Wayne State University funded research at the Archives Africaines and the Royal Museum for Central Africa in Brussels and Tervuren, Belgium. The Career Developments Chairs offered funds that freed me of teaching, allowing me the time for writing. The Department of History paid the costs of maps and reproduction of photographs.

Many people helped me during fieldwork in the Congo in the 1980s and the 1990s. The list is too long to mention all by name. I would like to express my gratitude to Professor Michel Lwamba Bilonda of the University of Lubumbashi, who helped identify former cash crop producers, most of whom will not see the result of our interactions. I will cherish the memories of Mugaza Wa Beya, Katayi Tende, and Lufundja, who shared generously their personal experiences and knowledge of colonialism. I am indebted to Big Brother Labama Lokwa, who, despite his failing health and busy schedule, took the time to process the interviews conducted in Kisangani in the 1990s. My gratitude goes to Hubert Lumbalumba Wana-Ti-Lawando of the University of Kisangani, who conducted the interviews in Kisangani.

Several scholars and friends read early drafts of the book. I am deeply grateful to Jan Vansina, who read the manuscript several times and provided hundreds of names. Elias Mandala, Nkasa Yelengi, and Chris Johnson commented on the entire manuscript. Melba Boyd read parts of the early draft. I learned from their suggestions and criticisms. I am deeply indebted to Thomas Spears, the editor of the Africa and Diaspora Series at the University of Wisconsin Press, for his insights and comments. Many thanks go to Walter Edwards, who shared his knowledge of linguistics. Monica Schuler was involved in this project from the time it took shape, and remained at the center of our academic discussions until her retirement in 2002, and she will find her imprints in the result. Among those who encouraged me to bring the project to fruition, I thank Marc Kruman, John Bukowczyk, Elisabeth Faue, Jorge Chinea, José Cuello, Ngoyi Bukonda, and Thaddeus Sunseri.

Naming Colonialism

Introduction

Naming and African Voices

I had obtained from the Niam-niam who accompanied our caravan an epithet which I never lost in all the subsequent stages of our journey. In their own dialect, these people called me "Mbarik-pa," [Balikpe] which would be equivalent to a name amongst us of "Leaf-eater."

G. Schweinfurth, The Heart of Africa

From the beginning of each European's stay in Africa, local people observed him carefully and gave him a name that he kept for his entire life. It would take an extraordinary event to change the name whose usage has passed so deeply into the culture of the white men who cite it next to the first and family names on legal documents and personal documents that show his marital status.

C. Van de Lanoitte, Sur les rivières glauques de l'Equateur

Every colonial official involved in cotton cultivation received a name. Some were called "lightning" because they shouted at Congolese farmers, others were named "scrapers of heaps" because they had checked if the seeds of cotton had not been negligently thrown away.

Françoise-Marie, "Lettre"

The naming of strangers was a long-established naming convention in Central Africa, which Africans creatively adapted to the colonial situation to identify individual Europeans and groups of Europeans. Despite the singularity of events and diversity of situations that motivated the naming of Europeans, the practice worked broadly the same way

3

across the village world. Africans first observed minutely Westerners' physical appearance, behavior, cultural practices, moral qualities and flaws, and the ways in which they carried out their tasks of establishing social relations of production. In the meantime, they took note of situations that Europeans individually and collectively created in their midst. From the familiarity of their village community with individual Europeans, Africans gained a comprehensive understanding of colonialism and its impacts on their individual and collective experiences. Africans then wove and translated their observations into names, which became not only the local identities for individual Europeans or groups of Europeans but also the semantic and political codes, which now informed and showed their perceptions, interpretations, and understandings of colonialism. By naming Europeans, Africans turned a universal practice into a local mnemonic system, which recorded and preserved the village's observations, interpretations, and understandings of colonialism as pithy verbal expressions easy to remember and to transmit across localities, regions, and generations.

In naming Europeans, Africans employed signifiers that described colonial material conditions directly, and riddles, allegories, proverbs, metaphors, metonyms, and symbols that attached symbolic meanings to their observations of colonialism and that, although hiding intended messages, indirectly described aspects of colonial daily life. Rather than letting Belgian officials have all the powers to silence their voices, Africans assigned meanings and significance to events and situations affecting their lives. The name of a European was thus an ethnographic and linguistic source that yields valuable evidence of African colonial experiences.[1]

Doing this research on names of Europeans to recapture local experiences of colonialism started out of a personal experience. When I was growing up, my grandmother Ofona Ekosa named my younger brother Lomelile *Ikeleso* because she thought that he was unlike her other grandchildren. Rebellious, he liked to play hard; obstinate, he always found ways to satisfy his caprice; shrewd, he always grabbed the attention of those who listened to his endless accounts of tooth pains. Whenever we asked her to explain what seemed to us innocent and meaningless, she always replied, "*Ikeleso* was a white man with a red face and who, ever furious, enjoined the entire village to collect rubber, kernels and copal. The white man brought more sufferings when he compelled people to grow itchy *ekonge* [the local name for *urena lobata*], a textile crop that his fellow white men of the Lomami Company needed to make sacks."

A talented storyteller, she told many tales about *Ikeleso,* who lashed men naked and took women hostages and walked house to house to look inside as he was collecting taxes, a burden that had people work hard, causing malnourishment and loss of weight, situations that convinced most people to believe that "Working for the tax man makes people thinner."[2] Her facial expressions and pitch of voice always conveyed an unspoken message that reinforced her common theme of the meanness of the colonial official. They always suggested to us that *Ikeleso* was execrable because he whipped men undressed until they bled, and because he took wives hostages until their husbands, who had fled the village to evade taxes and escape conscriptions and recruitments, returned home and surrendered to the colonial authorities.

The lingering memories of *Ikeleso* and the tales that contextualized and explained the name's multidimensional meanings developed into a broader and more coherent picture of colonialism after I conducted archival research in 1980. During the research, I discovered lists of names of colonial officials in African languages and broken French— loanwords—whose literal and figurative meanings were descriptions of material conditions, insults, mockery, moral indignation, criticisms, and praise of European officials. When I shared the findings with my mentor to figure out a way to use names as historical sources, he frowningly replied, "We are historians and we ought to stick to written documents because they tell us what happened and when it happened. I am afraid we cannot write history out of words and short phrases."[3]

The response underscored the challenge to elaborate a conceptual framework and methodological tools to tease out and interpret the meanings of diverse coded fragments of broader social and political messages embedded in the memories of repetitive actions recorded by Congolese villagers in the names of colonial officials. The response came as a surprise because at the University of Lubumbashi in the Democratic Republic of Congo, Jan Vansina's *De la tradition orale: Essaie de méthode historique* and *Kingdoms of the Savanna* had become classics and established oral traditions as valid sources and repositories of history and collective memory. One explanation to my mentor's reaction was that historians were accustomed to study history from elaborate texts—oral traditions for historians of the precolonial era and colonial archives for historians of colonialism. Despite the favor colonial archives enjoyed, they failed to provide relevant evidence to answer some questions about Congolese colonial experiences. In the 1970s, the limitations of colonial archives had become apparent to those scholars writing about the lives of peasants and workers. For example, while recognizing the value of "savoir archivé," B. Crine, an anthropologist then working for the Office National de Recherche et Développement, wrote in 1972 that the colonial archives were but the starting points for the study of the "avant-tradition zairoise."[4]

As women's studies and postmodernism entered African studies in the late 1980s, scholars expanded methodologies of oral sources to capture the voices of women missing from the colonial archives and revisited models of interpretations. Bogumil Jewsiewicki, shifting from economic history to cultural and intellectual history, collected the life histories of Congolese and paintings by local artists to tell colonial and postcolonial experiences of the Congolese. Johannes Fabian also commissioned paintings to capture local perceptions of colonial and postcolonial power.[5] Congolese scholars, proponents of *histoire engagée*, under the intellectual lead of Benoît Verhaegen, collected life histories and oral testimonies. Verhaegen and his group were promoting *immediate history*, a concept that transforms history into a weapon for social actions and change.[6]

Local sources thus have a long history in Congolese historiography as they did in historiographies of other parts of the continent where scholars have also explored the experiences of ordinary people. Focusing on songs, Leroy Vail and Landeg White captured perceptions of colonial power and forms of protests and resistance in Mozambique.[7] Popular culture was not the only source that carried African voices. Belinda Bozzoli relied on oral testimonies to recount life stories and experiences of black South African women, while through stories of vampires, Luise White discussed the place of rumor and gossip in historical reconstruction.[8] This research to re-create the experiences of Africans—peasants and workers—mixed oral and archival sources.[9] Supplementing archives with oral data, Elias Mandala aptly conceptualized the labor process, highlighting peasant autonomy and forms of rural struggles, and illuminating our understanding of work and control in a peasant economy. Through a meticulous exploration of archives and oral data, he recently produced a superb history of food and everyday life in Malawi.[10]

Looking back, my mentor's reaction highlighted the lack of methodological tools to decode the messages, and models of interpretation to understand the fragmentary evidence drawn from the meanings of names and coded in broader messages. The exchange temporarily dispelled my fascination with the topic. I studied the impacts of colonial administration on the Mbole people using colonial archives and oral sources.[11]

Even so, I continued meanwhile to collect colonial anthroponyms. And despite a firm interest in the names of colonial officials for historical reconstruction, I still wrestled with the questions of scope and ability of naming to record important details of colonial village daily life. Whether the practice was localized or widespread remained less well known until I conducted in 1987–90 intensive archival research and interviews on cotton cultivation. The research allowed the gathering of the hundreds of names of crop inspectors, cotton company administrators, and colonial state officials who carried out a mandatory system of cash crops cultivation.

The meanings of these names were descriptions of events and material conditions of the village world. They showed that the naming of colonial officials by Congolese peoples was a systematic recording of realities or interpretations of realities that underlay the relations between colonial officials and Congolese villagers, and showed beyond any doubt the significance of names of colonial officials as historical sources. Because the messages of names explained the workings of colonialism, I concluded that their use in historical research would provide an understanding of how Congolese villagers experienced colonial exploitative practices and disruptions of their lives from the perspective of men and women of the village.[12] I then understood that *Ikeleso*, the central character in my grandmother's tales of colonialism, embodied memories and observations of colonial experiences that provided reliable materials for the writing of histories of colonialism and everyday life in the village world.

In the end, changes in African historiographies brought the study of names of colonial officials to my research agenda. Although many scholars rightly associated postmodernism with the demise of the historian's craft, as eloquently stated by such a provocative title as *The Killing of History*, the literature nonetheless created an intellectual atmosphere that regenerated the enthusiasm to look at names of Europeans as innovative sources of collective memories and history. New thinking on cash crop producers' perceptions of social relations of production showed that, if contextualized, names of Europeans were important raw materials as insightful as songs, oral testimonies, art objects, photographs, ethnographic data, medals, objects of popular and material cultures, costumes, commissioned paintings by local artists, rumors, and written materials, which social historians have put to good use to analyze the fabric of collective life.[13] Besides, this study has benefited from a shift of emphasis from state formation and long-distance trade to social history, loosely defined as the history of ordinary people.[14]

The expansion of methodologies brought new models of interpretation. Africanists now debate subjectivity, historical imagination, the autonomy and multivocality of the text, and the multiplicity and multidimensionality of the meanings of its messages.[15] But the expansion of methodologies and the rise of new models of interpretations obscured as much as they illuminated. First, some colonial documents still silenced African villagers, women more so than men. The absence of African voices in these sources or historians' failure to detect them imposed limitations on the production of historical scholarship that covers all aspects of African colonial experiences. As a result, historical narratives based on these sources unwittingly relegated Africans to peripheral historical agents or denied them their agency altogether. A study of colonial medals that came out of an exhibit in 1996 exemplified such unfortunate cases. In this study, Marc Vancraenbroeck contended that colonial medals were a "metallic memory of history."[16] The phrase, apparently insightful, cannot serve as a methodological approach and theoretical framework because it overlooks the effects of colonial ideologies and unequal power relations on the ways medals were produced. If the book tells stories of Belgian officials in the Congo from 1876 to 1960, it silences Africans. The emphasis of colonial medals on Europeans denied the author the local voices he needed to illuminate the experiences of African colonized villagers and European colonizers, an inclusive way to capture the dynamics of colonial encounters and interactions. Out of 210 medals shown, most celebrate the "accomplishments" of the colonists. Only a few Africans and local scenes appeared on medals, and when Africans did, they had no say over the choice of the designs of medals and the meanings of embedded messages.[17] As repositories of collective memories, names of colonial officials talk about colonial situations and conditions of life and work more than do colonial medals, the ideological tools for promoting political and mercantile interests. Colonial anthroponyms allowed Congolese villagers to speak more loudly than colonial medals did.[18]

Second, the new interpretations resurrected old stereotypes about Africa and Africans. The focus on Africans' subordination to the colonial social engineering, hegemonic designs, and especially European models of thought, has inadvertently resurrected the old view of a helpless

Africa. Africa emerges not only as an object of economic exploitation, as underdevelopment theory presented it; now it is the object of the thought processes of others. The whole debate about "inventing Africa" hinges on the idea of a continent that entered the stage of modern history as a tabula rasa on which any Westerner could have written anything he or she wanted. Not the African village elder, with all the wisdom she or he had received from the ancestors, but the young European administrator or missionary did the thinking for the continent.[19] Like most previous paradigms that scholars have employed to recapture the African past, the new models of interpretations obscured as much as they illuminated. The study of colonial anthroponyms, however, testifies to the Africans' autonomy of thought and their power to observe and define the "Others" and thus challenges the trend.[20]

Once Africans minted a name for a colonial official, that name took on a life of its own and circulated across villages, administrative divisions, and ethnic groups, and reproduced across generations. Whether the career of a name as an established collective representation of an aspect of colonialism was popular and long or short and confined, it not only embodied ways in which Africans dealt with a colonial world of uncertainty, limitations, violence, and few opportunities, but it also kept its morphological form stable. The stability of the forms was, from a methodological view, one of the strengths of names as a source of African voices. The stability of forms does not stop the loss, distortions, biases, misrepresentations of colonial experiences, and the manipulations and change of meanings of names. Some morphological forms of names, though stable, hardly yield meanings and messages at first glance. This was true for local mispronunciations and onomatopoeias whose meanings faded when the contexts of their genesis changed and the stories they told became irrelevant to subsequent generations for their struggle against colonialism. The brevity and stability of the forms were as much an aid to the remembrance of names as were work songs, night dance lyrics performed during the full moon, and the village gatherings where villagers debated various situations that the names had recorded. Besides helping Congolese villagers preserve messages as social memory, the memorized wordings are the starting points for the study of popular etymologies. When the meanings of names are literal descriptions of situations on the ground, popular etymologies uncover clues to cultural, social, economic, and political contexts, which informed the meanings of names and social messages. Elucidating contexts and meanings based on archives or oral testimonies shed light on the larger economic and political structures, which defined the social universe in which villagers experienced colonialism. Briefly, the brevity and memorized wordings of the names of colonial officials make them the most stable voices of the village world transmitted across generations.

Congolese named colonial officials in various languages. Names therefore expressed different aspects of cultures in which they were embedded. The "embeddedness" of names in various cultures had consequences for the study of names as sources. A focus on themes of names, for example, would show shared perceptions of experiences of daily life under colonialism, indicate a cross-cultural understanding of colonialism, and explain the larger political and economic structures that shaped the experiences. Thus, the exploration of names supplements macro-analysis privileged by previous paradigms that produced "history without people" and denied Africans their agency. Names provide the inside view of colonialism. Ordinary villagers did not leave their own records of cash crop production, prices of commodities they bought from or sold to capitalist companies, taxes, imprisonments, and numbers of lashes they endured. Colonial officials recorded these data we access mainly in the colonial archives. Anthroponyms were contemporaneous mnemonic devices and records in which Congolese spoke about all these colonial practices. Listening to these voices adds much to the way historical truth is reconstructed because truth depends not only on who listens, but also on who speaks.[21] By focusing on a cultural form to decode African voices, the study of colonial anthroponyms moves the analysis to the intersection of structure and the colonial experiences of concrete people. Names provide insights into Congolese mindsets, the politics of memory, and collective consciousness, and all show Congolese understanding of large processes that affected everyday colonial life. An exploration of names is thus a methodological innovation. The naming of colonial officials mediated experiences of colonialism and enabled Congolese to express their concerns and sense of themselves in history and tell their experiences of colonialism according to their perspectives.[22] So naming is explored as not only a cultural form that conveys messages but also as a process that gives agency back to Congolese and represents colonial encounters as dynamic processes.

The values of names for historical reconstruction are as evident as their relative pitfalls are. As stated earlier, scholars have relied on interviews to capture the voices of the voiceless—women, peasants, workers, and nonliterate people. In some cases, verbal testimonies were and still are the only evidence to answer some questions pertinent to the lives of peasants, workers, and local elite. Conceptually, however, interviews conducted to produce verbal testimonies of the voiceless carry the unstated assumption that Congolese lacked the courage to speak to colonial officials about colonialism, and only after the collapse of the colonial regimes had they become able to express their ideas. To be sure, interviews appeared as rationalizations after events and often led to biases, manipulations, and the politics of memory, issues inherent to all reconstructions of the past based on documents produced in the present.

A further advantage of names as historical sources was that they were coined by Congolese in more than 280 languages. In many ways, the linguistic diversity was both a strength and a pitfall. The languages created enormous challenge, and the translations of interpreters were only shortcuts and partial solutions. In reality, the translations of names required a deep knowledge of local cultures as Congolese villagers drew many names from myths, metaphors, and legends, signifiers that referred to symbolic and multiple referents. As the old meanings of the signifiers were chosen to talk about new socioeconomic and political realities, they sometimes generated duplicitous messages. This situation complicates the decoding of meanings of messages. And short research trips for language immersions in different parts of the country were no substitute for adequate training in African linguistics and languages.

Briefly, it is inescapable to conclude that whether one regards the names of colonial officials as traces of social existence and the linguistic and ethnographic descriptions of colonial relations or the subjective interpretations of colonial encounters, they bear the imprints of colonial conditions and experiences of Congolese villagers.

Contexts and Interpretations of Names

More than three decades ago, Joseph Ki-Zerbo asserted, "Man [human] has made historic whatever he has touched with his creative hand."[23] Meanwhile successful uses of oral and ethnographic sources have challenged the Eurocentric view that *verba volant, scripta manent*. As noted earlier, creative methodologies have revolutionized Congolese historiography in the last five decades. Building on these achievements and insights, I first contend that whether preserved in the written documents— colonial archives, travel literature, and academic publications—or still spoken as word of mouth across the village world, individual and collective names of colonial officials recorded colonial experiences. They are valuable sources to re-create the experiences of daily life of Congolese villagers under colonial rule. However, the decoding of evidence from names and their interpretation requires an awareness of the shifting perceptions of colonialism held by the Congolese. Early encounters were rare events, and the successive ones discussed violence, the appropriation of material resources, and the control of African labor and minds. No surprise that the names of Europeans, including the categories that described the ways Europeans walked and talked and how they looked became among Congolese the topics of talk that were real and imagined.[24] A fruitful study of names requires therefore that one combs, as one ought to do with all studies of effects of colonial interactions on everyday life, through all available sources that yield details on colonial experiences in the village world. An exploration of available sources would place the meanings of names in their cultures and contexts and make the broader messages of names clearer, their interpretations intelligible, and the resulting historical narrative a thick and textured description of colonial experiences.

Decoding and interpreting messages of names called for an understanding of factors that affected the contents and changed the messages. Of these factors, the most important included the unending movements of colonial agents across administrative divisions and ways adopted by Congolese villagers to hide ugly and subversive messages in their day-to-day resistance against colonialism. No less important was also giving two names to one official and the maneuvers by colonial officials to change their ugly names, dynamics that, when overlooked, lead to distortions of the meanings of names and their broader political messages. Unlike these factors, which reinforce the weaknesses of names as sources, a few others illuminate the messages of names. Many colonial officials, for example, were not aware of their names, which their successors recorded in official documents long after the name-bearers had left the area. This situation was fruitful: Congolese villagers provided extensive comments that explained the literal renderings of names and the broader messages because they were now freer to spell out ugly meanings of names to the successors than they were in front of the bearers of names. A few others knew only the surface meanings of their names because Congolese villagers coded the messages in literary genres and figures of speech that hid their political messages and intentions to the outsiders. Once determined, a total or partial ignorance of the meanings of their names by colonial officials suggests a successful use of naming as hidden protests and counter-hegemonic strategy by Congolese villagers. The confusion circulated subversive messages and shielded Congolese villagers from the wrath of European colonizers. The colonial officials' ignorance of the meanings of their names also shows ways colonial officials manipulated names because many appeared dumb only to deceive Congolese villagers in order to collect candid inside views of colonial policies that they could hardly get from local leaders and state-appointed agents.

As with most sources, the names of colonial officials recorded contemporaneous information about events and situations they referred to and described without certifying the accuracy of the recorded information, let alone the certainty of its transmission across localities and generations. Several factors created the gaps between the meanings of names and the actual economic and political situations. Like people elsewhere, Congolese interviewees remembered their colonial experiences from the present, which has brought only misery. Indeed, wars, the precariousness of health care, political repression, economic ruin, and deprivation resulting from thirty-two years of mismanagement of national resources by the Mobutu regime, structural adjustment and globalization policies, and the incompetence of the two Kabila regimes have affected their present and the ways they remembered the colonial encounters and the meanings of names.[25] Two illustrations help explain the point. In 1986, I interviewed former policeman Lufundja Mbayo, who was compelled by the white man *Tuku-Tuku* to use violence against his Mambwe fellows in the 1950s. During the entire interview, he worried that I was an undercover government agent who had come to arrest him, although he was given every assurance I was a scholar and teacher. When he spoke, he nervously justified his past actions: "We were not mistreating our people; we were teaching them how to grow food to avoid famine. We only disciplined those who did not give money to their wives, spending it on alcohol or losing it to gambling, something the white man *Tuku-Tuku* vigorously forbade."[26] A professional historian, Lwamba Bilonda, remembered such situations differently and candidly stated, "The white man *Fimbo Mingi* ["Much whipping"] lashed men naked. He first tied their hands and then lashed their buttocks leaving scars, which the victims still have on their bodies until today. The white man *Fimbo Mingi* was wicked, but at least people sold their cotton and earned some money, things they no longer do today under Mobutu's regime."[27]

The two recollections highlight the influence of the present on the remembrance of the colonial past and vice versa. The hardships of the postcolonial decades and the justification of colonial violence make the colonial era a golden age. In reality, however, the recollections distorted the economic and political contexts that assigned accurate and truthful meanings to the names *Tuku-Tuku* and *Fimbo Mingi*. Besides the internal dynamics of the messages, the authoritative mediation of the historian who gathers, analyzes, and interprets them, affected the messages of names as much as the colonial and postcolonial conditioning. Despite the many conditionings, Congolese villagers were more vocal in these sources than they were in most colonial sources, where they remained silent or where, if they spoke, they did so through an overbearing missionary, a sympathetic colonial government official, or a chastising company administrator frustrated by an unsuccessful recruitment of workers.[28] The agency of African men and women is evidenced in their aptitude to assign multidimensional messages to specific situations. This strategy meant people knew what to say, and when and how to say it to colonial officials. As with all types of sources, a deployment of rules of historical criticism remains a requisite for the fruitful exploration of colonial anthroponyms.

As stated, names of Europeans yield a diverse body of evidence of colonial daily life in the village world. Specifically, they recorded the community commentaries about flogging, ruthless methods of tax collection, compulsory labor, mandatory cash crop production, village relocations, and sexual exploitation of local women since the conquest, which transformed the independent village communities into the colonial village world.[29] The end of the military conquests and early devastating colonial projects, particularly the end of rubber collection in 1912, did not bring an immediate qualitative change in the lives of Congolese. Violence remained a part of colonialism and the most enduring of the experiences that Congolese villagers recorded in names. Villagers continued to call the white men who executed the new projects by names similar to those they had given the builders of the Congo Free State. Illustrative of the continuity of violence were *Matcho Kali*, "Angry eyes," *Nkoi*, "Leopard," *Kimbwi*, "Hyena," which was translated metaphorically as "He who can eat me," and *Simba Bulaya*, "Europe's lion."[30]

The themes of such names carried messages and memories of violence, most of which, because of the repetitions of colonial practices they embodied, appeared timeless. In reality, however, the memory recorded in a name was seldom a static "ethnographic present." It remained stable for one generation only as new colonial conditions broadened the meanings of the cumulative message, and the experiences of successive generations diminished the significance of previous messages. To tease broader social meanings out of names and recapture generational evaluations of colonialism entails explaining political, economic, and social conditions that overwhelmed the lives of the village people, the name-givers. And names were chronological reference points, that, once understood as integral parts of historical developments, stamped out the timelessness in the observations and perceptions of repetitive events and characteristics of colonialism. Different categories of colonial anthroponyms and the multidimensionality of their meanings show that colonialism was neither static nor monolithic in African "minds" and lived experiences. Anthroponyms coined during the scramble for Central Africa, for instance, showed mainly cultural clashes.[31] Once the methods of colonialism were established and became repressive and diverted the labor of households and communities to undermine Congolese villagers' ability to eke out a normal living, Congolese developed negative perceptions of colonial rule. Names then underscored colonial abuses that were motivated by contemporary colonial projects.[32]

The omnipresence of expressions of violence in the corpus of names of colonial officials underscores the brutality of Belgian colonialism. Even so, violence was not the only theme resulting from the interactions between Congolese villagers and Europeans. In the eyes of Congolese, colonialism was not always terrifying and exploitative.[33] Congolese embraced new learning and technical skills that improved the quality of their lives and work; they admired Europeans who conformed wittingly or unwittingly to local ideals of masculinity and manhood; they appreciated the few colonial state officials who even symbolically promoted their interests and addressed their concerns. Congolese villagers expressed these perceptions in names from the beginning to the end of colonialism when they gave European officials such praise names as *Lubuku*, "Builder," *Mupenda Batu*, "He who loves people," *Mbavu Nguvu*, "Strong chest," and *Mondele Ngolo*, "Strong white man," names that I discuss in later chapters. Suffice it to say here that the foregoing names were metonyms for praise chosen by Congolese villagers to acknowledge the relations they considered beneficial and friendly.[34]

Praise names genuinely extolled colonial officials. But the meanings of praise names were also multidimensional, and in some situations they were only ostensibly praise and hid hostility and resentments toward colonial officials and colonialism. Understood as metonyms and metaphors of colonialism, praise names of colonial officials provide key details of a subtle counter-hegemonic discourse and expand the wide variety of concerns about which Congolese talked and which help analyze daily experiences.[35]

Although Congolese minted names of colonial officials, they were not the exclusive users of the social messages. As colonial officials realized the significance of the feedback of their names and their meanings on colonial policies and local perceptions of their personal character and the political behavior of the villagers, they turned the names into sources from which they learned valuable information about accusations leveled against themselves and colonialism. Broadly, colonial officials appropriated the feedback in two ways. Until the 1930s, the strategy consisted of incorporating the messages of names into cultural expressions, most notably annual agricultural shows that they staged to make Congolese villagers assimilate colonial ideologies.[36] Commonly, however, individual officials astutely built a pragmatic and usable reputation out of the message conveyed by the name to either mask colonial abuses or terrorize Congolese. Thus, European voices glossed over African ones and transformed the names of colonial officials into multivocal sources.

The awareness of the multivocality of names helps in decoding and interpreting messages. First, if an examination of cultural, social, economic, and political contexts identifies the voice of the colonial officials, their naming represents a political language, and not only a mnemonics that conveyed information about colonial experiences. This is a departure from structure-action dichotomy, which once privileged "history without subjects" over human agency or vice versa.[37] Second, the discovery of contradictions between the explicit and implicit meanings of the names alerts us to Congolese agency. This occurred when the explicit meanings described actual situations and the implicit ones pointed to criticisms of colonialism. Contradictions show how Congolese produced duplicitous messages to mitigate their criticisms of colonialism and avoid retribution.

Sources

The gathering of names used in this study spanned several years and was much like pulling a needle out of a haystack. Names are scattered in various sources, written and oral, including books, colonial reports and administrative correspondence, academic publications, novels, and oral testimonies. Europeans who encountered Africans in the nineteenth century not only recorded information about climate, rainfall patterns, vegetation, names of villages and rivers, population figures, and the resources of the areas visited, but also described artifacts, customs, hairstyles, and naming practices. Early explorers of the Congo such as Georges Schweinfurth, Hermann Wissmann, and Herbert Ward, early missionaries like Harris Johnston and George Grenfeld, and colonial state officials received names and discussed their meanings and the circumstances that compelled people to give them these names.[38]

As the colonial regime established methods and institutions for dominating local communities, interactions between Congolese villagers and Europeans intensified and the number of names of colonial officials increased. By the 1920s and 1930s, colonial officials regularly signed their Congolese names on official correspondence, unpublished manuscripts, books, and various government reports.[39] I gleaned many names used in this study from these written sources, housed in different archival depositories in Democratic Republic of the Congo and Belgium.

As they focused on unearthing local sources and restoring Central African voices in history, scholars of Central and South-Central Africa have rarely looked at these materials. The reason might be the time it takes to collect names. Notable exceptions are three texts. Jean-Luc Vellut published the first in 1982 in an edited collection, *Stéréotypes nationaux et préjugés raciaux aux XIXe et XXe siècles*. Using a sample of about fifteen names of Europeans, Vellut interpreted names as local representations of the white man.[40] Based on seventy names given to Catholic missionaries in Kasai from 1891 to 1959, the second study by T. K. Biaya defined the psychological motivations of the choice of names.[41] The third text was a two-part article published by E. Boelaert, H. Vinck, and C. Lonkama in *Annales Aequatoria* in 1996 and 2000.[42] Unlike Vellut and Biaya's studies, this two-part article is a huge repository of names gleaned from written sources and interviews conducted with former teachers, clerks, nurses, peasants, workers, traders, elders, and students in the areas most affected by rubber atrocities of the Congo Basin. I collected the bulk of names about the Congo Free State era from these sources.

Outside these cases, there are no studies fully devoted to the naming of Europeans. Scholars have instead commented briefly on names embedded in their documentations. Allen Isaacman, who extensively explored oral testimonies to study the political behavior of Mozambican cotton cultivators, and Leroy Vail and Landeg White, who analyzed praise songs to capture local protest against colonial power, commented in passing on names inscribed in the sources they studied.[43] There is evidence of the naming of colonial officials in Uganda and Tanzania.[44]

African writers of the 1950s used the memories of peasants and workers to publish novels in which the colonizers received collective and generic names, which, although not directly depicting situations in the Congo, were important to the argument that Africans deployed a common cultural practice to talk about shared colonial experiences.[45]

About one-third of the names used in this study came from interviews conducted in 1986 and between 1988 and 1990 with former cotton producers. I have earlier discussed the value, significance, and pitfalls of data gleaned from these interviews. But gaps in the data required more research, which was carried out in 1996 and 2000. Three years later, two research assistants conducted the last interviews by using a structured interview questionnaire. The new research threw light on the extent to which names derived from social stereotypes of gender and used by Congolese villagers to praise colonial officials voiced protest and praise simultaneously. Unlike previous ir..erviews that targeted mainly cotton producers, former policemen, and cotton monitors, the successive ones were conducted with cash crop producers, workers, academics, and retirees in the urban settings. Although Congolese satirized postcolonial politicians by giving them names, they still remembered names given decades ago to colonial rulers. This remembrance underscored the continuity of the practice.

Themes and topics that emerge from these names open up new areas of research as they enrich old ones. To be sure, names recorded African thoughts, actions, and structural constraints that shaped the colonial world. While Africans experienced limitations, violence, and few opportunities, colonial officials engineered plans to expand their own power.[46] Approaching histories of experiences of colonialism through colonial anthroponyms therefore recaptures many interconnections—the ways in which Congolese and colonial officials constructed, negotiated, and struggled over the real and symbolic boundaries of power, domination, and exploitation. This approach thus adds to a long academic tradition of recounting Congolese experiences based on local sources.[47]

To recapture these interconnections and re-create daily life inside the colonial village world, I have divided the book into seven chapters. This introduction highlights the relevance and significance of names as innovative sources of colonial experiences and their contributions to the writing of various fields of history.

Chapter 1 provides an overview of the dynamics of naming in precolonial Congo. Specifically, it broadly describes naming conventions, highlights important sociological conditions that affected the choice and meanings of names, and stresses the dynamics of naming and the ways in which names convey and even influence the essence of a person. The purpose is to prepare readers to understand the relation of precolonial naming conventions to the ways Congolese still deployed the same criteria of selection when they named individual Europeans and groups of Europeans.

Chapter 2 examines the contexts for naming colonial officials—the effects of colonialism on the village world and the ways in which they shaped the understanding of colonialism and the choice of names. Broadly, it describes the integration of the Congolese village world into the economies of the Congo Free State and Belgian Congo through rubber collection, compulsory cash crop cultivation, the supply of labor, and the ways local administrations squeezed cash out of the households through taxes and fines and appropriated corvée labor for constructing roads. The aim is to show the ways colonialism affected and defined the way of life in the village world.

Chapter 3 explores naming patterns, the meanings of names, the linguistic and sociolinguistic aspects of naming, the significance of naming patterns to provide ideas about names as sources of memories and histories of daily life of village peoples, and their understanding of colonialism. It contends that the meanings of names given to explorers, missionaries, officials of the Congo Free State, and agents of concessionary companies conveyed substantial information about colonial material conditions. Once subjected to the rules of evidence and contextualized, the seemingly disparate bits of testimonies woven into the meanings of names become valuable local commentaries on the nature and impacts of colonial rule on the daily life of the village people.

Chapter 4 explores the early names when political domination and extreme violence were scarce. The focus on the contrast between the two types of experiences explains new naming patterns, shows the totality of experiences, and expands the argument of the book that names are important sources of history of everyday life.

Chapter 5 documents critiques of colonialism and its practices by Congolese villagers. It argues that accusations of assaults on the village world, violence, exploitation of women, and the intrusion of colonialism into everyday life expressed suffering, anger, resentment, and protests. Although the chapter pays attention to different categories of names given to various groups of European professionals, it focuses mainly on names given to officials of the territorial administration and agricultural service. Territorial administrators, tax collectors, agronomists, and crop supervisors established several and consequential relations with the villagers. The chapter focuses on individual names that recorded and wove colonial situations into the themes of violence and assaults of colonialism on the village world.

Chapter 6 first centers on stories of true celebration of colonial officials and their actions and then looks at how Congolese villagers wove grievances of colonial practices into multidimensional meanings of names of praise to create strategic ambiguities, useful to their experiences with colonialism and its agents. In all cases, the analysis highlights the geographical distribution of the name, contexts, events, and situations that informed the meanings of names and explains the ways praise was connected to the character and actions of the colonial officials.

Chapter 7 documents the various ways colonial officials confronted local voices. The first part of the chapter is a brief discussion of the inevitability of negotiations. It sets the contexts that help to show why colonial government officials deployed their local identities to construct a discourse of domination. It argues that although Belgian colonialism was brutal, it could hardly work without some segments of the village world participating in the project. The second part of the chapter explores ways in which colonial officials used messages they decoded from their names as instruments of colonial policy. It investigates how colonial officials transformed messages of names of praise into paternalist discourse to woo residents of the villages into colonial economic and political projects and stave off perceptions of colonialism that belied the civilizing mission of colonial campaigns. Finally, it looks at ways colonial officials and agents retooled messages of violence to terrorize Congolese without using the corporal violence suggested by the explicit meanings of names.

A sample of names is included as an appendix and serves two purposes. First, it provides readers with a glimpse into various themes that show the interactions between colonial officials and agents and Congolese villagers. Second, it shows that just as Congolese villagers produced economic raw materials, they produced observations and comments, which historians can collect to write histories of colonial experiences.

1

The Dynamics of Naming
in Precolonial Congo

An Overview

The name of a black person evokes a whole past; it is something
vital and sometimes, it is even a jealously kept secret.
G. Liénart, "La signification du nom chez les peuples Bantu"

A detailed analysis of precolonial naming traditions of Central
Africa and the Congo is a monumental undertaking that falls beyond
the preoccupations of this chapter. This is not because such work is im-
possible to do. Designed to prepare readers to grasp the continuity of
precolonial naming conventions in naming Europeans, the chapter is
an overview and need not present cumbersome details. The influence
of precolonial naming conventions on naming individual Europeans
and groups of Europeans is shown by describing naming conventions
broadly, highlighting important sociological factors that affected the
choice and meanings of names, and underlining the ways Congolese still
deployed the same criteria of selection when they encountered the Europeans. It therefore stresses the dynamics of naming and the ways in
which names convey and even influence the essence of a person.

In the Congolese cultural universe, like elsewhere in Africa, individuals identify with their name. The oneness of name and person was expressed through verbal arts such as funeral oratory, proverbs, and riddles.
It was explicit in the sayings "Having a name is living" and "There will
be nothing where there is no name."[1] These assumptions not only under-
lie the relation of naming to cosmologies, mentalities, and collective
imagination but also show that nameless individuals were unimaginable.

That names defined persons and constituted their essence transpired in different types of collective behaviors and ideologies that underlay them. First, the first name of the newborn was hidden from the public and the external world to which he was known only by the second name, which did not define his essence and relation with the ancestors. The refusal to tell personal names of newborns and even adults to strangers so long as the intentions of the strangers were not known was a common practice many colonial census takers and health officers encountered and wrote about in the early years of colonialism. Second, the long-held conviction in the utterance of a name as a condition to bewitch the name-bearer was another widespread mindset that supports the idea that a name conveys the essence of a person. Third, the naming of guests after terms of friendship and alliance and after technical innovations and skills they introduced into the adopted group and the exchange of names during the rituals of adoption and blood brotherhood show the identity of the name with the name-bearer.[2]

Although Congolese naming customs and conventions varied and have changed over time, just as have the societies that created them, they were institutionalized and enduring practices. A child received a name at any time: before, after, or at birth. Although some names were gender specific, others were gender neutral and thus given to boys and girls. Many groups kept this first name throughout life; others like the Kongo kept it only until puberty, when they gave the child a second name during an initiation ceremony to replace the name received at birth.[3] Unlike the Kongo, the Ngbaka gave a second name to teenagers at a circumcision ceremony while they kept the name received at birth.[4] This naming custom shows that among the Ngbaka and others who followed similar naming traditions, males bore at least two names. While some societies surrounded the naming of children with elaborate rituals, others lacked special ceremonies to mark the occasion and create a sense of transition to a new cycle of life.

Renaming and name changes were in reality continuous practices throughout the life of a person. They occurred often and appeared vital because they altered the personality and restored harmony in the body and psyche of the name-bearer. Varying from group to group, reasons for the practices were philosophical, metaphysical, and psychological. Among the Basanga, a crying baby was believed to signal the refusal to bear its name and enough reason for a name change. The sickness of a teenager after the rite of passage was interpreted as a sign of ancestors' anger and resulted in a name change. From birth to the induction into

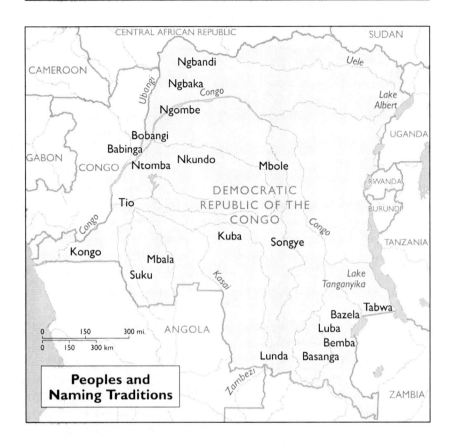

Peoples and Naming Traditions

manhood, the child played no role in the choice of his names, except twins who announced their names in dreams. Even the contribution of twins to their naming remained minor because twins received readily available pairs of generic names.

Unlike children who received names, ordinary Congolese adults re-named themselves under various circumstances. Faced with adversity, ordinary individuals changed their names when they discovered that their names were the cause of their misfortune. Sometimes ordinary in-dividuals changed names because they disliked unflattering meanings and derogatory connotations conveyed by the names they received at birth. But the most recurring reason for the change of names remained events and conditions of life, sociological factors that I discuss later in the chapter.

The commonest naming practice that added new names to the names of ordinary men and women was teknonymy, a practice that consisted in naming parents after their children. This naming pattern produced a uniform morphological structure, "Father of X" and "Mother of X" in which X represented the name of the child. In contrast to teknonymy, the naming of children after their grandparents and great-grandparents was widespread and deeply altered social relations among members of different generations. While teknonymy raised the prestige and social status of the parents, the naming of children after their grandparents or great-grandparents changed children to parents and ancestors of their own parents. Naming of children after their grandparents or great-grandparents also reversed expected behaviors between children and parents, a situation documented in colonial ethnographies.[5]

Naming newborn children was predominantly a father's right in societies with patrilineal and matrilineal descents. But like fathers and grandfathers, mothers and grandmothers named the child. Even where traditions did not allow a mother to name, she got the right of nomination under many circumstances, notably when she suffered a good deal during pregnancy and labor. Among the Bemba, who are matrilineal, grandmothers named newborns, as did grandmothers among the Mbole, who are patrilineal. Groups that followed a bilateral descent system gave a child two names at birth, one from the father's side and the other from the mother's. Parents and grandparents selected names for the newborns. The decision to name the newborn was, however, made only after a long consultation with oracles, witches, and mediums — experts believed to possess special powers to find a suitable name that would bring happiness, success, and protection to the newborn and revitalize the entire community. Where new names were added to the first names or the first names were dropped during initiation rituals, grandparents and initiation leaders were the name-givers.[6]

As stated earlier, babies experienced namelessness only temporarily because nameless individuals were unimaginable. Although a name identifies an individual, personal names of newborns were not revealed to the outside world because Congolese believed that the name defined the essence of the name-bearer, and if others knew the name, misfortunes would befall the newborn. The Babinga, for example, feared that revealing the name to outsiders would make the baby vulnerable to witchcraft. They used instead a second name that did not define the essence of the baby, an idea that shows once more the oneness of the person with the name.

Naming was not all about children in Central Africa. Leaders of different polities received titles and changed their names to explain new social status and political roles. They also received names of ranks that were given to ordinary individuals who, because of their talents and success, reached a position of leadership as big men, skillful hunters, and famous medicine men. Titles were particles accompanied by names of the domains. The list of the classic titles included *Mani* in the Kingdom of Kongo and *Ma* or *Mwe* in Loango, which were all variants of the word *Mwene*, a nearly ubiquitous word that meant "Lord." Before 1600, the term *mwene* followed by X means "possessor of X" in which X was the name of the realm. It was the individual title of the early chiefs who were the owners of their territorial domains and similar to the nineteenth-century local "chief of the land."[7]

When titles were given to a small elite group, the naming of ordinary individuals after rank was common in ancestral time. It started in the seventeenth-century slave trade among the Bobangi commercial elite who engaged in long-distance trade toward Pumbo. Of the corporate and collective names drawn from rank, *mokonzi* was exemplary. At first, the term designated an early riser who brought back game to the village, allowing the village to share and practice solidarity when unknown factors like inundation hindered such occasions. Gradually, the term was applied to anyone who became wealthy and influential in the village because of hard work. The term *mokonzi* thus became the pseudonym of a man who lifted himself and gained fame, prestige, and power by engaging in rewarding enterprise such as the long-distance trade toward Pumbo. Authority and prestige subsequently rested on the possession of material wealth. Once these representations were accepted by most people in the society, the word *mokonzi* became the name of rank for self-made men. Besides corporate names like *mokonzi*, Congolese coined generic personal names that connoted accumulation and display of wealth. Among the most common figured *Epanyabeka*, "He who displays his wealth," *Lohusabeka*, "He who boasts his wealth," and *Ndongabeka*, "Of the village of wealth."[8] These examples show that individual and collective names of rank praised the bearers of names, but sometimes such names were satirical comments about greed and social inequalities.

Women, like men, reached higher status and similarly received names of rank. Among the Mbole, when wives of house leaders distinguished themselves by good judgment and an aptitude to settle disputes, they received the name *Asele*. Witty wives received this name of rank to keep step with husbands, and they took the name after the husbands had paid expensive fees to equals who would perform the name-giving ritual. During this ceremony, *Asele* received the staff, the insignia of the new status and higher rank, and the title of "Mother of Lilwa," that endowed her with the authority to stop small and destructive wars.[9] Like with other names, *Asele* was passed to descending generations, and the transmission shows that not all bearers of the name *Asele* in the successive generations ever underwent the ritual of name-giving that was required to bear the name. *Asele* was the synonym of *Bolumbu*, the name of rank for Nkundo wives that was similarly passed on to girls of descending generations.[10]

What were the criteria for the selection of Congolese anthroponyms? Despite their diversity and without succumbing to the tyranny of taxonomy, Congolese anthroponyms might be divided into three broad categories. The first category includes names drawn from events and all types of philosophical, metaphysical, psychological, and material problems the family faced at the time of naming. Of the events that determined the choice of names in this group figured wars, epidemics, disease or sickness, famine, suffering, unsuccessful undertakings, the states of being orphaned and childless, and repeated miscarriages or deaths that often led parents and grandparents to name children after theophores, a practice of giving children names containing reference to deities. Among the Tutsi or Hutu, for example, Imana is the divine appellative. When families faced problems antinomic of death, they named their children *Habimana*, "There is a God," *Sebantu*, "The father of people," *Munyamana*, "This child has God's protection," *Ndagijyimana*, "I place this child under God's protection," and *Nshinyimana*, "I thank God." One can multiply examples endlessly, but this short sampling suggests that theophores show not only the relation of people with their gods but also concerns people confronted and for which they were seeking answers. Theophores, like other types of names, are sources of histories. Congolese also drew names from contemporary and past achievements of families and communities and told them as stories to help children emulate the lives of their homonyms. Centered on importance of wives and marriage, most were coined and given to children by women, and some expressed rivalries among co-wives, marital frustrations, and love. Parents and grandparents gave children names shown in dreams, which the Ngombe and Ngbandi interpreted as authoritative revelations from the ancestors.[11]

The second group included names derived from circumstances of birth, physical and moral personal qualities, and the personality and character of the child and ordinary adults who renamed themselves. When such names were received from previous generations, the qualities were those of the previous bearers of the names and used as teaching tools to inculcate the qualities into the children and commemorate events that preceded the birth or took place at the time of birth. These assumptions were at work when children received names after parents, grandparents, and relatives had observed children and consulted oracles and mediums.

Circumstances of birth were decisive in naming children. An umbilical cord wrapped around the body, the neck, and the head of a baby decided the selection of names. Among the Luba and Basanga, a baby entangled in the umbilical cord received the generic name of *Mujinga*. A breech birth among the Basanga typically generated the name *Tshela*, while a baby born holding one cheek with one hand earned the name *Kabungama*, and the premature baby received the name *Mubishi*, which means "unripe."[12] To this list of events and situations should be added the status of the health of child, the place of birth, the sibling order of birth, days of the week, and time of the birth. Although names drawn from these criteria were generic and provide information about repetitive events that hardly showed social change, they are important historical documents in the hands of a skilled historian.

The birth of twins, an event with sometimes awful consequences, cut the choice of names to few pairs of generic appellations. Everywhere twins received readily available pairs of typical names, some gender specific, others given to twins of either sex according to the order of birth. The Bemba and Basanga named twins *Kiungu* (First-born) and *Kapya* (Second-born). Luba-Kasai twins were given the names *Mbuyi* (First-born) and *Kabanga* (Second-born), while the Songye twins received the names *Ngoie* and *Mukonkole*. The Tabwa called twins *Kamona* and *Kisimba*, and the Yeke named them *Kulwa* and *Katoto*. The Mbole near the Lower Lomami River named the twins *Mboyo* (First-born) and *Kanga* (Second-born) or *Loola* (Sky, first-born) and *Leyali* (Earth, second-born) regardless of their sex.[13] Twins' names were selected by parents and grandparents after long consultation with oracles and mediums.

The pairs of twins' names in any group were usually few in number. Even so, Father Basile Tanghe, a Catholic missionary to the Ngbandi country in the 1920s, listed fifty-six pairs of names for twins, attributed to twins according to their sex and order of birth.[14] The sibling order of birth was important not only in naming twins, but also in naming twins' siblings and children the society considered atypical. Included here were children born after several siblings of the same sex, those with no siblings, and those born immediately after the twins. Like the twins, these children received generic names that tell their order of birth. The Suku, Ntomba, Mbole, and Ngombe, to mention just a few groups, named children born after twins *Landu, Mputu, Letuta,* and *Motutea,* respectively.[15] Therefore, the names of twins were seldom the great records of contemporary situations faced by the families, lineages or clans, and village communities.

Names drawn from sociological significance of events formed the third group of anthroponyms and included names of deceased members of the family given to the newborn to perpetuate the memory of these members as ancestors. Many of these names tell the stories of origin of the founders of clans, lineages, villages, and large groups, people reported in the traditions of migrations, and founders of different polities. The first bearers of these names are at the top of the genealogies, and colonial ethnographies and academic literature are replete with illustrations. One notes *Woot* for the Kuba, *Ngobila* for the Tio, and *Ilombo Okali* for the Mbole. So these names tell stories of early migrations and settlements. The group included titles, pseudonyms, and names of ranks that were highly suggestive.

Congolese, like other Central Africans, gave praise names to babies, ordinary people, leaders, corporate groups, and political institutions in societies with centralized and decentralized governance. The Kuba *ncyeem ingesh,* "songs of the nature spirits," praise the monarchy. The word *Kembe,* the identity of a group of Mbole of Opala, was an exaltation to bravery and a praise and means "Carriers of the arrows and intrepid warriors."[16] The two praise poems *Ndumbululu* (Kongo) and *Kasala* (Luba) extolled their respective lineages.[17] A common praise name for the Kuba king was "the great canoe in which the Diing and the Koong have crossed."[18] And Mbákám Mbomancyeel, who ruled in 1680, was praised as "the bow, the bowstring, and the arrow," while the Bemba praised Nkole wa Mapembwe, the second Lunda king, as "Nkole wa Mapembwe . . . stretch Lunda land. You are a real Luba chief."[19]

Anthroponyms extolled ordinary individuals as well. For example, praise naming was common among the Bayaka, Batanga, Luba, Mbala, Kuba, and Nkundo. A quintessential symbol of authority in the rainforests of Central Africa, *Nkoyi,* the term for "leopard" in many Bantu languages, was and still is a widespread praise name for ordinary individuals in poetry and sayings. The Luba of Ngandajika extolled the bearer of the name *Nkoyi* and addressed him with words of adulation: "Black leopard, which stands tall and surpasses all others." The Mbala gave individuals such laudatory names as *Anjombe,* "Strong," *Mobonde,*

"He who molds," *Bilikonda*, " Endless forest," and *Ebangala*, "He who planted the forest."[20] Individual or corporate names of praise played an ideological role the same as that played by initiation praise songs, dynastic poems, group mottoes, and political titles from which Congolese drew praise names for colonial officials.

As previously stated, anthroponyms were drawn from events and conditions prevailing at birth. Once passed down to the next generations, they conveyed little or no information about the societies, let alone the name-bearers. As a result, many anthroponyms show the gap between meanings and referents. Despite these gaps, Congolese anthroponyms were complete signs. Besides denotations understood by all the speakers of the languages in which they were coined, names had connotations, implied meanings that do not at first glance show the referents without the knowledge of the culture and customs of the society.[21] Even names derived from political titles or those received at initiation ceremonies, which were often group's mottoes and etiquettes, described accomplishments and personal qualities of the current bearers of the names. In various ways, Congolese villagers adapted the meanings of names to current bearers; one common way was to call names out on slit gongs, drums, and horns. These local instruments of communication afforded the users enough freedom for personal commentaries because most formulas used in these types of communication referred not only to the names of persons targeted by the message but also to their descents.[22]

At this point of the analysis, one can draw important conclusions relevant to the essential functions of a name in the Congolese universe. The discussion shows clearly that a name not only identified the individual and allowed him to establish private and official relations, but it also signified. The discussion also suggests that naming was a cultural form by which a community individualized members and converted foreigners into members of groups after they underwent a ritual that was often accompanied by blood exchange.[23] The discussion shows that names are pithy verbal expressions, carry memories, and therefore are important sources of history.

These naming traditions continued during colonial rule as Congolese drew names of their children from colonial situations and events whose disruptive or positive effects were deeply felt. Although colonialism was disruptive, exploitative, and repressive, it brought some opportunities for social mobility to a few Congolese who then translated their ideas of colonialism into names they gave their children. When a few

Congolese rose to the powerful position of *greffier* or prosecutor in native courts, they equated colonialism with progress and personal achievements and named their children *Sikitele*.[24] *Sikitele* is a loanword from the French *secrétaire*, which means "secretary." In reality, various connotations of *Sikitele* tell stories of colonial experiences. Besides embodying lived experiences and aspirations of upward social mobility, the name also expressed consciousness of internal social differentiations in social power, prestige, education, and accumulation of imports. Through *Sikitele*, some educated Congolese boasted of their newly acquired social status separating them from their fellows coerced to mandatory cash cultivation and unskilled manual labor. These meanings of *Sikitele* explain the resentment Congolese had and still have for manual labor, even if they are barely educated.

Congolese naming was affected by negative perceptions of colonial experiences as well. When they suffered injustices at native courts, the Mbole named their children *Tomilali*, a loanword from the French *tribunal*, which means "court." Drawn from injustices the Mbole faced at colonial native courts, *Tomilali* connoted anger toward local judges, most of whom were also state-appointed chiefs. Many appeals during inspections of the courts by European officials testify to the dissatisfaction and anger Congolese expressed by naming children *Tomilali*. Another typical name drawn from negative colonial experience was *Munyololo*. Coined and used by Kiswahili speakers, *Munyololo* means "chain" or "rope"; it was a symbol of enslavement reminiscent of the scenes of chained captives during the slave trade. Under colonial rule, the word referred to any condition of oppression that suppressed freedom, particularly scenes of handcuffed prisoners whose necks were tied to the chains or ropes. In 1988, Pene wa Pene described some of these conditions vividly, saying, "*Munyololo* reminds one of the image of persons tied with a rope around the neck while their hands were cuffed often behind the back; anyone who saw these people felt humiliation, indignity, and loss of freedom."[25]

The final illustrations are *Komanda* and *Kapiteni*, which were drawn from military ranks of colonial army officers who, until well into the 1920s, ran colonial administrations. At times, the reason to name a child after a military rank was but a mere visit to the village by a military officer. But the violence these military officers spread across villages assigned negative connotations to names drawn from military rank. Congolese named their children *Komanda* and *Kapiteni* after they had experienced a show of force during military operations conducted by the *Komanda*, "commander," and *Kapiteni*, "captain."[26] Names drawn from military ranks were therefore pithy expressions, which, once contextualized, tell stories of abuses committed during early colonial rule.

The story of Mbayo, a former mineworker of the Union-Minière du Haut-Katanga shows how naming recorded successive events that shaped the life story of the bearer of names. Named *Mbayo* at birth, the mineworker took a new name, *Panda Kilima,* a Kiswahili expression that means "Climb the hill" when he hired out to the company and worked for long years at Panda mines in Likasi. For a person who worked deep underground, the name was an accurate description of personal experience of work that consisted of descending into the ground in the morning and ascending in the evening. After years of hard work, *Panda Kilima* retired from the company and returned to his village, where he became a member of the chiefdom council. This new work earned him the name of rank *Tshikala,* which he proudly described as the highest social and political achievement of his life.[27]

Briefly, this overview of naming conventions in precolonial Congo shows that naming not only ended the namelessness of children but also worked as a mnemonic device and archive of history and the collective memories of families and groups. The naming of children and strangers allowed families and groups to record events and facts that were transmitted from one generation to another. Different naming conventions show that Congolese accumulated, changed, and dropped names at different moments of their life cycles. Although namelessness was only temporary, the overview suggests that names were not always shown to the outside world and that not all the meanings of names referred directly to personal situations of the bearers of names. Even when the meanings of names did not show referents explicitly, they still linked names to events, circumstances, and conditions of daily existence when considered in the broader social and political contexts. As Congolese peoples encountered Europeans in the nineteenth century, they adapted the preexisting naming conventions to the new contexts and situations to identify individual Europeans and groups of Europeans. Chapter 2 analyzes the contexts of the naming of Europeans.

2

Colonialism and the Village World

Contexts to Naming

The integration of the Congolese village world into the economies of the Congo Free State and Belgian Congo through rubber collection, compulsory cash crop cultivation, and supply of labor was repressive and exploitative, even if one takes the view that a few Congolese villagers benefited from the early ivory boom.[1] The local administrations squeezed cash out of the households through taxes and fines, and appropriated corvée labor for colonial public projects chiefly to construct roads of supposedly economic interest to the villagers. At the outset and under the pressure of private companies and the colonial state, villagers gathered wild products for which they received lower prices. Thousands took jobs for which the private companies paid them low wages.[2] The expansion of the cash crop economy, which the colonial state started to promote in 1917, depended on the building of a network of roads and railroads. But the construction of this infrastructure preyed on the labor of villagers and sharpened colonial assaults on the village world. Backed by native courts and prisons, cash crop cultivation, road construction, and labor recruitments for the colonial state and the private companies deeply affected and defined life in the village world.[3]

Colonizing the village world had, however, its antecedents—long-distance trade, explorations, colonial conquests, and political domination in the northern and eastern parts of the Congo. From 1870 to 1892, Congolese peoples in Uele, the Kingdom of Kazembe in southern Katanga, the inner Congo Basin, and Kasai encountered Europeans. In the north, "explorations," long-distance trade, and the Anglo-Egyptian political control extended into Uele, where different peoples traded ivory and slaves for copper coins called *mitako* with the *Jallaba,* traders who operated small firms called *Zeriba* in Uele and owned large commercial firms in Khartoum, the Sudan.[4] Even if one takes the view that trade was beneficial because it brought a few luxury items to local aristocracies, these interactions disrupted local ways of life more than they contributed to local societies. First, to prevent looting among rival bands, traders were organized into large parties of 250 to 3,000 members.[5] The size of caravans was enormous and subjected local groups to supplying large amounts of grains and labor for porterage. Demands for foodstuffs depleted food resources, infuriated local peoples, and caused conflicts, which sometimes escalated into wars. Second, traders interfered in local politics by supporting one ruler against another and raised political instability. Third, the Anglo-Egyptian administration that in the 1880s extended its sphere of influence and some political control over Uele, where it levied taxes in ivory and labor for porterage, further contributed to destabilizing local societies.[6]

As the Azande and Mangbetu in the north, the Lunda and other peoples of the Kingdom of Kazembe in southern Katanga encountered the Portuguese in the nineteenth century and exchanged ivory and copper for salt and guns. Portuguese explorations and unfair trade with the kingdom generated violence, which ended after the abolition of the slave trade.

Radical changes in the everyday life of the villagers were brought by the economic schemes of the "Congo Free State," whose mainstay was the collection of wild products. From the 1890s to 1912, the builders of the Congo Free State and concessionary companies compelled Congolese villagers to collect ivory, rubber, copal, palm oil and kernels, and hides. Although production quotas varied from district to district depending on the zeal of local agents, the organization of production was the same and represented the epitome of exploitation and violence. Householders in the Lulonga district, for example, gathered annually an unspecified amount of rubber and 180 kilograms of copal and kernels, products that required different labor inputs and time to harvest. To gather rubber, Congolese men spent weeks in the bush. They carried out the work at a time when they were most stressed and lived on wild roots and vegetables, a way of eking out a living that had previously supplemented subsistence farming. As a result, rubber companies exported tons of rubber, ivory, palm products, and hides while leaving behind emptied villages, particularly in the inner Congo Basin where heavy population losses occurred that disrupted and sometimes destroyed the village communities.[7]

Congolese villagers collecting rubber, Lusambo 1897 (AP.0.0.303, collection MRAC
Tervuren; photo F. L. Michel, 1897)

The collection of copal was as difficult as the gathering of rubber, although most studies have focused on rubber and the atrocities it engendered. A resin used in the manufacture of varnish, copal was found fossilized and buried deep underwater in marshes and riverbeds.[8] The collection of copal was similar to the gathering of rubber and started with the prospecting of fossilized blocs of copal buried deep in the ground or underwater. The first step of the work was done by men who used spears or wooden digging sticks searching to hit on the deposits of the resin. Once men discovered the fossils, they then called on women and children to dig, harvest, and carry the collected product home in dug-out canoes. The work carried out in the riverbeds and sludge was hazardous because men, women, and older children worked for over twelve hours a day, often with their bodies submerged in water to the waist. Where copal was buried in firm ground, the work consisted of digging, cleaning, and packing the resin in bags, and transporting loads first to the villages and then to the trading posts, which most villagers reached after walking three days.[9]

The consequences of the collection of rubber and copal on the village world were disastrous. First, the collection withdrew the labor of Congolese villagers from farming, gathering and hunting, and fishing while exposing the collectors to bad health risks. Many witnesses observed that the collection of wild products not only interfered with food production but also "was done under conditions harmful to population growth."[10] Second, rubber collection destroyed the workers. To escape rubber atrocities and harsh conditions created by the collection of rubber and copal, some villagers fled into the bush while others refused to collect the full amounts. In either case, the retributions were extreme. In the main theater of rubber collection, sentries lashed and killed villagers who failed to bring their specified quotas of rubber; some angry rubber agents burned down villages and destroyed standing crops and herds of goats to starve rebellious villages. Those villagers who fled into the bush faced hunger, and many died of starvation. Villagers endured the reign of terror by companies and colonial government soldiers for twenty-three years, as this practice caused atrocities of epical proportions that transformed rubber collection into the epitome of colonial terror. These stories intersect with the meanings of collective and individual names that rubber collectors gave the Congo Free State, the agents of concessionary companies, and the Congo Free State officials who ruled Upper Congo, Equator, and Lake Leopold II Districts from the 1890s to the 1930s. Thus, the organization of labor required for the collection of the products, combined with the meager reward and ruthless punishments, made the collection of rubber an exceptionally horrific story of colonial exploitation and repression.

The mandatory collection of wild products was the most spectacular economic exploitation of the Congo with extremely negative effects on the lives of Congolese villagers, but there had been others also devastating. The mandatory cash crop cultivation is a case in point. Although the Congo Free State had forced villagers to clear palm groves of up to 1.235 acres for each household in the Lower Congo since 1889, the colonial program of agricultural production started with the mandatory cash crop cultivation in 1917. To be sure, the compulsory cash crop production was the second project and sector of the economy that transformed life in the village world and that, compared with other sectors of the colonial economy, compelled the largest segment of an estimated population of six million to produce cotton, rice, corn, peanuts, coffee, tea, cassava, palm oil, beans, sweet potatoes, potatoes, *urena lobata,* and hevea rubber.[11]

Cultivating cash crops forcefully and intensively brought colonial rule and economic exploitation into daily life and removed control of the economic destiny from the Congolese villagers. Besides changing organizations of production and divisions of labor and creating intra-community inequality and intra-household differentiations, the cultivation of cash crops created and reproduced poverty in all parts of the Congo even though there were regional income variations of up to 70 percent in some years because of differences in soil productivity, bad weather, plant diseases, and local competition and economic opportunities.[12]

Until the Second World War, most villagers hardly benefited from cash crop production. Instead, they experienced ruthless brutality, the shrinking of local political autonomy, and impoverishment. The political domination and economic exploitation of the Congolese villagers were characteristically violent, making Belgian colonial rule and violence almost synonymous.[13] Despite waves of colonial campaigns of *mission civilisatrice,* Congolese villagers understood the conditions of exploitation and domination and at times rejected them openly by rebelling and resisting.[14] What compounded the precarious economic situation of the villagers even further was the colonial policy of phasing out indigenous crops that competed with mandatory cash crops for labor. Catholic missionaries still reported until the 1950s that the policy of eliminating sorghum in the northern part of the Congo, for example, severely affected the quality of infant nutrition.[15]

Besides growing cash crops, Congolese villagers participated in constructing roads and transporting colonial officials on hammocks and goods on their backs and heads until the 1930s and the 1940s, except in the Lower Congo where roads freed them of porterage sooner.[16] Constructing roads created an infrastructure that Congolese cash crop producers should have welcomed because the roads allowed trucks to cut down on porterage. Yet the roads generated resentment and anger.

Why the colonial road came to symbolize colonial oppression and exploitation is easy to tell. Work on the roads led to high mortality rates among road workers, village relocation, and loss of land rights and usufruct. Once they were built, the roads transformed villagers into easy prey to tax collection and labor recruitments and other colonial demands. Besides the violence deployed to extract corvée labor, the building of roads shifted the costs to rural households. Nowhere else was this truer than in the cotton-producing areas. The choice of cotton-producing areas is relevant for two reasons. First, although crops such as palm oil, peanuts, corn, and rice were important in some districts, cotton was the premier crop. Based on the number of households, cotton affected the village world more than any other crop. Households involved rose from 15,000 in just one year after its imposition to 105,556 in 1930. Ten years later some 700,000 households were cultivating cotton, and in 1959 as many as 874,000 households sold as much as 177,000 tons of seed cotton to twelve cotton companies.[17] Second, starting in 1936, an ordinance authorized the administration and cotton companies to withhold cash from cotton cultivators' pay to construct, maintain, and repair *routes cotonnières,* or "cotton roads."[18] The policy enabled cotton companies and the local administrations to divert huge amounts of money from Congolese households and place the sums year after year into the *Fonds de réserve cotonnier* and the *Caisse de réserve cotonnière.*[19]

The amounts of money withheld and the size of corvée labor expropriated resulted in an impressive number of kilometers of roads. While in 1921, 900 kilometers of *routes cotonnières* existed, this number increased to 13,000 kilometers of roads in 1936, in addition to 850 kilometers of railroad track.[20] The following year the administration and cotton companies made available 1.7 million francs to maintain 4,979 kilometers of roads and to build a road 1,098 kilometers long. In 1938, 2.27 million francs funded the construction of additional 6,077 kilometers of roads, and cotton funded a network of 15,000 kilometers of roads in 1940. Between 1940 and 1948, the *Caisse de réserve cotonnière* provided 164 million francs to maintain existing cotton roads and construct new ones.

From 1949 to 1955, the same *Caisse cotonnière* shouldered the 165-million-franc expense of road maintenance, contributed 20 million francs to the colonial state for the construction of new roads, and inaugurated a five-year program to replace old bridges and wooden ferries with metal ones and construct new roads for 211 million francs. In addition, the *Caisse* purchased tractors, graders and tippers for 30 million francs, and placed the equipment at the disposal of local colonial authorities to maintain cotton roads. The overall contribution of the *Caisse* to the construction of roads amounted to approximately 616 million francs.[21] The roads reduced porterage in cotton-growing villages located along the roads. But the producers who resided away from the roads and marketplaces were still subjected to porterage; and producers knew that the monies spent on roads came from their labors, making the expression *routes cotonnières* a metaphor for exploitation.

Outside cotton-growing areas, the colonial administration also subsidized roads through corvée labor. Congolese villagers continued to bear these costs well after 1933 as they were still required to maintain and construct roads the administration tagged *routes d'intérêt local,* the roads of local interest. The heaviest burden of the construction and maintenance of local roads fell on underpaid road workers and villagers, and the latter regularly worked on these roads without pay because the system allowed territorial administrators to classify most roads in the category funded by villagers, and because the colonial government did not adequately fund local roads. In 1927, a road worker in Kasai District toiled one kilometer of road to earn thirteen francs. The pay was below the annual income of peasant households in the local economy and worth a kilogram of ginned cotton on the world market.[22] And yet the unrewarding work exposed Congolese people to exhaustion, diseases, and death. The construction of a road in Lubefu in the Sankuru District shows the kinds of risks road workers faced. Out of 6,381 workers recruited in 1926, as many as 210 died in three months because of harsh conditions of work, malnutrition, and diseases, situations of hardship that contributed to the rumor that "the white men's work was eating peoples."[23] Constructing roads assaulted the village world as much as producing commodities did. It went hand in hand with the compulsory village relocations that compelled villagers to build new homes and to travel long distances to find farmland, fish, and game, and many in the end lost the ancestral land, the most valuable asset of the village communities. Congolese villagers along the road became easy prey at the hands of policemen, labor recruiters, and tax collectors.[24]

Withholding household income, appropriating labor for the construction and maintenance of roads, and compulsorily relocating villages along roads infuriated rural dwellers, watered down the potential benefits of colonial roads, and transformed the colonial road into a symbol of colonialism and a target of resistance. Colonial annals are replete with many public expressions of protests and resistance against road construction and village relocation along roads. A striking example occurred among the Lele of Kasai in 1933. After they had first agreed to settle in the new villages along a new road, the Lele later resettled in the old villages once the official left the resettlement. In explaining the Lele's refusal, the official, like most of his counterparts, overlooked the disruptions of the village world caused by the village relocation and concluded that the abandonment of the new villages was motivated by "Lele's love for raffia palms, valleys, and graveyards of the ancestors."[25]

The bond of affection with familiar environments and shrines fuelled the opposition of rural dwellers to the relocation of their villages. But it was heavy colonial demands, unpopular policies, and the incursions of colonial roads on the village world, more than the affection they had for the ancestral surroundings, that caused the Lele to leave the new settlements. The meanings of names that Congolese derived from their experiences of work on the colonial roads showed the effects of colonialism on local response. The different meanings of the colonial roads painted a complex imagery of domination, oppression, and exploitation that individuals and groups experienced when they worked on building the roads and when they transported colonial officials on hammocks before and after the roads were built.

The construction of roads made colonialism abusive, created misgivings about promises of economic progress, swelled the hearts of Congolese villagers with anger, and stimulated resistance. To maintain colonialism, the entire prison system and whips became the cornerstone of the mandatory cash crop cultivation and the construction of roads. These instruments and institutions of repression supported the local administration, native courts, and labor recruitment.[26]

The beating of individual villagers was an alternative to punitive expeditions, punishments that occurred when large numbers of male villagers fled the village to avoid the mandatory cultivation of cash crops, the payment of taxes, and the hiring out of labor to private companies. Although beatings inflicted pain on the body, the outcomes of military operations were killings, indiscriminate arrests and imprisonments, which Congolese regarded as the extreme forms of injustice, the disruption of families, and destruction of the village world.[27]

Besides enduring beatings and punitive expeditions, Congolese villagers who failed to comply with colonial policies were sent to prison. Despite variations in repression, the conditions inside all types of prisons were grim. Prisoners were not only overworked, a condition of oppression they endured regularly as peasants and workers, but they also were underfed and beaten. Overwork, flogging, and undernourishment were important themes that frequently emerged out of stories of daily life in prisons. And prisoners were forced to defecate and urinate inside the prison houses when they talked to each other at nighttime, sneaked lovers inside prison cells, and insulted prison overseers. A magistrate inspecting prisons in Niangara in 1949 observed, "Prisoners were whipped for sneaking women, making nightly noise and defecating inside prison cells."[28] Defecating inside prison became both a punishment and a reason to be whipped. Mugaza wa Beya, a Mambwe man who spent three months in the Kalemie Central Prison in the Tanganyika District of the Katanga Province in the late 1950s, recalled in 1986 that the prison inside resembled a "barrel of shits."[29] Rare prison fires, which ended with the painful and slow deaths of chained prisoners unable to escape the prison house and flee, and the high mortality rates in prisons made a prison sentence a potential death sentence.

As in the construction of roads, the building of railways required constant supplies of labor from adjacent communities and beyond. To be sure, the demands for labor went far beyond the railways and disrupted the village world. The Matadi–Kinshasa and Ilebo–Bukama railways are cases in point as they disrupted the village world and epitomized the ruthlessness of the colonial state. Like any project undertaken under the Congo Free State rule, the recruitment of labor for the construction of the Matadi–Kinshasa railway was extremely violent, led to the mistreatment and death of laborers, and spread the horrific reputation of the colonial state to every corner of the Congo. According to most colonial government statistics, some 1,800 African and Asian workers lost their lives to the project.[30] As with any government statistics, this figure should be accepted with caution and might be well below the actual number of people killed. First, to prevent claims of compensation by families of victims, the company administration mishandled the counts of dead workers. Second, workers who survived accidents and malnutrition in the workplace but died shortly after their return to their villages were not counted. Third, Protestant missionaries recorded a high mortality rate for African workers. Because most Protestant missionaries were not subjects of King Leopold II, they were candid eyewitnesses to the abuses of his enterprise in the Congo and provided more horrific testimonies of demographic repercussions of the railroad construction than could government sources. Although testimonies of these missionaries sometimes exaggerated the impact of the railroad on demography, their descriptions of the colonial state as people's "torturer" were not far-fetched or entirely divorced from the contemporary conditions. In 1929, a German Protestant missionary portrayed grimly the methods of construction and the plight of workers: "The methods of railroad construction in the Belgian Congo are truly medieval. Indeed, between 15 and 20 percent of people recruited die during the trip. Work-related mortality reaches 37 percent a year. On the way home at the end of their contract, an untold number of Blacks also die because of exhaustion and deprivation during the trip. By fear of this forced labor, peoples often flee their villages. An overseer calculated that each kilometer of railroad took about 1,200 lives."[31]

Besides the collection of wild products and peasant agriculture, mining was the sector of the colonial economy whose negative effects were felt from the outset of colonial rule across the village world. Starting in 1905 and 1907, public and private capital created the three major mining companies in the northeast, southwest, and south of the Congo.[32] At first a part of the rural world, the mines quickly created huge demands for labor and foodstuffs. Although in theory creating economic opportunities and a temporary escape from colonial demands and exactions, mines reinforced colonial constraints and dislocations of the village world.

I am using as a paradigm the northeastern mines where the mining of gold started at Moto and Kilo in 1905 and 1911, respectively, to illustrate how the mining industry affected the village world. From the outset, this state-owned company faced a labor shortage that it overcame with brutal methods of recruitment. One of the first methods of labor recruitment the colonial administration employed in the early years to supply workers to the Moto and Kilo mines was the forced labor of prisoners as workers and Congolese policemen as recruiters. The unpopular second method consisted of compulsory relocation of villages closer to the mines and the burning of villages and outright killings of Congolese villagers who openly refused to hire out to the mines.[33] As with most colonial projects, the colonial administration depended on local leaders for the recruitments of workers. To strengthen the power of these leaders in recruiting workers, the colonial administration provided them with guns—*albini*, a policy that encouraged violence as much as did the recruitment of policemen as recruiters. The implementation of this policy varied from one chief to another, as did its repercussions on the communities. Chief Goli represented an extreme case in the misuse of the new militaristic power given to local leaders. Indeed, the participation of Chief Goli in the recruitments of workers for the mining company in 1915 led to a confrontation that resulted in the massacre of "150 people of whom women formed a third . . . and whose necks were sawn off by knives to preserve ammunitions, when the heads of small babies were smashed against the ground and turned into pieces."[34] This incident illustrates one of the scenes of extreme violence brought to the village world by the demands for mine labor. It was the epitome of violence caused by recruitments that enabled, along with similar other conditions, the mining company to expand its workforce, which increased from 500 workers in 1905 to 3,357 in 1915 to reach 14,520 workers in 1924 and the peak of 18,897 in 1947.[35] The expansion of the company workforce deprived local communities of strong members who became porters, seasonal migrants, and workers. Such ruthless methods of labor recruitment compelled Congolese villagers to make long and exhausting journeys to the mines, where they faced shortages of food, harsh working conditions, and atrocious punishments.

The life stories of recruits who took jobs as porters, seasonal migrants, and regular workers show the conditions of recruitment, work, and daily life, and these stories dominated village life and shaped local perceptions of the mining industry, colonial capitalism, and colonialism. It is easy to portray the plight of Congolese who were forced to join the mining workforce. Until the mid-1920s, recruits were forced into the workforce; they freely took a job for wages only on exception. Before trucks were used in the 1930s in Orientale Province, recruits were divided into teams of 40 members and walked between 2.5 and 250 kilometers before they reached the workplace. At their departure, the recruits received a small food allowance and a daily small amount of salt, a meager cash incentive, and a food ration that fell short of covering their needs during the journey. What made the journey hard was the lack of food and the fact that recruits usually carried a load of fifty kilograms on their head or back. Complicating their access to food and good nutrition during their journey to the work site was the refusal of villagers along the roads to sell their foodstuffs, as they feared that huge sales could deplete household food reserves. Therefore, the recruits depended mainly on the daily rations they received from the recruiters, which consisted of dried plantains, sweet potatoes, and a spoonful of salt. This ration was too poor a diet and as a result caused malnutrition and death.[36]

During their journey, the recruits walked long distances during the day and slept during the night in awful dwellings and most often in the open air without blankets. Some succumbed to exhaustion and died because of the lack of food and protection against the chilly weather in the high altitude of the Ituri District. Dead recruits did not leave behind testimonies of their experience of exploitation and oppression, which could have provided us with their perspective on the situations they endured. But their oppressors who witnessed horrible scenes of death along roadsides or learned about them did leave testimonies, and detailed conditions of death are found in many inspection reports. A traveling prosecutor observed the Medje porters, and according to his account of November 1924, he saw "at least five new graves" alongside a 120-kilometer road between Mongbalu and Moto. The prosecutor attributed the five deaths to hunger and diseases the recruits contracted during the journey to the mines when they slept in appalling dwellings or in the open. A company physician supports the story of the prosecutor in his medical report, stating, "Physical exhaustion and malnutrition were the main causes of these deaths, and those of other recruits and porters he had examined at the company's hospital in Mongbalu."[37]

The recruits' experiences did not change drastically when their job status changed and they became migrants with short contracts of two or three months. To the contrary, their plight worsened, as they stayed longer in the camp where standards of living matched harsh conditions of work. An important disadvantage was the lack of access to adequate food. The migrants were not entitled to rations from the company and depended instead on their wives. As husbands left the village for the mines, wives now carried out husbands' domestic chores besides their own. Overworked, the wives could supply food only irregularly, and sometimes they could not at all. Because the mines were located far away from villages, even kinship networks and ethnic webs could not help recruits to secure food. These factors sharpened the vulnerability of migrants to undernourishment and bad health.

The inefficiency of porterage to supply the needed foodstuffs to the mines meant that although regular workers were entitled to food rations and supposedly were better off than seasonal workers, they also suffered food shortages and undernourishment. In 1911, for instance, 2.5 percent of the company's 200 new workers at Moto died of starvation. One can imagine the situation to be worse for seasonal mineworkers whose wives and children could supply only two-thirds of their food in 1913. The food situation remained precarious in 1917. Colonial officials reported then, "foodstuffs are rare in the mines . . . workers cannot meet their nutritional needs even with the money they received for food rations."[38] The shortage of food and the malnutrition of workers were magnified by the insensitivity of the mine managers to differences in the eating habits of a culturally and ethnically diverse workforce. So the one-fits-all diet was adopted by the mine managers were conducive to hunger even when food became plentiful in the 1950s.

One cannot explain the food scarcity in the mines in 1917 by the "war effort" for the First World War alone, because the shortage of food continued after that. In reality, porterage by men, women, and children was not a reliable means to transport the food needed for a large workforce. In 1920, Ituri District officials estimated that feeding 5,000 mineworkers and their families required 160,000 porters, who would be mostly women coerced to leave their villages for more than ten days at a time. The 98,700 porters who supplied foodstuffs to the mines were far fewer than the number of workers needed for the job. These few carriers could not meet the food needs of regular workers, who were consuming about 4,000 tons of food annually.[39]

Faced with food shortages and the ruthless brutality of labor supervisors, workers routinely ran away from the labor camps. "Desertions" triggered more violence and complicated the workers' access to food and quality of nutrition. Colonial archives and oral testimonies are replete with stories of violence against fugitive workers. An untold number of fugitive workers shared the experience of Mbianga, who, caught and beaten up by overseers, was taken to the company's hospital in Mongbalu but died two days later. Out of 300 workers who ran away in 1924, as many as 50 were captured and returned to the mine camps where they faced angry and vengeful supervisors who denied them wages and rations.[40] As the administration authorized extreme violence to discourage disobedience and overseers withheld wages and rations, hunger and malnutrition became parts of daily life for recaptured workers. Many of the 112 workers incapacitated by malnutrition out of 190 workers the company laid off in 1925 were crippled because of the policy of holding wages and rations and because overseers forced them to "work harder, constantly accusing them of bad will and laziness."[41]

Rooted in the company's need to tighten control over disgruntled workers and encouraged by inducements given to overseers, the practice of denying workers wages and rations caused violence, malnutrition, and poor health that became common occurrences. It also caused many migrants and regular mineworkers to select bad future employers. The practice often forced fugitive migrants to work as porters, an option that was as harmful to health as work in the mines.[42] In brief, porters, migrants, and regular workers hardly enjoy good health in the mines because of shortage of food supplies and because of inadequate medical care. The company's main hospital, for instance, had only 80 beds for 6,378 workers. As stated earlier, the incentives given to labor supervisors and the lack of infrastructure partly explain the mortality rate of 12 percent in the mid-1920s among migrants in the mines.[43]

In sum, the journeys to the mines tell stories of hunger, disease, exhaustion, food shortages, beatings, and deaths. These stories, just like people who produced them, traveled back and forth between the village world and the mining camps. As told in the villages, they hardly extolled economic gains and thus negatively shaped the understanding of mining and colonialism.

Early forms of colonial economies changed profoundly the village life, but so did the colonial legal system that regulated the colonial social order in the village world because it attacked traditions and threatened the mechanisms of social and cultural reproduction. Carried out through local legal systems since 1886 and formally organized in 1926 when the colonial government created the native courts, the colonial justice system was intended to regulate conflicts among Congolese villagers and to set up colonial social order.[44] Although native courts settled intra-community and intra-household conflicts and disputes, they became key colonial institutions of domination and repression at the hands of colonial officials and, to a lesser degree, Catholic missionaries. The tax collector resorted to native courts to mobilize financial resources; the census taker and health officer relied on them to establish population figures and find out the health status of the population in *chefferies*, important elements for allocating labor to different capitalist groups; chiefs and agricultural monitors used the institutions to carry out their tasks and rid themselves of subjects who challenged their authority. The institutions helped missionaries as much as colonial government officials and Congolese auxiliaries. To be sure, they assisted missionaries in their campaigns against polygyny, "superstition," and all cultural practices they deemed repulsive. An analysis of transcripts of native courts in cotton-producing *chefferies* of the Lower and Upper Uele shows that 80 percent of cases brought to the courts between 1932 and 1958 dealt with colonial demands rather than with intra-community conflicts. The most virulent of critiques against native courts was Grevisse's *La grande pitié des juridictions indigènes*. Published a little over two decades after the creation of native courts, it pointed out massive failures echoed by many prosecutors in various reports.[45] The indictment of native courts that follows is a vivid illustration and case in point: "Our judicial apparatus is . . . unsuitable for the country, incapable to ensure the respect of the law and fight crimes. It is destructive to the native it intends to protect."[46]

The transcripts of native courts in the Lower and Upper Uele Districts show that many reasons motivated state-appointed chiefs and agricultural monitors to use the native courts in punishing Congolese villagers. They included disobedience toward a colonial officeholder, refusal to plant crops in straight lines and to care for them, the unauthorized hiring out of villagers to private companies, "laziness," the smoking of hemp, "vagrancies," and attempts to escape from prisons.[47] The data show that regardless of their status and rank in the colonial administrative structure, chiefs, headmen, agricultural monitors, policemen, and ex-soldiers were treated in the native courts as harshly as ordinary villagers were, although the colonial administration depended on these auxiliaries to carry out its economic and political programs. Congolese interpreted these prosecutions, which gave a predominantly repressive character to native courts, as the direct assaults of colonialism on the village world.

State-appointed chiefs, like other Congolese subaltern agents, were both abusers and victims of native courts. Inspection reports of different territories detailed the ruthlessness of native courts at the hands of local leaders. Chief Bongo, who ruled over the Mango-Medje, rendered in 1938 a sentence the prosecutor described as "iniquitous," while others reported that the verdicts of native courts were "excessive," "brutal," and "demoralizing."[48] The headman Duangapa sentenced Aboyo in 1952 to fifteen days in prison and fined him 50 francs for refusal to obey him. As the inspector commented in the report, the refusal to obey was actually a pretext because the headman had designated Aboyo to load cotton into a truck, a job the company workers could have carried out.[49] Chiefs also targeted ex-soldiers who thought of themselves as civilized and threatened their authority and prestige. The tensions between the two groups had their roots in the politics of appointment of Congolese auxiliaries. In fact, throughout colonization, the colonial administration often appointed ex-soldiers to the position of *Chef de secteur* in time of crisis of succession, arguing that they were disciplined and westernized, and it was remarkable that many who were appointed carried out their job to the liking of the colonial administration. Nevertheless, the ruthlessness of native courts rarely spared ex-soldiers. The sentence of seven days in prison and a fine of 300 francs received by an ex-soldier in the 1950s at Nguru court because he failed to make his cotton field into a clean garden is an excellent illustration. The fine was heavy since it represented half the annual income of most households in the area.[50] In a village world with limited economic outlets outside compulsory peasant production, seeking a job outside the village world was an economic opportunity and an escape from chiefs' abuse of power, and many villagers sought and took service under private companies for these reasons. Since most of these jobs were unauthorized, initiatives to seek jobs outside the village world resulted often in imprisonment and heavy fines. Chiefs' harsh sentencing of villagers was motivated by generous production premiums and incentives they received from the state and private companies for their work as front men in agricultural campaigns and labor recruiters. For these reasons, Chief Ukwa, who ruled over the Bokoyo chiefdom, sentenced a villager to seven days in prison and a fine of 50 francs for failure to prepare the field of cotton.[51]

Besides chiefs, agricultural monitors came down on cash crop growers by using native courts. As shown by innumerable cases, the explanation of their ruthlessness resided in the inducements, the lure of salary increases, and the desire to expand their authority and power. In 1938, for example, a court in Ango sentenced a cotton grower to fifteen days in prison and fined him 25 francs for slapping a cotton monitor.[52] Colonial officials harshly punished public attacks of Congolese subalterns because such acts undermined the colonial authority. As late as 1958, the court sentenced Masanga to fifteen days in prison and ordered him to pay a fine of 30 francs for verbal threats against an agricultural monitor who wanted to delineate his paddy field. Two weeks in jail was too harsh a punishment for a man too old to do the work, and it seemed to have been designed to frighten the villagers and keep them working despite the rising nationalism of the 1950s.[53]

The sentences made by native courts for cases brought by chiefs and monitors appeared excessive because they all punished the accused twice. They simultaneously inflicted physical pain and impoverished the householders financially. In a case in which an agricultural monitor sued a villager for refusing to cultivate cash crops in the 1930s, the court sentenced the accused to fifteen days in prison and ordered him to pay a fine of 100 francs, money that represented over 30 percent of annual income of most households in the area. A similar case brought to the court for insult to a European territorial agent in the mid-1940s resulted in the sentence of fifteen days in prison, six lashes, and a fine of 100 francs. One can multiply illustrations of these punishments endlessly. The few cases analyzed here show the extent to which colonial officials and Congolese chiefs and monitors transformed the native courts into instruments of repression for colonial economic purposes.[54] Most examples show that the harshness of punishments depended not on the merit of the cases brought to the courts but the rank and race of the colonial official.

Besides repression, native courts represented the best colonial avenue for negotiations where the debates helped colonial officials to figure out the attitudes and intentions of Congolese villagers toward colonial policies. Congolese villagers did not express all the views of colonialism at the chiefs' councils and native courts, however. During the entire colonial period, native courts competed with local systems of conflict resolution for primacy, and this duality of institutions prevented the colonial administration from monitoring all the information inside the local communities. Conflicts over theft, larceny, bridewealth, and domestic abuses were brought to native courts while families, kinship groups, and closed associations settled the same kinds of conflicts to maintain or restore social harmony. Because of the role of closed associations as alternative and independent courts, and because of the secrecy in the ways these institutions settled community and household conflicts, some key information about the communities and the households escaped local administrations. Although these situations gave the leaders of these institutions some bargaining power in dealing with the colonial administration, deficiencies in the control of information worried colonial state officials and private employers and forced negotiations because the household was the most important unit of production of the mandatory cash crops and the reproduction of the labor force. Whatever the role of the native courts as avenues for negotiations, they were nonetheless repressive, and the accusations by Congolese against them were strong.[55]

Historians of colonial Congo have conventionally represented Belgian colonialism as an edifice held up by three major pillars: the colonial state, private companies, and the Catholic Church. Catholic missionaries carried among Congolese villagers many projects that were as diverse as their personal attitudes. On the positive side, Catholic missionaries from the beginning founded schools and dispensaries to provide education and health care to the villagers. A concordat between the Vatican and the Congo Free State in 1906 granted Catholic missions the right to build schools in exchange for land. The program had roots in the 1876 Brussels Conference, one objective of which was the supposed introduction of civilization into Central Africa. This came as soon as 1886 when religious orders flooded over the colony and created schools that became the vehicles of cultural change. Catholic missionaries' projects then became more disruptive as schools seeded doubts in the minds of Congolese villagers about themselves and their culture. From the mission stations, the discourse of Catholic missionaries penetrated the village communities, influenced sexual behaviors, and transformed the space and the culture of local people.[56] It was at the mission station dispensaries that most Congolese for the first time received *kinini*, a loanword from the French word *quinine*, to treat malaria, castor oil to get rid of worms, and mercurochrome to heal their wounds.[57] Where Catholic missionaries did not own any clinics, they ran and worked in those owned by private companies and the colonial state.[58] Catholic missionaries' involvement in education and healthcare shaped local receptions and interpretations of their discourse on important aspects of everyday life such as traditions, gender, sexuality, and biological reproduction.

Individually and collectively, Catholic missionaries denounced in their ecclesiastical regions the atrocities of rubber collection by bringing to light the wars waged against villagers, the unsanitary conditions in which Congolese villagers collected the wild products, and the ruthlessness of rubber agents. Congolese villagers appreciated these actions that contributed to regenerating Congolese population. After the collapse of rubber by 1912, Catholic missionaries still denounced the abusive and ruthless methods of recruitment of workers pursued by the colonial administration and private companies. Catholic missionaries were unyielding critics of the mandatory cash crop cultivation, particularly where it caused nutritional deficiencies. Catholic missionaries employed their membership in advisory institutions such as the Commission for the Protection of the Natives to influence colonial decisions in a wide range of areas that affected the everyday life in the village world.[59] From the outset, Catholic missionaries offered a safe heaven to women whose behavior challenged existing social norms. This group of women consisted of widows who, because of the widespread practice of levirate, could end up in polygamous unions and female adolescents who had objected to arranged marriages and had run away from the authority of family and lineage.[60]

On the negative side, Catholic missionaries were fierce adversaries of Congolese cultural practices, values, and institutions they deemed repulsive. Catholic missionaries campaigned for abolishing bridewealth, polygyny, methods of breast feeding and long intervals between births, public expressions of indigenous religions, traditions, gender ideologies, and any institutions that shaped sexual behaviors and practices and social and biological reproduction they deemed obscene, repulsive, or immoral.[61] They moreover targeted postpartum sexual abstinence, methods of abortion, and gendered divisions of labor in colonial agriculture. These campaigns undermined and disrupted the dynamics of local cultures more than they allowed their reproduction, and they alienated men and women of the village world, particularly the elders who were the keepers of traditions. Catholic missionaries attributed low fertility to polygyny by arguing that polygyny upset sex ratios in the village communities because young women, the most productive segment of marriageable women, married fewer old men.

The empirical evidence supports the claims of missionaries about the negative effects of polygyny on marriage patterns. The money economy in 1912 raised bride price in the 1920s and 1930s, and the rise of bride price hurt unmarried young men. Until the 1930s, many unmarried young men in the inner Congo Basin and Uele could not easily find wives, a situation that forced many to postpone marriage. The Catholic clergymen, who since the 1890s pressured the colonial government to outlaw polygyny, saw their initiatives come to some concrete fruition in 1914 when the colonial government enacted a decree that ordered polygynous men to pay taxes on every new wife they married after the first. However, the victory was partial because taxes on new wives were not set high enough to discourage men from marrying more wives. The failure of the legislation to decrease polygyny had other causes deep in the colonial economy. The legislation started reducing polygyny after the government created in 1926 native courts that Catholic missionaries used to fight polygyny, which diminished in some areas in the 1950s.[62]

Although Catholic missionaries pressured the government to enact anti-polygyny legislation, they were convinced that a permanent solution for producing high birthrates lay in changing local ideologies that underlay biological reproduction. This conviction meant changing local traditions and gender ideologies, and the ways they went about changing traditions relating to reproduction varied enormously. While many Catholic missionaries awaited the colonial government interventions to outlaw the practice of polygyny, others relied on persuasion and used skillful conversations to "awaken women's conscience of moral value and self-respect."[63]

One practice that Catholic missionaries attacked and hoped to wipe out by using persuasive conversations was postpartum sexual abstinence. This practice allowed women to breastfeed babies for at least two years and antedated, like abortive practices, Belgian colonization. Catholic missionaries attacked long spaces between births because they believed that such spaces were the cause of polygyny and the root of low fertility. In seeking to abolish abortive practices and traditions regulating births, Catholic missionaries sought to shorten birth intervals and raise fertility. A part of a discourse of modernity, Catholic missionaries' campaigns weakened these traditions and practices. But the discourse of Catholic missionaries was hardly authoritative because it alienated at any given time at least some segments of the village world, and therefore their efforts were not entirely successful. First, the pace and radicalism of changes caused local resistance. Second, the integration of households into the mandatory cash crops production and the dynamics of regional colonial economy countered missionaries' campaigns and actions. The mandatory cash crop production encouraged production-oriented polygyny and inter-household differences in three ways. Without colonial investments in agricultural technology that would cut the need for family labor, polygyny proved useful to the peasant economy because it allowed polygynous men to expand the pool of household labor. Mobilizing labor for production increases generated more household income, enticed men to the practice of polygyny, and forced the colonial state to tolerate the institution. Until the stabilization of labor in the mid-1920s, the expanding mining industry, which required a large workforce, created migrations that resulted in sexual imbalance as men left the village temporarily for work.[64]

I have discussed colonial conditions that defined life in the village world. But although the scale of domination and the appropriation of labor and wealth had been small on the eve of European colonialism, domination and exploitation were not new realities for Central Africans in general and Congolese in particular.[65] The history of the collection of tributes and labor in the kingdoms and empires of precolonial Congo is now well known. In the archaic period of the Kuba kingdom, the *meshoosh* collected tributes and supervised the labor of the Cwa. The collection of tributes and taxes on special goods and services expanded afterward to support a rising network of title holders.[66] The Lunda empire offers another illustration. Here, the *cilool* served as tax collector at the beginning and was later replaced in the nineteenth century by the *kak-wata*, who constantly traveled with a militarized retinue in the dry season once a year to collect tributes.[67] In places where decentralization was the principle of governance, agricultural products and select game accrued to the leaders of dominant houses. The words, proverbs, symbols, and metaphors that captured these exploitative systems became readily available to describe colonialism and assign meanings and significance to the broader messages conveyed by names that Congolese villagers gave colonial officials.[68]

The antecedents to colonialism and colonial practices had a deep impact on the ways Congolese villagers perceived colonialism and named the colonizers. In naming the colonizers, Congolese villagers prompted naming conventions that became a creative mnemonic method of recording colonial situations on the grounds I discuss. Anthroponyms given to colonial officials are thus points of entry into various aspects of history of the Congo under Belgian rule. But to tease the fragmentary evidence out of names to re-create the totality of social life requires the description of naming, the process that produced the names.

3

Naming, Colonialism, Making History, and Social Memories

Discourse on colonialism tended to portray colonial encounters as a one-sided process marked solely by military campaigns directed against groups to colonize.[1] Although bellicosity was the epicenter of the colonial encounters, as this widespread image suggests, Congolese groups and Europeans were constantly engaged in many interactions. Some interactions were started to size up each other's strengths and weaknesses, while other interactions were designed to build reciprocal cognitive views, determined first by earlier understanding of self and others and transformed by the reality of interaction.[2] The stereotyping of Congolese villagers by Europeans and the naming of Europeans by Congolese villagers, though not always concomitant processes, illustrate the dynamics of colonial encounters and interactions.[3] As early as the 1870s Congolese started naming the Portuguese, Italian, and German explorers, the Sudanese traders, and the Anglo-Egyptian officials they encountered. The practice intensified when, from the 1890s to the 1950s, the officials and agents of the Belgian colonial government established the methods, rules, and institutions for dominating the village communities, and agents of trading companies signed commercial deals with leaders of different local polities. As Congolese villagers named Europeans, they followed local customs and naming patterns that articulated and interpreted various situations created by European explorations, trade, conquests, and colonialism.

This chapter contends that the meanings of names given to explorers, missionaries, officials of the Congo Free State, and agents of concessionary companies conveyed substantial information about colonial material conditions, and that the seemingly disparate bits of testimonies woven into the meanings of names, once subjected to the rules of evidence and contextualized, became valuable local commentaries on colonial rule and its impacts on the daily life of village peoples. The chapter therefore explores naming patterns, the meanings of names, the linguistic and sociolinguistic aspects of naming, the significance of naming patterns to decode ideas about names as source of memories and histories of daily life of village peoples, and their understandings of colonialism.

At the beginning, from about the 1890s to 1914, only local leaders, Congolese servants, office watchers, soldiers, and workers at mission stations, trading stations, and military posts observed closely the Europeans and gave them names.[4] The reason only a handful of Congolese close to the Europeans named them was the paucity of Europeans in the villages. The scarcity of Europeans in the village world denied ordinary villagers the details of encounters, leaving those Congolese in colonial posts to do the naming. The r ne *Sukuma*, an imperative in Kiswahili that means "Push!" is a good example. In the 1890s, Congolese guards in Nyangwe gave the name to Captain Losange, who spent about four years there building ten office houses and a cemetery for Europeans, accomplishments that remained unsurpassed until the 1920s. These accomplishments came, however, with a high price tag for the Congolese who experienced the ruthless brutality at the hands of the officer, whose behavior was expressed accurately by the meaning of the Kiswahili verb *Sukuma*. Congolese guards gave him the name because he used the word for all purposes whenever he interacted with them, a practice that earned him a bad reputation. It is documented that "whenever a Black passed by the office where Losange worked without removing his headdress, he yelled out to his guard 'Sukuma ye' [Push him]. And whenever he saw Congolese taking a break during work hours, he shouted, 'Sukuma nyama' [Push the beasts]."[5] The name *Sukuma* recorded local observations of early power relations and the methods used by the heads of posts to deal with Congolese villagers. When broadly contextualized, the name expressed anger and resentment.

Like Congolese guards in Nyangwe, Kiswahili-speaking prisoners at Kasongo Prison named its supervisor Bosoni *Yamba-Yamba*, which means, "Defecate, defecate." The expression *Yamba-Yamba* is reduplication suggestive of the frequency and intensity of actions and behaviors described by the name. Thus, the word-by-word translation of *Yamba-Yamba*, "Defecate, defecate," becomes "Frequent defecator" and defines the situations created by the name-bearer. Bosoni received the name in the 1900s because he built a central prison house, Kasongo Prison, and followed policy of denying prisoners latrines, ordering them to "defecate inside the prison house."[6] Like many colonial practices, ordering prisoners to defecate inside the prison house was an extreme form of oppression that they translated by reduplicating the verb *Yamba*, "to defecate." Reduplication and the story of oppression attribute a wider semantic field to the name and suggest that the name tells obliquely a larger story of prisons. To be sure, Congolese disliked, insulted, and only ostensibly revered supervisors of prisons. The widespread use of *Yamba-Yamba* shows that it was a common reference to colonial officials' lack of control over bodily waste, a familiar mockery of colonial government officials. So *Yamba-Yamba* exemplified a surreptitious discourse about the colonial prison and its supervisors and offered a glimpse into the material conditions inside these "houses of repression" where Congolese endured smells of defecation and urine as daily concerns.[7] The naming of colonial agents and officials of the colonial administration by Congolese working for institutions of repression recorded early forms of oppression, harsh punishments, and indignities, concerns shared by all residents of the village community.

The naming of Europeans by ordinary villagers became common when private companies sent out agents to recruit workers, and European traders set up shops in trading posts. It spread farther as hundreds of thousands of subaltern agents traveled up and down villages to compel Congolese villagers to collect rubber, kernel, and copal, agricultural officers enforced mandatory cultivation of cash crops after 1917, territorial administrators carried out administrative organization, and tax collectors crisscrossed the countryside to gather taxes. As colonialism intruded into the communities, naming patterns diversified and recorded complex colonial relations, the mechanisms of colonial power, and every aspect of everyday life in the village communities.[8] The rising intrusion of colonialism into local communities also enabled Congolese to observe Europeans more closely, to experience the oppression and repression of colonial rule, to find out grim motives of Westerners, and to realize the loss of freedom and power for independent decisions. As a result, the Congolese villagers grew accustomed to the Europeans, their knowledge of colonialism widened, and the naming patterns now closely associated with actual colonial situations with Europeans and colonial policies developed.

From the beginning to the end of colonization, Congolese named Europeans collectively and individually. And when naming individuals and groups of European officials and Catholic missionaries, Congolese villagers distinguished the subaltern agents from the superiors. They gave the former the names *Mwana Mputu*, which means "Child of Europe" in Lingala, and *X Kakese*, which translates as "Little X, Junior X" in Ciluba; they named the last *X Mukulu*, which means "Boss X" in Ciluba, *Bwana X* and *Bwana Mukubwa*, "Mister X" and "Big boss" in Kiswahili, *Mfumu X*, "Chief X," and sometimes *Bula X*, which means "X, breaker of" in Kikongo.[9]

Whether the collective naming of colonial officials and agents was done by local leaders and Congolese with close ties to Europeans or by ordinary villagers who experienced the brutality of colonialism away from the daily surveillance of Europeans, naming associated groups of Europeans with outward symbols and uniforms they wore, the tasks they compelled the Congolese villagers to carry out, and the typical work they did, particularly the ways in which they did it. The criteria of selection included, therefore, besides the physical characteristics and appearances, the economic, social, and political situations that affected everyday life in the village community and shaped the meanings of these names. As Congolese villagers named colonial officials collectively, they created as many categories of names as the professions of different groups of colonial officials and professionals.

The typical collective name for any colonial government official of Belgian Congo was *Bula Matari*, which means, "Break rocks!"[10] Kikongo speakers coined the name after a charge of dynamite was detonated in the Lower Congo during the construction of Vivi Road in 1882. They gave the name *Bula Matari* first to Henry Morton Stanley, the British naturalized American who crossed Central Africa (1876–79), and who later took a job under Leopold II as the general administrator of the Congo Free State. As colonialism intruded into the village communities, the pace and ways of everyday life changed, and Congolese villagers everywhere now gave the name *Bula Matari* to the colonial state and all colonial officials and agents. From being an imperative suggestive of a colonial language of command, the semantic field of *Bula Matari* broadened to include the totalitarian power and violence of the colonial state.[11] It is the single collective name whose meanings have not withered away from the Congolese collective memory. Even today, *Bula Matari* still reminds Congolese of the ruthless brutality of colonial officials that they consider the supreme evil of Belgian colonialism.[12]

All the collective names of colonial officials seldom expressed the brutality of the colonial state openly. The name *Mondele Mboka*, which was given to the heads of administrative posts in the countryside, was an

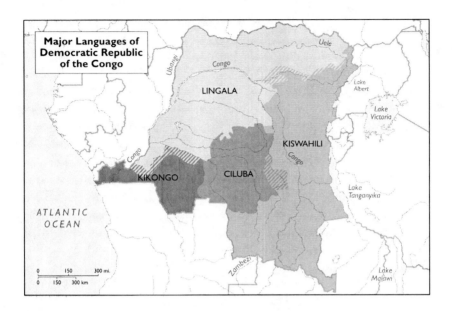

example. To set up colonial rule and carry out economic projects, the colonial administration organized since 1891 old local polities into *chefferies* and *secteurs* ruled by Congolese chiefs. Besides these local leaders, the colonial administration stationed low-ranking officials across the countryside at strategic outposts. Integrating local polities into the colonial administrative structure and European agents in the posts created colonial situations that were interpreted differently by Congolese villagers. In Lingala-speaking districts, the head of the outpost was named *Mondele Mboka*, which means "Village white man." Like most collective and generic names, this meaning of *Mondele Mboka* was never universal and static because it had explicit meanings, which were often laudatory and implicit, and which were figurative and duplicitous. Low-ranking officials in the outposts at first lured some local leaders who hoped to raise their prestige with the possession of imports and consolidate their power by acquiring guns and gunpowder.[13] Understood against these backgrounds, *Mondele Mboka* means "Native son," a connotation that implies harmonious political relations. This representation of colonial relations echoed the wishes of colonial agents in their reports and administrative correspondence.

Despite the material rewards and political inducements, local leaders soon came to despise the colonial officials who, after defeating one ruler after another, reformed local structures and principles of authority,

severely cutting access to low administrative posts.[14] These circumstances and the actions of this group of colonial officials assigned to
Mondele Mboka negative and surreptitious connotations. As subaltern
agents to the territorial administrators, the heads of outposts assisted
them in organizing *chefferies*, recruiting labor, building roads, collecting
taxes, and expanding cultivation of cash crops imposed on the households in 1917.[15] These actions transformed any *Mondele Mboka* into an op-
pressor and exploiter and pitted him against villagers who then assigned
ugly connotations to his representation. Moreover, the negative perceptions of colonialism held by different communities across districts reinforced ugly connotations of *Mondele Mboka*. Until the 1930s, Congolese
villagers in the Aruwimi and Maniema districts and in districts of Katanga Province, to mention only a few areas, considered the collection of
rubber, the cultivation of cash crops, and work in the mines as akin to
slavery.[16] Such negative perceptions of the work forced on villagers by
colonial officials assigned negative meanings to *Mondele Mboka*. And even
when Congolese praised *Mondele Mboka*, they often did it to mitigate their
negative criticisms of colonialism and its negative effects on the village
world because colonial officials seldom tolerated open criticism.

Catholic missionaries were an important segment of the colonial social aggregate whose collective representations were as diverse as their
actions and personal attitudes toward Congolese villagers, local institutions, and cultural practices. They received, like state and private company agents, collective names whose selection was determined by physical characteristics such as their long beards and white soutanes, moral
flaws, and aspects of their work that assumed a public character. Out of
these criteria emerged the staged collective representation of the Catholic missionary as a beneficent "other." This image of Catholic missionaries has its first explanation in that they provided education and healthcare to Congolese villagers. A second explanation was that collective
names of praise that underlay the image beneficent "other" were received at the mission stations that were already under the authority and
influence of Catholic missionaries.

A common collective name Kiswahili speakers in Eastern Congo
gave to Catholic missionaries was *Padiri*, a loanword from Spanish *padre*
and which means "Catholic priests." In Orientale Province, Kiswahili
speakers named them *Mupe*, another loanword from the French syntagm "Mon Père," which means "My father." Lingala and Mongo
speakers named them *Sango*, which, like the preceding collective names,
means "Father." Still, in many areas Lingala speakers called Catholic

priests *Nganga Nzambe* while Ciluba counterparts gave them the collective name *Ngangabuka*. *Nganga Nzambe* and *Ngangabuka* mean "God's healer."[17] As discussed earlier, names in lingua franca were given to the bearers at the mission stations that were under the control of missionaries. Most were self-representations of Catholic priests as beneficent "others" expressed in ways that justified their claims and right to unquestioned authority and respect from Congolese villagers.[18] But whatever the benevolence of Catholic missionaries, their representations were ambivalent as eloquently illustrated by the meanings of their individual names discussed later in this chapter.

Congolese scarcely interacted with geologists and mine prospectors. Yet they rarely escaped the disastrous consequences of situations created by the works of these professionals. To be sure, the discovery of mineral deposits created the mining industry, which often resulted in the mandatory relocations of villages, massive confiscations of land, disruptive recruitment of labor, and heavy requisitions of food from the villagers.[19] These conditions overwhelmed the collective imagination and found expression in the names given collectively to geologists. The naming of geologists was widespread and occurred even in places where the prospecting and discovery of mineral ores did not lead to the mining industry. Congolese villagers and mineworkers in mineral-rich Katanga Province, for example, wove their observations of these conditions into the Kiswahili collective name *Bwana Maibwe* they gave European geologists and mine prospectors. The expression mainly means "Mister stone." In Orientale Province, where a large gold-mining industry started in 1905, Lingala-speaking villagers gave geologists and mine prospectors the generic name *Monganga na Mabele*, which means "Earth healer." At first glance, these names simply identified a group of European professionals. As with many collective names, however, these had many meanings and carried ideological loads. First, where charges of dynamites were detonated, rumors and stories of the white men harming and polluting the land quickly spread, transforming names derived from prospecting to disparaging comments about this group of European professionals. For Congolese who knew stories of prospecting, "Earth healer" meant "Earth polluter." Second, because some myths associated metal workers with the symbolic low social status, and because the mining economy caused social disruptions, the names *Bwana Maibwe* and *Monganga na Mabele* were condemnations of geologists and scornful criticisms of negative effects of the mining economy and its related industries on daily life.[20]

Colonial officials who were not geologists but worked in any area of soil and land received names with negative connotations. Van Kerckhoven, the head of an expedition to secure the possessions of the Congo Free State at Lado in 1892 and later the district commissioner of Aruwimi District, was named *Bula Matende*, "Dynamiter" and "Break rocks," by the Kikongo speakers in the Lower Congo because he was in charge of constructing Vivi Station, where charges of dynamite were detonated under his watch.[21]

As these examples show, collective names originated in situations that dominated an era and overwhelmed the totality of the colonial experience of the givers of names. Only in rare cases were they drawn from single events, actions, and behaviors of individual colonial officials.[22]

Besides collective names, Congolese overwhelmingly gave individual names to traders, military officers, missionaries, administrators, agents of private companies, and colonial government officials. The individual names were drawn from personal actions, behaviors, and the ways in which each European official carried out colonial policies. Naming colonial officials individually was the most comprehensive pattern of nomination that afforded Congolese villagers the means to represent and record all aspects of experiences of every day life in the village community. This was reached by creatively using various naming customs and linguistic devices such as reduplication, suffixation, onomatopoeias, local mispronunciations, morphological congruencies, praise, and double naming. The reasons Congolese villagers gave personal names to individual Europeans besides collective ones are easy to tell. First, the naming of strangers was a naming tradition in the Congolese cultural universe that hinged on the idea that only a name makes possible the life of individuals.[23] For this reason, I chose the term *name* over *nickname*, which I had considered at first. Second, a personal name differentiated situations of oppression and exploitation each European created from those created by his predecessors, contemporaries, and successors. Third, Congolese villagers gave each European an individual name because in stark contradiction to Congolese anthroponyms that were complete signs, Western family names were meaningless.[24]

In naming individual Europeans, Congolese villagers often gave them a temporary name at first, which they later replaced by a meaningful one to show actual colonial situations. The replacement of the first name occurred after the European bearer visited villages frequently, interacted with men, women, and children, and stayed longer in their midst. Based on close contacts and the familiarity of Congolese villagers with a European, they scrutinized his physical appearance, behavior, cultural practices, moral qualities and failings, work, and the relations that he had established with local communities. Sometimes the change took place after an extraordinary event occurred during the term of office of the colonial official. Congolese villagers then replaced the temporary name with a personal identity that better articulated the effects on daily lives of the event and policies carried out by the bearer of the name. The naming custom was common in the village world. Harry Bombeeck was named at first *Mwana Mputu*, a generic name that means "Child of Europe."[25] Bombeeck later received from a local leader the name *Bombeki*, a loanword from Bombeeck.[26] The change of name occurred after the son of the local leader took service with the agent, who had also shared game with the leader and the entire village. The violence of colonial conquests transforms the taking of a job with Harry Bombeeck and the sharing of the game into exceptional moments that illuminated colonialism. Broadly considered, the context shows friendly relations between the local leader and the company agent and transforms *Bombeki* into a positive appropriation of Bombeeck. Briefly, then, many local mispronunciations allowed Congolese villagers some right to European family names to which they assigned connotations that articulated local representations of colonial situations.

Harry Bombeeck was an agent of the Société Anonyme Belge (SAB). The scope of his power was without any doubt small, and therefore the change of his name was less spectacular in showing broader changes taking place in the village community. In contrast, the scope of power of the district commissioner was enormous because the district was the largest territorial structure until the First World War. The change of the name of District Commissioner Gillain shows stunningly how the change of a name mirrored the change of actual colonial political relations. Commissioner Gillain was first named *Kabalo*, which means "Horse," because he rode a horse. The official later received the name *Tshombe Bululu*, a syntagm that means "Bitter cassava leaves." Changing names was a longstanding custom in precolonial Congolese societies and depended on personal circumstances and events that affected the society at the time of the naming or renaming. The change from *Kabalo* to *Tshombe Bululu* resulted mainly from the internal dynamics of this tradition. The shift of meanings from a description of an amusing scene of riding a horse to the bitter taste of the cassava leaves was drastic and corresponded to the radical change in the relations between Congolese villagers and the official. Introduced in the seventeenth century to cope with food shortages during the Atlantic slave trade, cassava became a staple food in Central Africa in the nineteenth century. Despite the welcomed addition of the crop to local diets, the choice of the poisonous variety of the crop to name the district commissioner was surreptitious and carried a negative connotation. Between the first and second naming of the district commissioner, relations had grown excessively repressive, oppressive, and exploitative, escalating into the mutiny of Congolese soldiers in 1895 at Luluabourg. The bitter taste of the leaves of cassava symbolized deteriorating relations of colonial domination and assigned to the name an ugly connotation that was corroborated by the reputation of harshness and meanness earned by Commissioner Gillain, who was partly blamed for the revolt of Luluabourg that left eleven European military officers dead.[27]

Like colonial state officials and private company agents, Catholic missionaries received individual names. The criteria for the selection of individual names of these members of the Catholic Church, one of the three pillars of the Belgian colonial edifice, included, besides physical attributes and characteristics, their fierce campaigns against local institutions and cultural practices that represented the most infuriating aspects of Catholic missionaries' work. The conditions so created were first talked about intensely, then scrutinized, and finally transformed into individual names of Catholic missionaries.

From 1891 to 1959, Congolese in Kasai gave to Catholic missionaries individual names with multidimensional meanings. In his study of individual anthroponyms given to Catholic priests in Kasai, T. K. Biaya analyzed a corpus of eighty names, some laudatory, and others negative and conveying criticisms of the behaviors of individual missionaries and of the ways in which they assaulted cultural practices and institutions that underlay their beliefs.

As Congolese elsewhere appreciated some aspects of the work of colonial officials and gave them individual names of praise, Congolese in Kasai extolled Catholic missionaries for the ways they carried themselves and performed their works, particularly the aspects of works that did not focus solely on evangelization. Father A. Lippens was named *Ciswa-bantu*, a compound name that means "He who loves people." The priest received the name when he arrived in 1915 because he shared with the parishioners basic imports such as clothes, notebooks, and medicines, and even money. He did many good things associated with love until his death in 1958, and the name-givers highlighted his generosity. Similarly, Father A. Demunster received the name *Cimpanga* when he arrived in Kasai in 1906 and kept it until his death in 1950. The name means "Bull," and the priest earned it because he was strong and worked all day long. Congolese based their choice of the name on his physical traits that were simultaneously metaphors for authority and power: he had the strong and hairy chest and the beard that were symbols of authority, still power, and industrious character.[28]

Catholic missionaries received praise for generosity and moral qualities that Congolese admired. But they were criticized as much for immorality and attacks on Luba culture and institutions as they were praised for their good actions. This naming tradition was widespread, and the list of illustrations is long. Fathers F. Van Nimmen and J. Van Uden received the name *Cibalabala*, which means "Wild cat." The name was drawn from the method the two priests used to assault local cultural practices and was similar to the way wildcats attacked their victims. The priests would come by surprise in the night as wild cats, moving constantly and stealthily, to destroy fetishes, shrines, and sacred drums and to attack ancestral religious practices. The Luba translated their criticism of Catholic priests' actions aimed at wiping out polygyny into *Cibutama*, a clear derivation from the verb *butama*, which means "to hide." Father R. Bearts who lived in Kasai from 1908 to 1924 received the name because his method of evangelization focused not only on the conversion of men and women into Christianity but also on the fierce fight for abolishing polygyny. As Congolese converts elsewhere, new converts in Kasai refused to abandon long established social and cultural practices at once. After the blessing of their marriage by the priests, for example, many husbands faltered and took back the wives they had divorced under pressure from the priest, and every time the priest's visit was announced, villagers fled into the bush with their families. Informed about the practice, Father R. Bearts then feigned leaving the village and returned back to surprise polygynous men and their wives. The campaign against polygyny was fierce, as shown by the frequency of names given to priests. Like Father R. Bearts, Father L. De Brandt lived in Kasai from 1911 to 1937 and received the name *Kabangu*. The syntagm *Kabangu* derives from *ka-bangu* and means "Small scar," a meaning that the prefix *ka*, a diminutive, precisely conveyed. But *Kabangu* also referred to a traditional device of torture used to force witches to confess witchcraft. Father De Brandt received the name because he used the device to punish those converts who fell short on their quest for inner perfection and returned to polygyny and old ways of life. So *Kabangu* referred specially to the attacks of the priest on polygyny.[29]

West of Kasai in Kwango, Father Adolphe De Meulemeester earned around 1910 the name *Mfumu Mantese,* a syntagm that means "Prince who has things to say."[30] What were the things the priest was saying? Against whom was he saying them? The meaning of the name and the details provided by a report written in 1911 by officer Achten show that the Catholic missionary fulfilled the role of a colonial government official, which offers some answer to the meaning of the name: "Father De Meulemeester (Mfumu Mantese) summoned Pululu Kusu to a meeting at the farm-chapel and reprimanded him for bad roads. As Pululu smiled, the Father took the smile to be a laugh at him, got him held by his catechist Sappo Sappo, and beat him several times on the face; he then grabbed him by the shoulders, and kicked him. [. . .] Pululu Kusu had over all his body twenty-three noticeable wounds caused, according to their appearance, by the whip."[31]

It was customary for colonial officials to curse Congolese when whipping them publicly. The excerpt above shows that the priest engaged in the same practice. The transcripts of native courts also show that the Catholic missionaries took Congolese villagers to court for practicing polygyny, refusing to pay taxes, and neglecting cash crop production, a task usually carried out by territorial administrators and subaltern state agents. Given these circumstances, one may infer that "the things to say" were not only Christian teachings that derided traditions, local cultural practices and political institutions, and the ancestral ways of life, but also the colonial government demands carried out by Father De Meulemeester.

The geographic growth of missionary work on evangelization was unequal and depended on the objectives and commitment of religious orders, and local response. In the 1930s, Catholic missionaries of the Congregation of Montfort reached the Mbole country where they encountered fierce resistance to evangelization. The resistance, which was mainly directed against the destruction of sacred insignia and drums of Lilwa, the Mbole initiation association, created constant suspicions for every action taken and words spoken by Catholic missionaries, as well as their relations with women and children. In the mid-1950s, for example, the Mbole named a missionary *Ipipola,* an onomatopoeia that connoted copulation. Stories are still told today that the priest received the name because he was suspected of flirting with catechumen at the mission station in Opala.[32]

Many colonial officials and Catholic missionaries received individual names that were drawn from European family names, most of which Congolese could not pronounce correctly.[33] These loanwords were pronounced according to local phonology and adapted to the sounds patterns, rules, and morphological markers of local languages. Some of them have lost their meanings; others remain daunting to decode; still others carry meanings that tell stories of everyday life. Illustrations taken from several districts of the Congo make all these points plain. In 1889, Lieutenant Pierre Ponthier, who later became a commander, arrived in Basoko, the seat of Aruwimi District, where Likatu, the leader of Bango people at Yamangandu, named him *Loponge*. *Loponge* was a loanword from the family name Ponthier, which, at first glance, has no meaning. But archival and oral data provide details that shed much light on the mnemonic function of the term. The war of conquest of the area waged by Lieutenant Pierre Ponthier, like most wars of conquest elsewhere, caused the dispersal of the group and the killing of Chief Likatu's brother-in-law. Although archival data do not help in uncovering the primary meaning of the loanword, tales of colonial conquests told in the area and collected in 2003 show that *Loponge* was the mnemonic code and a chronological reference to stories of colonial encounters and their key events. In sum, people no longer remembered the name of Chief Likatu and the death of his brother-in-law, but *Loponge* was still conspicuously a powerful memory of early colonial encounters dominated by wars, killings, and heroic local resistance.

Two other local mispronunciations, *Vandebuluki* and *Vandebunduki*, were among the most creative political codes and mnemonics minted by Congolese villagers, and they captured the collective memories of rubber collection and its wars and killings. In Lake Leopold II District, now Lake Mai Ndombe, rubber collectors called Léon Van den Broeke the names *Vandenbuluki* and *Vandebunduki*, two mispronunciations of the same name spoken in different parts of the district. Sometimes the terms were used interchangeably. Analyzed one hundred years later, *Vandebuluki* and *Vandebunduki* carry at first glance vague meanings and political messages. The sociolinguistic analysis shows that they have not been entirely unintentional. To begin with, *Vande* in the local mispronunciations *Vandenbuluki* and *Vandebunduki* has no local semantic equivalent and refers solely to the bearer of the name. In contrast, *Buluki* and *Bunduki* are morphological congruencies in Lingala and many other Bantu languages and respectively denote "witchcraft" and "a gun."[34] They may have simply been local mispronunciations of the family name Van den Broeke. But because all referred to the instruments used for destroying individuals and the village community, they cannot be explained alone by the inability of Congolese villagers to pronounce the word *Van den Broeke*. More important, the naming pattern "X + verbal theme," "X + adjectival theme," or "X, nominal theme" offers a new key for decoding the meanings of the two local mispronunciations. The verbal, adjectival, and nominal themes in the naming pattern suggest actions and habituated behaviors of the name-bearers, and because *Bunduki* means "gun," the syntagm *Vandebunduki* must translate as "Vande, the gunman."[35] The mispronunciation *Vandebuluki*, whose nominal theme *buluki* means "witchcraft," carries a negative connotation. A key cultural concept in the Congolese universe, witchcraft is the power to destroy humans or to consume another person's essence. These sociocultural contexts help translate *Vandebuluki* as "Vande, the witch." This translation conveys the idea of evil power associated with witchcraft.

The conditions of work and the harsh punishments suffered by rubber collectors in Lake Leopold II where the names were coined corroborate the linguistic analysis and reconstructed meanings. Like many parts of the inner Congo Basin, Lake Leopold II was a theater of atrocities where rubber collection represented the epitome of early colonial violence. Sentries killed those who refused to collect rubber, whipped those who failed to bring the exact quotas of rubber, and burned houses and crops of those who fled the villages. The overwhelming brutality makes *Bunduki*, "Gun," and *Buluki*, "Witchcraft," metonyms for killing and social disruption, some salient characteristics of rubber collection. Broadly, then, the oppressed rubber collectors conveyed through the mispronunciations of the family name Van den Broeke the accusations of violence, killings, and social disruptions caused by the collection of wild products.

These examples show that it is daunting to retrieve the figurative meanings and the political messages of the names that were loanwords and morphological congruencies. In some other instances, however, the meanings have become either simple references to Europeans or anecdotes without any social significance. Ciluba speakers in Kasai named Legat *Bwana Leke*, which means "Mister Leke," and *Mukalenge Leka*, "Prince Leka," while they named Bugschlag *Kasongo Bushila*, a syntagm that means "Tall and lean." The Kuba named King Albert of Belgium *Alube*, which means "King Albert." The name *Alube* also means a brand of cigarettes, but the context does not link the name to excessive smoking, which was perceived as a vice and subject to criticisms by villagers. Kimbundu speakers named a Portuguese trader established in Kasai since 1881 *Kashabala*, a loanword from his first name Gaspar.[36] The task of decoding the meanings of such names is complicated because one cannot recover the tone and pitch of voice and the facial expressions of Congolese name-givers, important details that could suggest and corroborate the meanings of names and elucidate the broader social and political messages. The loss of such details that accompanied local mispronunciations of the family names of colonial officials and missionaries denies the researcher important clues to decipher the meanings and broad messages of some names drawn from loanwords. And because Congolese could not pronounce correctly the names of some Westerners in the first place, one may reasonably assume at first glance that local mispronunciations of European family names did not carry meaningful messages. Still, ethnography and linguistics in many cases help decode important inside comments about colonialism from loanwords and morphological congruencies.

The naming of Captain Nicolas Tobback, one of the conquerors of Orientale Province, offers an excellent illustration that shows how data and important messages about colonial rule and officials can be extracted from loanwords. The inhabitants of Stanley Falls used the name *Tumbaku* for Captain Nicolas Tobback, who was second in command of the post in 1889 and who became its commander two years later.[37] *Tumbaku* was a loanword from Tobback, which means "tobacco" in Kingwana, a dialect of Kiswahili spoken in Stanley Falls. Despite its linguistic status—an alteration and loanword—the name had meanings rooted in local interpretations of smoking and its effects. The first message of *Tumbaku* speaks about the work ethic of colonial officials. Indeed, although smoking a pipe was a pleasant way of spending an evening in Central Africa, smoking all day long was associated with laziness and irresponsibility. And heavy smoking produced stale and unclean teeth, unhygienic conditions that generated ugly satires that still permeate local folklore and popular songs. Because Captain Nicolas Tobback smoked tobacco all day long, the denotations and connotations of *Tumbaku* depicted the negative effects of smoking captured in such satirical names as *Alangwi Likaya*, a syntagm that means "Drunken smoker." Although drawn from a socially accepted form of leisure, and therefore suggestive of praise, *Tumbaku* became a metaphor for a sticky mouth and stained teeth and a satire against a lack of work ethic Congolese perceived in Westerners.[38] These meanings of *Tumbaku* were critiques and a rejection of Europeans and their cultural practices. Indeed, jeering at and mispronouncing someone's name were a challenge to fight in Central Africa just as they were in other parts of the continent. Given many rebellions and forms of hidden protest, *Tumbaku*, like other local mispronunciations of European family names, expressed criticisms of colonialism and the lack of work ethic, which Congolese villagers still talked about in the 1940s and the 1950s and continue to do today in the countryside and cities.[39] In a conversation I had in 1986 in Lubumbashi with former Mambwe cotton cultivators from Kongolo, they all stressed that by mispronouncing the names of colonial officials and agents, they wanted to convey subversion: "We mispronounced the names of white men who inspected our fields to show them our anger. They came carrying long cords, measuring the length and width of the fields, and asking women to line up seedlings. We were tired of being told to do things we already knew how to do or things we did not want to do anyway."[40]

To decode the messages from local mispronunciations, they should be tied to the political and economic conditions and subjected to local cultural interpretive norms of which they were seldom independent.

The personal family name of a European sometimes became his local name only because it was a morphological congruency. When Professor Jan Vansina told the Tio and Vili his name, they named him *Va-nsina* after a fashionable Loango song, "Va-nsina, nsina, nsina." *Va-nsina* is an imperative in Tio and Vili and means, "Sit down."[41]

Congolese drew many individual and collective names from physical characteristics, particularly fatness, beauty, tallness, shortness, posture, gait, infirmities, and body parts of Europeans. The sample used for this study shows that Congolese drew 30 percent of names from physical characteristics, most of which were in Lingala, Kikongo, Kiswahili, and Ciluba. The popularity and spread of names in the lingua franca show that they were received in places already under colonial control or influence where Europeans encountered Congolese for the first time. As colonial officials traveled, their names accompanied them to distant places where Congolese villagers appropriated and employed them as loanwords to name other Europeans who fulfilled similar colonial roles. Only on rare occasions were the traveling names translated into local languages. From the 1890s to 1900, this naming pattern was at work in places and regions as far away from one another as Ituri in the north of Congo, Yambinga and Aruwimi in the center, Tanganyika in the southeast, and Kasai in the southwest.[42] The Kiswahili name *Bwana Mukubwa* means "Mister tall." It was part of a pattern described earlier and designed to differentiate superiors from subaltern agents. In this perspective, *Bwana Mukubwa* connotes "Big boss" or "Superior." It had its synonym in the Ciluba compound name *Kasongo Mule*, which means

"Tall and lean." This group of names was widespread and often conveyed praise to colonial officials. Many officials and Catholic missionaries who received individual names drawn from physical characteristics and appearances were plump, handsome, tall, or short, and the names meant just what officials and missionaries looked like. A good example is *Mundele Kikufi*, a Kikongo syntagm for "Short white man."[43] Yet, names derived from looks and other physical descriptions of the body had multidimensional meanings ranging from praise to criticisms of greed, abuse of power, mockery, and insults. As discussed later in chapter 7, descriptions of the body could be duplicitous and insulting to the name-bearers. Briefly, figurative meanings were subversive interpretations of the harsh realities of colonialism, including the ways in which each individual official carried out colonial policies.

Threats of death, severe warnings and orders, and insults that colonial officials repeated in menacing voices with harsh words when punishing Congolese were selected as individual names of colonial officials, which were again loanwords and which, if broadly interpreted and contextualized, expressed the accusations of violence.[44] The commonest of these threats spoken by colonial officials when ordering Congolese to kneel and watch their speech and actions were two French expressions, *attention*, a warning given by mean-spirited officials to remind Congolese that a mistake or disrespectful misbehavior would result in harsher corporeal punishments, and *à genoux*, spoken to have Congolese kneel when they were caught fulfilling assigned tasks negligently.[45] Regardless of the circumstances under which colonial officials employed the expressions, they wounded the manhood and sense of worth of Congolese men and in the end emasculated them. Congolese villagers captured these indignities and conditions of repression in *Bajunu* and *Ataso*, two loanwords drawn from the French expressions and criticizing the ritualized scenes of domination and humiliation created by officials who ordered the kneeling of individuals.[46]

Colonial officials rarely forced women to kneel. Instead, they took them hostages, chained them, and exposed them to the sun standing up or sitting down, scenes reminiscent of the caravans during the slave trade, slavery, and similar punishments such as *ombi*, a form of imprisonment in the societies of the rainforests of Central Africa that consisted in attaching a heavy pierced trunk of a tree around the ankle of the prisoner.[47] Common from the early years to the heyday of colonial rule, the taking of women hostages was designed to compel fugitive husbands who had evaded taxes and cash crop cultivation to return and face imprisonment, lashing, and fines. The punishment in the end caused as much humiliation, shame, and indignity as orders given to Congolese men. The *ombi* shamed and infuriated its victims because it was a traditional means to restrain lunatics.

Although the custom of naming colonial officials after verbal threats conveyed multiple political messages, oral testimonies clearly show that it mainly expressed resentment and pledged vengeance against brutal colonial officials. Congolese villagers asserted that while drawing names from the vocabularies of domination that colonial officials had coined, they wished "the maltreatment the threats purported to inflict to fall on colonial officials."[48] And although the colonial government had militarily weakened Congolese men when it outlawed the bearing of traditional weapons, no Congolese man acquiesced submissively to orders and warnings given by colonial officials.[49] The naming of colonial officials after instruments of colonial domination conveyed mainly the accusations of colonial assaults on the village world and was seditious.

Onomatopoeias devised by Congolese from imported goods and items of European behavior and speech were names well represented in the sample of the study. Drawn from the motorcycle's rumbling, *Tuku-Tuku*, documented in colonial archives and oral testimonies, was among the commonest. In the 1890s Congolese in Stanley Falls named Victor Rue *Tuku-Tuku*, while in the 1950s the Mambwe cotton producers gave the name to an agronomist.[50] In all cases, the colonial officials received the name because they rode motorcycles. The term means "Motorcycle" in Lingala, Kiswahili, and other Bantu languages. To rural cash crop producers, however, the name meant situations of oppression caused by officials who rode motorcycles, as the example of the Mambwe testifies. The Mambwe named an agronomist *Tuku-Tuku* because he visited their villages riding the motorcycle to check if they had worked the cotton fields. During these visits, Mambwe producers who refused or failed to carry out agricultural tasks to the liking of the motorcycle-riding agronomist were harshly punished. Many were imprisoned in the Tanganyika Central Prison, where they cut wood and fetched water for colonial officials and did public works. Others were publicly whipped and fined. As a result, *Tuku-Tuku* became a metonym for hardship and violence. In the late 1980s, more than two decades after the independence of the Congo in 1960, two Mambwe, Mugaza wa Beya, a former cotton producer, and Lufundja, an ex-policeman, still associated the name *Tuku-Tuku* with jail sentences, whipping, and public humiliation that the Mambwe cash crop producers in Kongolo suffered during colonization.[51] When cross-checked with oral and written sources and contextualized, as this example shows, onomatopoeias yield evidence of material conditions prevailing in the rural communities and local reactions to new manufactured goods. In brief, onomatopoeias tell much about colonial conditions and the attitudes and ideas of Congolese villagers about colonial modernity.

Congolese drew names as much from praise-worthy moral qualities as from moral failings and lack of achievements they observed in European officials, particularly character flaws and poor job performance. This naming pattern was a Congolese response to European cultural chauvinism of the nineteenth century, eloquently expressed in one of the three objectives of the Brussels Conference of 1876: the claim of introducing civilization into Central Africa by Europeans.[52] The paradoxes from which Congolese drew this group of names of colonial officials and missionaries sprang from three situations. First, European traders, colonial government officials, and Catholic missionaries carried themselves as if they were all-powerful and exempt from physical infirmities and moral flaws. Second, they openly claimed that Congolese villagers were uncivilized and therefore had no religion and no culture, and that to move them to the stage of modern history, their cultural practices and social and political institutions had to be transformed if not abolished altogether. Third, they held up to ridicule accumulated local wisdom and knowledge. In this ideologically charged context, the territorial administrator and the Catholic missionary became the experts in finding healthful environments where they could relocate villages for fighting diseases and cultivate cash crops for staving off poverty. And when Congolese villagers scrutinized colonial officials and Catholic missionaries and found them physically challenged, politically weak, and notably incapable of making smart choices while allocating land for cash crop cultivation, they gave the self-proclaimed experts names that captured these deficiencies and paradoxes.[53]

Names expressing these paradoxes were as widespread as the practices they recorded and represented. Because Shaw committed scandals, Lingala speakers named him *Nsoni Mingi*, which means "Very shameful." The nominal syntagm *Nsoni Mingi* and many similar names expressed mainly moral indignation toward those colonial officials who claimed that they had come to the Congo to civilize peoples but who could not civilize themselves, committing acts of immorality that Congolese villagers found horrifying. In the first decade of the nineteenth century, the Mongo named an agent *Nkoso*, which means "Parrot."

Naming children and individuals after animals was a common naming tradition that produced names whose meanings were determined by what the animal represented in the culture. As a result, names drawn from names of animals carry loads with multidimensional meanings. "Parrot" carried a negative connotation, and Congolese coined it to insult the colonial official who was less witty and more talkative. It also designated colonial officials who not only spoke senselessly but also lacked the economy of words and the art of listening, the cardinal rules of wisdom. The Kongo of Kazu-Zimba-Kindunga sector accused an agent of this deficiency in 1918 when they named him *Matuba*, a nominal syntagm that means "Words." The official received the name because he was a "blabbermouth."[54] In brief, Congolese gave such names to colonial officials to talk about the lifestyles and various practices that were not locally ethical or commendable.

Criticisms of moral deficiencies covered diverse themes, one of which was the leadership of colonial officials, which Congolese villagers questioned from the beginning to the end of colonization. In the 1890s, the Azande named Hinde, the colonial agent who pioneered rubber and ivory collection in Uele, *Molanda*, a Lingala term for "Follower." This denotation of *Molanda* was an open critique of failed leadership. The agent received the name because he was always waffling when the Azande villagers asked him to raise prices of rubber and ivory. Like village people in the 1900s, peasants in the 1930s and 1940s continued the naming custom to question the leadership of colonial officials and agents. Luba cotton producers in Kamina named such officials after the reduplication *Awaya-Awaya*. This reduplication described the state of confusion and lack of direction shown by colonial officials. The name was given to colonial officials "who easily bend in the direction of winds," and the aim was to ridicule their leadership.[55] The same theme was stressed by the Kuba who gave colonial officials the name *Tshiwaya-waya*, which means, "Balance in breeze." Because the name was given only to those colonial officials who were easily swayed to change their opinion, the representation was again an open attack on their leadership. Briefly, accusations of failure of leadership and moral deficiencies mean that naming afforded Congolese as much freedom to express moral indignation and grievances as songs and paintings, cultural expressions that scholars have used in their studies.

Giving to one colonial official two names, one official and flattering, another secret and critical, was a common naming pattern deployed to cloak contemptuous messages and disguise messages of protest and insult to avoid retaliation. The first of the many factors that underlay double naming was bilateral descent, a kinship system that allowed the father's and mother's sides to name the child, which was adapted to the colonial situation. Showing the interplay between meanings and the material conditions of everyday life, the second factor was the constant need to adjust the meaning of a name to current situations that changed from what they were when Congolese gave the name to a European. This dynamics explained also the change of names of colonial officials. The third and last explanation of double naming was the need to mitigate stark comments about horrendous conditions created by an unfriendly colonial official who would respond to an aggressive accusation with harsh punishments.[56] Thus, giving one colonial official two names was, like drawing names from stereotypes of feminine gender, a way of communicating differing messages to Congolese villagers and European colonial officials. By creating duplicitous messages that disguised the intentions of Congolese villagers from the officials, this naming pattern dissipated the fears of retribution and disseminated subversive comments about colonial rule across the village world.[57]

Typical and vivid examples were *Kamuziki* and *Kelelo* that were given to J. G. Bolle. Appointed district commissioner of Lake Leopold II twice in the 1890s, Arthur J. G. Bolle was first named *Kamuziki*, which means "Little music." He was given the name because he created a band that accompanied him during his tours of the district. Because Belgian rulers held a wide misconception that the songs, dances, enthusiasm, and smiles were expressions of joy and implicit approval of colonial policies and because the band had greatly excited Congolese, the official might have mistaken his name for praise of his policies. The linguistic analysis interrogating the contexts of the genesis of the name suggests, however, a critical and condescending perception of the official and explains the broader message of resentment and protest carried by the name. The name *Kamuziki* was obtained by the prefixation of *ka-* to *muziki*, a loanword from the French word *musique*. A diminutive, the prefix *ka* means "insignificant" and "little" and conveys a message of condescension, mockery, and insult despite the enthusiasm people showed to the music played by the band. When Congolese later named the official *Kelelo*, a loanword from the French word *clairon*, which means "bugle," they reinforced this unfriendly attitude toward the official.

To be sure, *Kelelo*, the bugle, was one of the first colonial wind instruments European explorers and colonial government officials introduced into Congolese villages, and Congolese assigned multidimensional meanings to it. During European explorations, the sound of the bugle announced Europeans.[58] After the scramble for Central Africa and the military conquest of the Congo, it signaled the rising of the colonial flag, the ritualized performance of political domination, and the stringent discipline that Congolese villagers experienced most intensely during the tours of their village communities by itinerant colonial government officials. This discipline intensified in the 1920s when officials forbade nightly dances and established rigid schedules of farming, a system of social control similar to the firm type usually set up in prisons, military camps, and colonial outposts. Like the role it played in these controlled institutions and places, the sound of the bugle warned villagers at dawn, "wake up, it is time to go to work for Bula Matari," and ordered them at dusk, "stop all the noise, the white man is about to sleep."[59] Because Congolese despised such orders, *Kelelo* expressed protests against colonial timetables and economic projects ʳhat disrupted local time use and impinged on social and economic pursuits such as bridewealth negotiations, mourning, initiations for boys and girls, fishing, hunting, and collecting wild vegetables and mushrooms.[60]

In the end, the names *Kamuziki* and *Kelelo* epitomized two differing perceptions of colonialism held by Congolese and colonial officials. In the minds of colonial officials, *Kamuziki* meant local enthusiasm for colonial entertainment and implied the collaboration of Congolese villagers to colonial plans. For the Congolese, *Kamuziki* expressed mockery instead. Colonial officials believed also that *Kelelo* produced a sound symbolic of colonial power and political domination while in the minds of Congolese it meant the micromanagement of time, an aspect of colonialism that Congolese considered the worst kind of domination and oppression. But *Kelelo* was a stronger criticism of the ways the colonial administration regulated the daily life than *Kamuziki*, drawn from a form of entertainment staged by the official to overcome local resistance to early economic exploitation.[61] The shift from *Kamuziki* to *Kelelo* accompanied changes in colonial relations that had grown more domineering, exploitative, and oppressive.

The multidimensionality of the meanings of *Kamuziki* and *Kelelo* become plain when compared with the meanings of similar names that Congolese drew from other sounds they associated with European presence and colonial authority.[62] Between the 1890s and the 1940s, colonial government agents earned the names *Ngonga na butu* and *Soso aleli* in Lingala. The first syntagm, which means "Nightly talking slit gong," described colonial agents who ordered local leaders to announce government instructions on slit gongs late in the night to allow full coverage. The second name, *Soso aleli*, means "Rooster has crowed" and identified those colonial officials who enjoined local leaders to wake up their people at dawn to answer roll calls and go to toil on public projects or mandatory cash crop fields.[63] Although the response of Congolese villagers to the cash crop economy was not uniform and changed over time, research shows that they were hostile to mandatory cash crop production and unpaid labor on public projects because the last were exploitative and encroached on domestic economy, and because rituals of life cycles and village life became less flexible. Briefly, names drawn from sounds that regulated time and set the rhythms of daily life criticized the rigidity of colonial work calendars.

Many symbols were used to coin names that generate opaque and duplicitous messages. The choice resulted partly from naming traditions and partly from the struggle of Congolese villagers against colonialism. Congolese villagers who constantly struggled against the oppressive and exploitative relations were not willing either to show entirely or to hide all their concerns from colonial officials. This naming pattern afforded Congolese the means to articulate anonymously rural grievances and concerns and express hostile views of colonialism to colonial officials without showing their personal identities and therefore attenuating the fears of retribution that inhibited straight talk and truth telling. Interviews conducted with Congolese villagers expressed this point strongly. When asked why Congolese could not tell colonists every thing they had on their mind, Lwaka Mukandja, the son of a cotton grower from Kongolo, replied, "My father told me that there were moments when, angry, they did not think of what the White man might do or how he might react to the truth. Men remained men and stood against him. Yet there were times when all what they thought of was their family; everybody in the village knew that insulting a white man openly was somehow begging for harsh punishment. The hatred of the white man like *Paipo* who had rotten and ugly stained teeth, and who smelled almost like a rotten fish could not fade if men told him the truth in the face."[64]

Briefly, Congolese villagers coined some names to deliver equivocal messages to skirt retaliation from brutal colonial officials, while they minted others to make colonial rulers aware of hidden protests against repressive methods of maintaining colonial social order.

Many collective and individual names were reduplications. Reduplications were, in oral literatures and languages, repetitions of a solitary word twice to signal superlatives. They represented, from the 1890s to the 1950s, 30 percent of names in the sample and stressed the intensity of labor demands, tax hikes, and the extent of the intrusion of violence into daily life. A reduplication such as *Longo-Longo* in Logo, which means "Tall, tall," tells a story that offers some glimpses into terrifying mal-treatment of migrants before the policy of labor stabilization in the mid-1920s. It shows that although the meanings of reduplications were not always explicit, they offer a strategic entry point into investigating exploitation, domination, and repressive colonial practices. The name *Longo-Longo* was coined by Logo workers at Moto mines and given to a white labor overseer. White overseers had broad power over regular and seasonal workers whom they regularly misused. The word-for-word meaning of "Tall, tall" assigned to *Longo-Longo* sheds little light on the reputation of evil that the labor overseer earned and that arose from his mistreatment of Congolese migrants and workers. Only a cross-check of evidence suggests the implicit meaning of *Longo-Longo* that explains the bad reputation and misuse of power by the overseer. The archival data show that he beat and deprived captured fugitive migrants of ra-tions and wages and sometimes starved them. The last punishment killed a worker in 1910, and the first two left many workers undernourished, weak, and vulnerable to diseases.[65]

Briefly, the meanings of reduplications, like those of onomato-poeias, were glossed over, and the political messages they once carried were altered and sometimes lost. To reconstruct and sometimes retrieve them, one should combine a careful reading of archival and oral sources with a study of popular etymologies to illuminate the contexts of their genesis.

Congolese villagers gave to colonial officials and Catholic mission-aries individual and collective praise names drawn from good looks, moral qualities, and actions deemed progressive by the community. Many extolled colonial officials and their actions and policies. But a great many names in the sample of this study conveyed only ostensible laudatory messages because they circulated duplicitous messages.[66] This is illustrated by the following example. Kiswahili speakers named colo-nial officials who were quiet *Pole-Pole*, a reduplication that means "Very calm." Many officials who received the name were quiet, rarely em-ployed violence, and "carried themselves as real human beings." As a result, they were admired by villagers. The name, however, also had the surreptitious meaning of "Slow walker." A meaning such as this changed the naming pattern into a skillful linguistic tactic designed to hide resist-ance and skirt retaliation.

Conclusion: Naming, Colonialism, Community Voice, and Agency

Despite the influence of preexisting naming traditions and frames of reference on the naming of Europeans, the meanings of names of Europeans show that Congolese defined the messages fully aware of what was happening in their lives and communities. The meanings of some names were easy to tease out because they described overtly the material conditions at the time of the naming. Other names cloaked meanings in imagery, allegories, proverbs, metaphors, metonyms, and symbols, hiding intended messages. Although messages were conveyed through various literary devices and genres, they even so referred to aspects of colonialism and the daily life of Congolese. The cloaking of local perceptions of colonialism in names of colonial officials was as effective a hidden struggle as conveying anti-colonial messages through rumors, surreptitious songs, and deceptive smiles, well-known hidden resistance that left colonial officials perplexed and worried, and at moments powerless. Names given to colonial officials described the thought processes of Congolese rural dwellers, in addition to aspects of their social life.

Understood against local backdrops, each name represents a lived collective experience or its interpretations. Each is valuable for historical reconstruction because each is potentially apt to reveal the social universe where Congolese lived, worked, contested, and negotiated the boundaries of the colonial world. Whether the meanings of names were objective descriptions of Congolese experiences or subjective interpretations is irrelevant because they were held as "historical myth" by Congolese. From this perceptive, any name was "a communicative phenomenon located in the social matrix within which the discourse is produced and understood, towards which there is a social orientation, rendering the text interpretable by a community of users."[67]

Congolese did not record every experience of daily life when naming European explorers and colonial state officials; neither did they narrate through names all the happenings in the village. Nonetheless, the practice was ubiquitous and recorded not only various colonial events, scenes, and circumstances but also conditions of work and life and the mindsets of Congolese, elements that formed the basic structure of relations between Congolese and colonial officials. The naming of Europeans thus generated a repository of raw materials about colonialism over a long period spanning from the time of European explorations in the 1870s to the end of colonization of the Congo on 30 June 1960. This discussion shows that in naming individual and groups of Europeans, Congolese villagers merged differing perceptions of colonialism into one collective voice, which, as it took hold in the village community, became the lenses through which they interpreted their integration into the colonial world. It also shows that the naming of colonial officials allowed Congolese to assign meanings and significance to colonial events and situations that affected their everyday lives. The names of colonial officials are therefore important and relevant raw materials for reconstructing the local understandings of colonial experiences. A focus on names opens the enquiry into stories, the collective memories, observations, and perceptions of colonialism and sheds light on various aspects of colonialism that restructured everyday life. These views become even plainer in the following chapter, which centers on the names of European traders and explorers and early agents of colonial state and concessionary companies.

4

Early Naming, Explorations, Trade, and Rubber Collection

The Brussels Conference of 1876, which launched "explorations" to Central Africa, brought Portuguese, Italian, and German explorers to interact with Congolese, whose cultural, economic, and political ideas were different from their own. These explorations only diversified the interactions of Congolese with foreigners because Congolese in Uele were already interacting with Sudanese traders and Anglo-Egyptian government officials. While explorations and trade represented one extreme in the continuum of relations, brutal conquests and integration of Congolese villages into rubber concessions were the other. The explorations, trade, and rubber collection affected the relations between the two groups and the perceptions they developed of one another. Explorations, trade, and rubber collection became important criteria for selecting names and meanings of names that Congolese, following local naming conventions, gave Europeans. Focusing on naming as a recording technique of experiences and names as sources of history and the collective memories explains representations of these relations. The analysis looks at the names that people gave to Europeans in Uele, the Kingdom of Kazembe in southern Katanga, and the inner Congo Basin between 1870 and 1892.

Why devote a separate chapter on the early names after the preceding chapter has centered on the naming patterns and customs? The answer to the question is twofold. First, there were undoubtedly wars and confrontations during explorations and long-distance trade in nineteenth-century Central Africa. Yet, this was not a time of systematic political domination. Second, integrating Congolese into the rubber concessions that followed the explorations and trade represented the most violent era and the most brutal economic exploitation in the Congo history. During this period, Congolese gave Europeans names with meanings and connotations that show striking contrasts, and focusing on the contrasts shows again that names recorded all types of memories and stories of the village communities.

Explorations, Trade, and the Naming of Europeans

From 1870 to the 1890s, few European explorers and traders entered the village world, and those who ventured to the villages and sought protection from local leaders received names. This section focuses on these names coined during the explorations, trade, and conquests in the northern and southern parts of the Congo. Because the explorers and traders were not the direct agents of systematic political domination and economic exploitation in the eyes of the residents of the village world, they received names that sometimes set them apart, except for colonial rulers and company agents who represen'ed colonialism and its practices. This difference in representation of groups of Europeans shows that naming recorded all types of relations, and that names are therefore important sources from which researchers can tease out important information for writing histories of daily life experiences.

The "explorers" were among the first European strangers the Azande encountered in the second half of the nineteenth century. The story of the encounters between the two groups is not linear. Sometimes the explorers followed in the footsteps of traders; sometimes they moved simultaneously with them as they entered Uele in the 1870s and 1880s. To the Azande, George Schweinfurth, a German botanist who visited their country from 1870 to 1872, was *Balikpe,* which means, "Leaves eater."[1] They named Giovani Miani, an Italian explorer who visited their country in 1872, *Balikuhe* because it means "He was eating raw and bland food." When the explorer reached Mangbetuland, the Mangbetu named him *Nafranki* because "He has white beard and long hair." When another Italian, Gaetano Casati, encountered the Azande in 1881, they gave him two names, *Nabira* and *Sato.*[2] The same Azande gave the name *Koja* to Guillaume Junker, another German "explorer" who stayed in Uele from May 1879 to December 1883, longer than any other European ever had. Whereas oral accounts collected in the 1920s and 1930s identified *Nabira* as a cultural hero, *Sato* (Casati) and *Koja* (Junker) were local mispronunciations and loanwords and hardly conveyed information of any social significance at first glance. Yet, the memory of *Koja* that the Azande still had in 1892 when research to find his tomb was undertaken was of a king, which shows that the hosts had affection for their guest.[3]

Meanwhile, the Ango-Egyptian administration extended in the 1880s its sphere of influence and some political control over Uele, where it levied taxes in ivory and labor for porterage and thus contributed to the political destabilization of local societies.[4] Of the Anglo-Egyptian officials the Azande and Mangbetu encountered, Eduard Schnitzer was the most famous as governor of Aequatoria Province and known locally as Emin Pasha. In Uele he earned the name *Eminimbi* created by the suffixation of *-mbi* to Emin, a process that assigned a negative connotation to the name.[5] The suffix *-mbi* or its variant *-mbe* in Bantu languages means "bad." So the word-for-word translation for *Eminimbi* becomes "Emin, the wicked." This connotation of the name associated the governor with stories of horrors, plunder of ivory, and the kidnapping of slaves committed by predatory traders and preying Anglo-Egyptian government officials in Uele. These practices likened Anglo-Egyptian officials to traders. In the nineteenth century, the long-distance trade from the Sudan had extended into Uele, where local peoples traded ivory and slaves for copper coins called *mitako* with the *Jallaba*, traders who operated small firms called *Zeriba* in Uele and owned large commercial firms in Khartoum, the Sudan.[6] By any measure, this trade contributed little to local societies and the accumulation of wealth by local peoples. Instead, it created demands for grains and labor for porterage that depleted local food resources, infuriated local peoples, and caused conflicts that sometimes culminated in wars between the two groups. Moreover, traders interfered in local politics by supporting one ruler against another and thus raised political instability in the area. The invention of the term *Eminimbi* and its meaning shows that although Anglo-Egyptian government officials and traders shared the color of skin with "explorers," Congolese peoples did not lump all these Europeans in the same category. They distinguished explorers or travelers who seemed harmless from plundering traders and officials of the Anglo-Egyptian administration who preyed on them. The connotation of *Eminimbi* thus shows that the encounters seldom benefited the name-givers.

The message conveyed by *Eminimbi* was a loud voice of protest against exploitative taxes. But what can one learn from names given to explorers whose economic and political motives were not open and not perceived by local people as grim and exploitative?

Cultural clashes, the results of misunderstandings attested to in the travel literature of the explorers, characterized encounters of European explorers with Congolese in the second half of the nineteenth century. Although European explorers' views expressed in the travel literature were detailed, Africans left commentaries about the encounters in the names that they gave Europeans and that found their way into the travel literature.

Because Europeans were not yet imposing political domination systematically, names depicting physical appearances and cultural practices such as the eating of raw and bland food were mainly manifestations of cultural clashes and, second, the perceptions of Westerners' supposedly low cultural attainments. Names derived from such notions as white beards, which symbolized deference, age, authority, and wisdom, and long hair, a symbol of high social status, were still predominantly descriptions of the bearers of names informed by collective imagination. In reality, the unfamiliarity of the Mangbetu with European cultural practices generated as much curiosity and clashes as the deformation of their craniums and artfully elongated heads stunned Europeans.[7] The Europeans who did not conform to local standards of behavior and etiquette shocked the Azande, Manbgetu, and others. Giovani Miani and Gaetano Casati received two names from two different peoples. Because the double names of these explorers were not synonymous, they show local ideas about Europeans and their actions and local conditions of encounters. Although the European imperialism was yet emerging, and cultural clashes still shaped the naming of Europeans, some names of explorers derived from local notions and values already carried a discourse questioning unequal trade in ivory and slaves and the extraction of labor for porterage.

The name *Balikpe*, a term that means "Leaves eater," is a good illustration of a name with subterranean meanings. The Azande derived the name from Schweinfurth's habit of spending time in the bush eating raw leaves. At first glance, the name seemed to convey little or no political message. Yet, it summed up local suspicions about the imagined harsh conditions of the white man's country, as Schweinfurth wrote in 1871:

> During our travels, I had obtained from the Niam-niam [Azande] who accompanied our caravan an epithet that I never lost in all the subsequent stages of our journey. In their own dialect, these people called me "Mbarik-pa," which would be equivalent to a name amongst us of "Leaf-eater." It was a designation that reminded me very vividly of my professional brother David Douglas, who fell a martyr to his devotion to Nature, and who was known amongst the North American Indians as "the Grass-man."
>
> My Niam-niam interpreter Gyabir, as I learnt some time afterwards, had given his friends some marvelous accounts of the way

in which I was accustomed to eat whatever I found growing. He used to relate that I had a habit of dismissing my attendants and getting into a dense thicket where I imagined that I was unobserved, and that then I used with great haste to gather and devour enormous quantities of leaves, and he added that this was the way in which, one day after another, I groped after my ordinary food. Others contributed their observation that I invariably came forth from the woods with an exhilarated expression and quite a satiated look, whilst they were conscious of nothing else than the cravings of hunger . . .

The dominant idea, which seemed to be impressed upon the natives by my botanical ardor, concentrated itself upon their conviction as to the character of the country where the white man has his home. According to their belief, the land wherein the white men spent their lives could show neither grass nor tree, and consisted of nothing better than sandy plain and stony flat. Those amongst them who had been carried away as slaves in the ivory expeditions and had returned again from Khartoom had brought strange accounts of the grim desolation and utter drought of the Moslem lands over which they had passed and what, they asked, must be the condition of the still remoter countries of the Frank, of whom they only knew that he kept the Turk supplied with cotton-stuffs and guns.[8]

Briefly, the examples show that besides describing personal qualities and cultural practices that Congolese observed in early Europeans, early names of Europeans in Uele tell a great deal more. They show mainly cultural clashes and, to a lesser degree, ideas about emerging exploitation and unfair trade interpreted through local metaphors, a situation that was a prelude of resistance to relations of exploitation and domination.

As the Azande and Mangbetu, who encountered Italian and German explorers and Sudanese traders and officials of Anglo-Egyptian government in Uele, peoples of the Kingdom of Kazembe in southern Katanga—Lunda and others—met different groups of Portuguese in the nineteenth century and gave them names that also recorded local views of local conditions that resulted from the encounters—violence and unfair trade. A Portuguese merchant, Manoela Caetano Pereira, was named *Mwendo-Mwendo* when he visited the Kingdom of Kazembe in 1796. The name *Mwendo-Mwendo,* a reduplication, means "Travel, travel." Early colonial officials who conducted an ethnographic survey in the 1890s translated it as "Voyage at the foot of the world."[9] This opaque syntagm is explained by widespread stories of the slave trade, which tell us that trips to the coast represented travel "at the foot of the world" where captives ended inland journeys and started the middle passage. The meaning was part of a larger story of the effects of the slave trade interpreted through Central African cosmology, notably the idea that the sea represented the meeting of the sky and earth, and the separation of the worlds of the living and the dead.[10] For Central Africans trapped in the slave trade that was still going on in the nineteenth century, and who still ended up in Angola and Sao Tomé until the first decade of the twentieth century, "Voyage at the foot of the world" meant the trip to the place of death. In 1870, Manoela Caetano received another name, *Luanda,* a place of his origin in Angola that was once a major market for slave trade.[11] Identifying a person by his place of origin and group was a widespread naming pattern in Central Africa by which the political and economic role and the reputation of the region shaped the meaning of the name. As collective representations, *Mwendo-Mwendo* and *Luanda* covered the theme of the predatory trade that the Portuguese still had with southern Congolese groups in the nineteenth century despite the end of slave trade.

The governor of Tete in Mozambique, Lacerda, followed in the footsteps of Manoela Caetano Pereira to the Kingdom of Kazembe. Although I did not find Lacerda's name, he was followed by Mayo-Monteiro who was named *Miere-Miere,* a reduplication that means "Many knives."[12] According to the colonial documentation, the people of Kazembe kingdom gave Mayo-Monteiro the name *Miere-Miere* because he was a "ferocious and wild warrior."[13] This translation finds support in the life of Mayo-Monteiro and the economic conditions of nineteenth-century Central Africa. Mayo-Monteiro was a military officer and traveled to the Kingdom of Kazembe during the abolition of the slave trade, which Portuguese traders tirelessly strived to circumvent. He may have also received the name because he brought many knives as means of payment and exchange. In South Central Africa, moreover, a knife was a weapon and an emblem of authority, and it implied violence, an attribute of power explicit in the living symbols of authority such as the leopard, eagle fish, and python, which were all predators. So the name depicted local conditions of the nineteenth-century slave trade that still triggered violence and disrupted local societies.

Briefly, the names of European travelers and traders and the Anglo-Egyptian colonial government officials were interpretations of interactions between local peoples and Europeans in the region between 1870 and the 1890s. They also show the significance of naming as a technique of recording historical evidence.

Rubber Collection and
Early Naming of Europeans

Rubber collection dominated the economy of the Congo Free State from the 1890s to 1912 and changed the conditions of everyday life in the village world. The victims of this exploitation and oppression recorded their collective imagination in the names they gave Europeans. In the concessions of the Anglo-Belgian India Rubber Company in the Upper Congo, the Lulonga and Busira rivers, and those of Anversoise in the northern band of the Congo River, these anthroponyms described atrocities and horrendous conditions created by rubber collection. They interpreted colonial encounters and the collective experience of Congolese victims under King Leopold II's colonial regime of destruction and terror.[14]

The victims of rubber collection in the Upper Congo named the Congo Free State *Ipanga Ngunda*, a nominal syntagm that means "He who destroys the country."[15] This collective name is a metaphor for the horrors of rubber collection and its destructive impacts on the village world. Any name of an individual agent or a group of agents suggesting any association with rubber always referred to the harsh conditions of rubber collection, the brutal methods of torture deployed by the agents of the Congo Free State and the agents of concessionary companies who were determined to raise rubber quotas and hinder local resistance by rubber collectors.[16]

The political career of *Ipanga Ngunda* as a collective representation of the Congo Free State ended in official documents as the Congo Free State and the new Belgian Congo came to favor *Bula Matari*. The collective and generic name *Ipanga Ngunda*, as many others, could have satisfied the stereotypical idea shared by most political and economic planners that "the black respects only the person he fears."[17] Advocates of force as the most effective instrument of social control could have chosen any of the many names coined during the reign of terror of King Leopold II as the official and collective representation of the colonial state. They chose *Bula Matari* as the most accurate representation of the Congo Free State to explain its horrific attributes and the prevailing asymmetrical power relations between the victims and their killers for many reasons.

King Leopold II and his Congo Free State officials shied away from names suggesting the abuses of rubber because they provided evidence of atrocities of rubber collection to the campaigns against King Leopold II, especially during the Commission of Inquiry in 1904 and after the publication of reports and books critical of his regime. To be sure, Congolese provided testimonies during the Commission of Inquiry, referring to company and government officials and agents by their local names; all depicted harsher punishments and the ravages of rubber on daily life. The reactions of colonial officials, ranging from changing their names to forbidding Congolese victims from testifying, attested to the intensity of these tensions. Mutilated by company sentries, Ekabo and Epondo, for example, "were retained in Coquilathville for precautionary measures taken to stop them from fabricating legends that discredited the State."[18] What the official called "legends" were stories of the negative effects of rubber collection on Congolese, which were sought by proponents of the campaigns against King Leopold II.

Besides economic and market conditions, mainly the fall of prices of rubber on the world market and the production of better-quality latex in rubber plantations of Southeast Asia, the stories of rubber atrocities told by Congolese contributed to the collapse of the "rubber economy" and the shift from it to peasant cash crop production.[19] The report of the British consul Roger Casement, Edmund Dene Morel's *Red Rubber*, and Arthur Conan Doyle's *The Crime of the Congo*, which graphically detailed the killings, sufferings, and torture of the Congolese, sharpened the international pressure on King Leopold II and his officials. Edmund Dene Morel, the founder of the Congo Reform Association, Roger Casement, and, to a lesser degree, American writers such as Mark Twain and Booker T. Washington were the most outspoken and fierce adversaries of the Congo Free State and King Leopold II. The writings of these writers shaped the context in which outsiders read stories of genocides, massacres, and mutilations that were taking place in the Congo because of rubber.[20] The international criticism was one of the reasons the Congo Free State chose *Bula Matari* over *Ipanga Ngunda*. The collection of rubber and the construction of the Vivi Road both generated names, despite the difference of degree in social disruptions and demographic losses and decline. Contemporary colonial campaigns claimed that despite its atrocities and high human costs, the road created an infrastructure and economic opportunities for needy Congolese. The intensity of international pressure against rubber atrocities restrained King Leopold II and his officials from choosing *Ipanga Ngunda* or a similar collective representation of the Congo Free State in part because they supplied Westerners with evidence of the atrocities of the rubber wars and the Congo labor system.

Besides collective representation of the Congo Free State as destroyer of the country and people, rubber collectors coined generic names for company agents and colonial state officials in charge of rubber collection — collective names with embedded and thus opaque meanings. In the concession of the Anglo-Belgian India Rubber Company (ABIR) along the Busira River between the 1890s and 1912, for example, villagers named these ruthless oppressors the "white man of the rubber vine."[21]

This syntagm exemplified a group of names that derived their meanings from the economic projects that overwhelmed the experiences of Congolese villagers. Although the meaning of the "white man of the rubber vine" was implicit, the association of the name-bearers with rubber, the symbol of killings and violence, shows that the "white man of the rubber vine" mainly referred to the harsh conditions of an entire era and was therefore a critique of the new conditions. We are afforded glimpses into the multidimensionality of the meanings of the name and similar names by a conversation between the Yela people and Lieutenant Grégoire in 1911 about widespread stories of "white men of the rubber vine" across the concession of ABIR. The stories show local conditions of exploitation and the hatred for the negative effects of rubber collection on family and village communities, and explain the meanings of "white men of the rubber vine" explicitly. The Yela, particularly the youth, told the officer that the "white men of the rubber vine" caused the crisis of biological and social reproduction and bemoaned the departures of kinfolk to work for Anglo-Belgian India Rubber Company. They contended that the temporary migration of kinfolk to the company stations caused labor shortages in the households, the subsequent overwork of wives left behind, and the decline in childbirth. The conversation showed the Yela's hatred for a widespread practice of holding as hostages the men who brought foodstuffs to officials of the company at the stations. To gauge the opposition of the rubber collectors, Lieutenant Grégoire crisscrossed the concession interviewing many Yela rubber collectors and drew a conclusion that elucidates the meaning of the name: "The widespread image of the white man of the rubber vine held and talked about everywhere in the concession smells of bad will and resistance."[22]

When rubber collection was abolished in 1912, the "white man of rubber vine" was replaced by generic names derived from the names of cash crops that the colonial government imposed in 1917. Indeed, when rubber collection ended and the colonial government imposed the cultivation of cash crops, Congolese started naming agronomists, crop supervisors, and territorial administrators who brought new cash crops after the names of the crops they introduced into the village world.[23] The general conditions that overwhelmed the collective experience shaped the meanings of such collective names that every linguistic group coined, and that were subtexts to conditions of exploitation brought by cash crops. Kiswahili speakers named these colonial officials *Muzungu wa Pamba,* " White man of cotton," while Lingala speakers called them *Mondele na Loso,* "White man of rice," *Mondele na Kawa,* "White man of coffee," and *Mondele na Mbila,* "White man of palm oil tree." *Ondele W'Ekonge* was the Mbole phrase for "White men of *urena lobata*," given to any colonial official involved in promoting the production of the textile that the Mbole producers sold to the Lomami Company that enjoyed monopsony to buy the fiber for manufacturing sacs.[24]

If translated raw without an investigation of contexts, such names do not tell the stories of cash crop cultivation—its organization and systems of social control, and the ways in which individual colonial officials carried out agricultural policies and dealt with producers, let alone the perceptions of colonial rule held by the producers. Although they were generic and their meanings implicit, names drawn from the names of the cash crops provide subtexts that help decipher their connotations and broad social and political messages. Everywhere in any rubber-producing district, rubber still reminds people of severed hands, killed members of the village communities, burned homes and destroyed crops, and women taken as hostages. Because most peasants until the *paysannat,* an agricultural scheme that aimed at creating a prosperous middle class after the Second World War, interpreted the mandatory system of cash crop cultivation as akin to slavery, the seemingly straightforward and descriptive names were surreptitious accusations of the negative effects of cash crops, which other local voices excavated from many sources and corroborated.[25]

Besides collective names, rubber collectors gave agents of rubber companies individual names whose meanings and connotations reinforced and intersected with those of collective names. With a few exceptions, individual names captured only the violence and ravages of rubber on individuals and communities. In places where villagers suffered the horrific punishments of seeing their homes and crops burned, the oppressors received the names *Tumba Lombe,* "Home burner," and

Lilanga'atumbe, "Garden destructor." And those who faced angry and brutal agents coined the term *Etumba Mbilo,* "Office that resembles a battlefield." Congolese villagers everywhere described agents who excessively employed the whip *Sikoti,* a loanword from the French term *chicotte,* which means "hippopotamus-hide whip."[26] Congolese rubber collectors expressed escalating brutality of the rubber regime when they named *Bola-Bola,* "Beat, beat," an official "who punched people," *Ebuka-Buka,* "Breaker of things into pieces," or any official "Who crunches people"; all were reduplications. "He who destroys things" received the name *Ekuma.* Rubber collectors highlighted experiences of killings by naming any official "Who shoots people" *Ikoka,* and "He who kills" *Liboma.*[27]

Putela depicted these conditions in his answer to the Commission of Inquiry on 28 December 1904 in Bikoro: "My village is Bombanda and it produced rubber for the white man *Etumba Mbilo* ['Office that resembles a battlefield']. One day, soldiers came and started war against us because of rubber. They killed my mother and father, and I received a bullet in my neck and fell down to the ground. . . . Soldiers thought I was dead and cut my right hand . . . to show it to the white man." On 16 February 1905, the headman Betela told the Commission of Inquiry: "On the orders of the white man *Panzi* (that is, Fievez) ['Lying side,' allusion to death], soldiers were sent out to fight wars against people who refused to bring rubber; he told them, . . . to have proofs that you are not telling lies and that you had fought war, I want you to bring me the hand of each individual you kill. Severed hands ought to equal the bullets you fired."[28] Yela testified on 7 May 1905:

> A long time ago, *Likoka* ["Shooter"] fought war continuously against peoples in Tumba. Do you know why? He found the rubber that people collected too little although the entire village worked and brought rubber several times a month to the post. There were two other whites. *Bonginda* who remained always at the post and *Besolo* who walked up and down the region with *Likoka.* . . . These whites always arrived in the villages unexpectedly. One morning, I heard gunshots. After hesitation over what was going on, I came out and fled into the bush. Soldiers were already scattered across the village, and one of them who has come close to me fired at me. I was hit on my left thigh that the bullet pierced. I fell on the ground. The soldier, who fired on me hurried and with a knife, cut my right hand despite I begged him and cried. When he was doing this, another soldier wanted to cut my left hand. He had started cutting it when the first soldier told him that the white man

was only counting the right hands. The second soldier left me without cutting my hand while the first soldier who had then finished
his job wounded me on the back and left off. I became unconscious
and did not know what happened then. I regained consciousness in
my home where my brothers had taken me. By then the white man
and his soldiers had already left.[29]

Congolese villagers in the concessions of the Anglo-Belgian India
Rubber Company and Lomami Company in the Aruwimi District suffered similar rubber atrocities. From Opala and Lokilo down to Ilambi,
agents of the Lomami Company collected as much as 1,500 kilograms
of rubber a month.[30] There are no statistics to argue specifically for the
decline of population because of rubber. Nonetheless, the names of officials explain the demographic repercussions of rubber collection by
pointing out the sources of malnutrition and conditions of work that
caused ill health, morbidity, and death. The Mbole forcefully captured
the impact of rubber collection on daily life in the widespread expression *wando wo limolo,* which means "tax-caused loss of weight." By referring to the burden of taxes (*limolo*), the expression underlined overwork,
which, once combined with lack of food and exhaustion in the bush, resulted in undernourishment and emaciation. These two conditions had
the Mbole rubber collectors believe that "working for the tax man
makes people thinner."[31] Stories about rubber collection in the area illuminate the meaning of the expression further. Wenga Asomo, toothless
and in his eighties in 1980, remembered, "To gather rubber, men spent
weeks in the bush without food, feeding on tender leaves of ferns and
palms, wild berries and roots. Brave men refused to collect rubber and
fled into the bush to hide from overseers."[32] An interviewee who did not
reveal his name recalled, "people walked backwards to fool sentries who
hunted them down, and many came back almost walking dead men
because they had lost much weight." Perceiving rubber collection as "a
work that ate people" in the Lower Lomami River underscores the
demographic impact of rubber. To be sure, whether Congolese men
fled into the bush to escape the collection of rubber or went to the bush
to harvest it, the outcomes were invariably undernourishment, emaciation, exhaustion, and death.

A last illustration of the close relation of rubber to names in the
Lower Lomami River was *Limende,* a name that the Topoke, the Mbole's
northern neighbors, gave to an agent of the Lomami Company posted
at Yahisuli on the bank of the Lomami River. The agent earned the
name *Limende* because he hunted the Topoke, who escaped the collection

of rubber and punitive expeditions by fleeing into the marshes where they built hiding places. The flights frustrated the agent so much he then lamented, "Topoke refuse to work by melting into the marshes because they think that the work reduces them into slaves; they hate to work like they did during the occupation of their country by the Arabs."[33] Even without precise translation, the context allows the argument that *Limende* tells the common story of conditions of exploitation and repression caused by the collection of rubber. Talking about rubber across the Lower Lomami River Valley through *Limende* was similar to literary genres such as sayings and proverbs, which omitted explicit details to explain situations assumed to be known to everybody. All the insiders deemed any added explanation of *Limende* redundant because of its association with rubber collection, the metaphor for violence.

Briefly, despite differences in the circumstances Congolese encountered agents of concessionary companies and officials of the Congo Free State in the inner Congo Basin, the meanings of names of officials overwhelmingly underscored the negative effects of rubber collection. Rubber-drawn names were thus local voices talking about and against violence and population depletion, salient features of this unprecedented system of exploitation, which started when Congolese entered the Congo Free State economy dominated by the concessionary companies.

5

Naming and Belgian Colonial Rule

This chapter documents critiques of colonialism by Congolese villagers through naming. It argues that accusations of assaults on the village world, violence, exploitation of women, and intrusion of colonialism into everyday life expressed sufferings, anger, resentments, and protests. Although the chapter pays attention to different categories of names given to various groups of European professionals, as discussed in chapter 3, it focuses mainly on names given to officials of the territorial administration and agricultural service. Territorial administrators, tax collectors, agronomists, and crop supervisors established more than any other groups of colonial government officials many and consequential relations with the villagers. The two sections of the chapter focus on individual names that wove colonial situations into the themes of violence and assaults of colonialism on the village world. Analyzing individual names that were perceptions of colonial situations prevailing in a larger area elicits consistencies and changes in the workings of colonialism.

Scholars have documented and gauged the exploitation of Congolese crop cultivators and their resistance.[1] To evaluate the revolutionary political behaviors of Congolese cash crop producers, a number of works have looked at the fines resisters paid to colonial treasuries and days of imprisonment and lashes they received. These quantitative data showed the exploitative conditions of the colonial system and economy. Yet the analyses overlooked a contemporaneous discourse of villagers lamenting and contesting colonialism by contrasting wealth accumulation by capitalist segments with losses Congolese villagers incurred while selling their crops and their labor force. The analyses do not express, as much as names do, the inside views of the producers about the effects of low prices and high taxes and fines on the economic security of the households. Exploring assaults of colonialism on the village world by looking at the meanings of names given to colonial officials is thus a

92

strategic entry point into the inside views of colonial aggression and violence, and fills the gap.

To show the relations of naming to colonial rule and experiences of colonial life, the chapter first explores the accusations of colonial assaults on the village world. Second, it looks at critiques of violence by concentrating on native courts and prisons, whippings, cash crops, roadwork, and exploitation of women. It also investigates names, which, although seemingly less loaded, denounced such colonial practices as the confiscations of food. The chapter contends that the accusations of colonial violence and assaults of colonialism on the village world were laments of suffering and expressions of discontent and anger. Yet, references to historical memories and the ambiguities of messages of names transformed many accusations of assaults and violence into voices of protest against colonialism and its representatives.

Names and the Evil of Belgian Colonialism

A typical accusation of colonial officials as evil and colonialism as assaults on the village world was the name *Ndoki*, which means "Witch." The Congolese gave Elter the name when he was the station chief in Kasongo because of his use of exasperating stereotypes designed to deny them justice: "Whenever a Congolese was accused of a crime and brought to his court, Elter who was deaf asked his elderly guard Kumbwa to repeat what the accused said. The guard then leaned closer to his ear and shouted, 'he is saying that he is innocent.' Elter then imperturbably pronounced the sentence. 'If you say that it is not you, then it is you.'"[2]

Elter's trial procedures were partly rooted in a widespread stereotype about Congolese shared by most colonial officials. He believed that "all the blacks are liars. So the truth is always the opposite of what they say."[3] Congolese's reference to *Ndoki*, an antisocial individual associated with evil powers in their cultural universe, meant that Elter's trial procedures disrupted social harmony and caused the decline of natural order and even the ruin of individual life force. The outcome of the trial procedures was that Congolese accused of committing crimes and brought to his court rarely escaped imprisonment, whipping, payment of fines, and public humiliation, and all fed the negative perceptions of colonialism.

Congolese also interpreted Elter's trial procedures as partly motivated by his infirmity. Colonial officials propounded ideologies and carried out their tasks in ways that subtly or openly showed to the villagers that white men were physically flawless and all-powerful. When colonial officials failed to live up to their self-imposed ideals and standards and fell short on local canons of physical strength and beauty, as routinely happened, Congolese mocked and insulted them. In a Belgian colonial world where physical force was an important asset to carry out colonial policies, insults to physical defects were not just mockery of personal limitations. They struck a mighty blow to the powerful myth that maintained colonialism. Elter's hearing impairment was thought of as the source of his harsh treatments staged to compensate for his crippled condition and the symptom of the weakness of the colonial social order.[4]

Colonial officials were aware of the accusation of meanness and the protest that Congolese expressed through *Ndoki*. First, they wrote detailed reports on witchcraft accusations, witch finding, witches' executions, and witches' evil powers. The rituals of purity performed to rid the community of the evil powers of witches through "witch finding" suggest that Congolese expressed popular protests through the name *Ndoki*. Second, every colonial official who went to the Congo received and read the government confidential handbook that defined *Ndoki* as "All those who have the power to harm."[5]

Force and threats of force were the instruments of social control in colonial Congo. Everywhere, the whip supported the local administration, native courts, labor recruitment, and the entire prison system. From the beginning to the end of colonization, the beating of individual villagers alternated with punitive expeditions against entire villages, which the colonial administration deployed when most inhabitants refused growing mandatory cash crops and paying taxes. Congolese also suffered punitive expeditions when most able-bodied men of a village ran away from a labor recruiter, a tax collector, an agronomist, or a health officer. Military operations resulted in indiscriminate killings, arrests, imprisonments, the burning of houses, and confiscating foodstuffs, which Congolese villagers equated with the disruption and destruction of their world. These actions reinforced the perception of colonialism as the quintessence of violence and injustice, which Congolese translated into generic names.

The Ekonda named an agent *Efanja*, "He who disperses people," and *Ekanga-kanga*, "He who arrests people arbitrarily and indiscriminately" during the Congo Free State. A colonial official in charge of tax collection and road construction in the area along the Lomela River, which the Congo Free State had subcontracted to the Société Anonyme

Belge (SAB) earned the name *Ekanga-kanga* because he arrested the villagers arbitrarily even when only a few refused to comply with his orders and carry out the tasks of collecting rubber.[6] This category of names expressed virulent critiques against the failure of the colonial regime to dispense justice, and each name in it represented accusations and stories of collective punishments. Reduplications such as *Koma-Koma*, "Strangler," *Bola-Bola*, "Ruthless beater," *Malu-Malu*, "Rush, rush," and *Wai-Wai*, "Big troublemaker," were parts of local views of injustices.[7]

Injustice was not the only colonial assault on the village world that motivated critiques expressed in names of colonial officials. From the producers of cash crops came such virulent accusations of the aggression of colonialism on the village world as *Nkake* in Lingala and *Mangbe* in Azande, two names that mean "Lightning," "Scrapers of the heaps," and "White cannibals," also graphic descriptions of violence.[8] These collective names were popular and given to colonial officials who fulfilled the same or similar roles. In Buta, an area of cotton cultivation in the Lower Uele District, cash crop producers gave these names to crop supervisors, agronomists, and territorial administrators from 1919 to the 1940s. Written and oral sources show that colonial officials earned the name "Lightning" because they assaulted village communities. Congolese villagers everywhere thought of lightning as an animal that "strikes only when enemies [witches] sent it,"[9] an idea that shows that the name expressed anger at the colonial officials for their destructive actions toward the village world.

As "Lightning" and *Ndoki*, "Witch," expressed aggression against the village world, the Congolese villagers gave the name "Scrapers of the heaps" to agricultural officers who checked heaps of refuse to see if the seeds of cash crops had been wasted. The broad message conveyed by the name derived from the cultural meanings of witch and the act of "scraping the heaps." Central and Southern-Central Africans thought of witches as evil doers who searched through the heaps for household refuse and fragments of excreta left by individuals they wanted to bewitch. The implicit message in "scraping the heaps" was the widespread suspicion that colonial officials were witches who possessed evil powers and watched everything that happened in the community. Congolese cotton producers developed the suspicion as they observed white overseers and agricultural officers searching for cottonseeds in the heaps to see if they were wasted.[10] Chronologically, the trauma of military defeat had already caused Congolese villagers to develop the perception of Europeans as witches whose medicines were more powerful than theirs. It was reinforced in the heyday of colonialism once institutions of domination enabled colonial officials to carry out policies reminiscent of typical actions of witches.[11] The discovery of cottonseeds in the heaps by white overseers resulted in the flogging and imprisonment of the producers, days of forced labor in public projects, and fines.[12] In Congolese eyes, these punishments were similar to the evils of witches, and these conditions transformed the first suspicions of officials as witches into reality.[13] Through the name, villagers thus accused cash crop overseers and agricultural officers of evil policies.

Colonial officials received names that, although expressing Congolese villagers' fears of violence, articulated accusations of "white man cannibalism" and the resentment of villagers. Examples of accusations of *man eating* and *man killing* included *Chakundia,* "He who can eat me," the reduplication *Koma-Koma,* "He who can strangle me," and *Kimbwi,* "Hyena."[14] Beyond the literal meanings, which underlined the meanness of colonial officials, such names denounced the demographic depletion of the early years of colonialism caused by rubber collection, punitive expeditions, and ruthless recruitments of workers for porterage and the construction of roads and railroads.[15]

The meanings of the names of colonial officials that accused colonialism of evil show that through names, Congolese conveyed various messages to alert the communities to the dangers they faced from bad colonial officials. When rubber was the mainstay of the colonial economy, the Mbole named an agent *Liamamba,* "Millipede," which, in their cultural universe, presaged misfortunes. The proper course of action prescribed by the culture to avert misfortunes was to throw away or burn alive the millipedes. Colonial annals are replete with stories of the killings of colonial officials, which left persistent stereotypes about Congolese cannibalism and insatiable thirst for blood.[16] Despite killings of colonial officials and rumors of cannibalism, the bearers of the name *Liamamba* and similar anthroponyms such as *Lokonga,* "Venomous snake," *Bambenga,* "Red pepper," *Bolemba,* "Stupefying vine for killing fish," *Ikuka,* "Bitter shrub," and *Likoke,* "Prickly tree," were not burned alive or eaten alive. These names highlighted the meanness of the officials, warned members of the community to potential trouble, told stories of violence as metaphors and metonyms, and expressed protest, as did the name *Ilanga,* which means "Enmity."[17]

Congolese leveled accusations of assaults on the village world against the colonial administration when it created *chefferies* (chiefdoms) and *secteurs* (sectors), the territorial divisions where colonial officials made contacts with local leaders to carry out political, farming, and labor policies.[18] First established in 1892, local administrations transformed local polities to control people, promote cash crop production, and make labor recruitments easier. The new administration and the successive administrative reforms changed the functions of lineages, villages, and kingdoms in ways that made the entire process synonymous with colonial aggression on the village world. More important, these changes came with many political demands and compulsory farming policies, which raised pressures on village economies, and generated rural radicalism.[19] The colonial administration countered resistance with military operations that resulted in burning villages, destroying household gardens and herds of goats, and killing rebels, and these forms of violence shaped Congolese perceptions of colonialism coded in names. Two examples — one taken from the Bazela, and another from the Mbole — show how Congolese perceived colonial *chefferies* and administrative reforms as assaults on the village communities.

Between 1913 and 1918, P. Wautier established a local administration along the banks of the Lower Lomami River in the Mbole area to ease the collection of kernels, copal, and rubber and the recruitment of labor and production of palm oil for the Lomami Company, a concessionary company created in 1892.[20] Relocating villages, gathering independent lineages into small *chefferies*, and the new economic demands disrupted the area in an unprecedented way that the Mbole recorded by naming Wautier *Liombo*. *Liombo*, the Mbole term for "broom" or "flywhisk'" carried a political message because it was a local symbol of authority and because it also was associated with a taboo against hitting someone with the flywhisk. It was believed that to hit a person with a broom destroyed his life force, depleted his health, and weakened his entire community's strength. Because P. Wautier changed the rules of access to leadership, the legitimate procedures of access to authority, the Mbole interpreted the process as the sweeping away of the social order.[21] The rising power of colonial agents following the administrative reform of 2 May 1910 corroborated this interpretation. Already in the 1920s, colonial officials had gained much power to restrict the freedom of villagers by forbidding public expressions of healing rituals and nighttime dances. Claiming that such cultural expressions encouraged laziness and contributed to the decline of commodity production, colonial government officials viewed the policies as the needed steps toward modernizing rural societies. The Mbole resentfully regarded them as the source of subjugation, the demise of their way of life, and the loss of initiative to control the pace of everyday life and guarantee the social and cultural reproduction of their village communities.[22] At first a symbol of political authority, the meaning of *Liombo* then shifted to a powerful accusation against political destabilization and social disruptions.

The illustration from the Bazela also highlights concerns about colonial interventions seen as assaults on the principles of legitimizing authority. The Bazela in the southern part of the Congo gave to the colonial agent Wilson the name *Nyoka*, "Snake," during the conquests of Katanga from the 1890s to 1916. Wilson earned the name because he intervened in the succession struggle of the ruling lineage.[23] The accusation expressed protest against the appointment to office of a puppet candidate by the administration, which overlooked legitimate procedures. Across Central Africa, *Nyoka*, "The snake," was a mysterious creature that instilled fear. But the Bazela's reference to *Nyoka* was not a simple story of fears and therefore mere expression of submission. Instead, it exemplified the anger and resentment of villagers against the assaults of colonialism on the principles of legitimacy of authority.

Administrating the village world required control and scrutiny of the villagers and pitted them against colonial agents, agricultural officers, and tax collectors. Of the typical names that referred to colonial social control and surveillance were those that connoted "severe looks," "the evil eye," and the harshness of colonial officials. Oral and written sources recorded *Miso Minei*, "Four eyes" or "Thief," *Miso Nkoyi*, "Leopard's eyes" or "Anger," and *Matala-Tala*, "Mirror" or "Eyeglasses" or "Scrutiny," all in Lingala. Also documented were *Adamiso*, "Knowing eyes" or "Control" or "Anger," in Baso, and *Matcho Kali*, "Angry eyes" or "Harshness," in Kiswahili. The examination of each of these names shows that besides word-for-word meanings, they all had multidimensional social meanings, most of which criticized the tight control and assaults of colonialism on the village world and its residents.

A substantive derived from the verb *kotala* that means "to look" and "to watch" in Lingala, the reduplication *Tala-Tala* was widespread from the beginning to the end of colonization. Congolese villagers named territorial administrators and crop overseers *Matala-Tala* because they wore glasses, and in many instances the name meant only "eyeglasses" and "mirror." Besides this word-by-word meaning, *Matala-Tala* meant also "witchcraft" and "scrutiny." In Buta, for example, cotton cultivators gave the name to crop overseers and agricultural officers because they believed that *Matala-Tala* were artificial eyes that allowed these officials to magnify their sight and scrutinize what was going on inside the village communities.[24] The name was the semantic equivalent of "Scrapers of the heaps" previously discussed. Although this meaning of the name had already circulated widely at the time of the military conquests, it became in Buta and elsewhere stereotypical for colonial officials who tried to micro-manage the agricultural labor process, and all the social and cultural pursuits they suspected of subversion—dances, rituals, playing cards, and initiations of boys. According to Sister Marie-Françoise, *Matala-Tala* referred not only to the general assault on the village world by cotton cultivation; it also implied protest against the elaborate system of social control that enabled colonial officials in the 1930s to micro-manage work in the fields and to set the rhythm of daily life in the village. The theme was also stressed by Kiswahili speakers. For example, a colonial official who organized the Mbole area south of Kisangani to expand cash crop cultivation in the 1920s earned the name *Matcho Kali,* a Kiswahili syntagm that means "Angry eyes." The name carried many more layers of meanings such as "Severe look," and the firmness of the official who was expanding the mandatory cash crop cultivation and thus economic exploitation.[25]

Briefly, the names of colonial officials drawn from the notion of eyesight meant "scrutiny," "anger," and "malice." When giving these names to administrators and crop supervisors, Congolese crop producers accused them of totalitarian and evil powers and expressed the sense of being under constant surveillance, conditions that they regarded as the epitome of political repression.[26] These names show that Congolese identified domination and oppression with policies that suppressed rituals and political expressions, and the slow and yet steady shifts in the local ways of life, situations that caused an intolerable humiliation. Congolese also read exploitation in low wages, depressed prices of agricultural commodities, and alienation of labor, and all formed predatory economic practices.[27]

Unique among the names of colonial officials expressing outrage at predatory assaults of colonialism on local communities was *Nzoku*, which means "Elephant." In many traditions of Central Africa, *Nzoku* was a recurrent symbol of enormity, abundance, and excess. Under colonial rule, it became a metaphor for a wide range of referents. Sometimes it was a praise name and referred to the celebration of the strength of colonial officials, a common naming pattern discussed later in the chapter. Frequently, however, *Nzoku* meant the size of colonial exactions and destruction and the sense of exploitation. Irrespective of the peculiarity of

events and situations that prompted the choice of *Nzoku,* in over twenty
cases in which Congolese peasants used *Nzoku* to designate colonial officials, the name was a metonym for bad political and economic policies
with disastrous outcomes.[28] In such instances, *Nzoku* identified colonial
officials who went beyond authorized means when carrying out policies
such as village relocation, road construction, and the cultivation of new
crops; all disturbed harmony in the households and communities and
undermined domestic economies in an unprecedented way.[29] Mbali
Ndolo, a former cotton producer in Buta, affirmed in 1989, "Cotton supervisors were elephants; they harmed our land and phased out our
crops. They usually left behind parasites and leeches that sucked our
blood."[30] Mbali Ndolo was using powerful metaphors that he explained
in the interview. Parasites and leeches symbolized agricultural officers
and Congolese monitors who, during the agricultural campaigns, remained longer in the village to monitor scheduled farming tasks and
thus depended on the village for foodstuffs. Here *Nzoku* meant excessive
demands for foodstuffs, especially the demand for poultry, whose consumption was regarded by the households as a source of prestige and social status rather than the main source of protein.[31]

More often than not, *Nzoku* connoted the sense of emptiness that
came with the decline of food security. This decline was the result of
colonial officials' decision to phase out old food crops in order to end
competition for labor with mandatory cash crop cultivation. This name
also expressed the accusation of fewer ways of finding food, caused by
the interdiction on intercropping that the colonial government imposed
and enforced until 1954. Colonial archives are replete with examples of
the name *Nzoku,* which conveyed multiple layers of meanings of colonialism, all referring to colonialism as a system of predation. In the 1940s,
Tetela farmers of the Sankuru District named agronomists "Those who
come to measure the fields."[32] The name was called out on the slit gongs
to announce the arrival of these officials. The Mbole of the Stanleyville
District named any colonial official who played the same role *Atila
Okondo,* which means "He who does not let land lie fallow."[33]

While the name "Those who come to measure the fields" was a clear
description of the most basic task agronomists performed, the syntagm
Atila Okondo, "He who does not let land lie fallow," was a metonym. It
referred to agricultural officers as they shortened the land-and-fallow
system because of cash crop cultivation. It also conveys the idea that
people who do not farm have no resting fields on which they may rely in
time of hunger. The name attacked the exploitative dependence of

colonial officials on villagers for foodstuffs, which was seen as aggression on the village world. The accusation that the mandatory cash crop production shortened the land-and-fallow system, the main way for land renewal that established usufruct, expressed the main concern about the colonial assaults of mandatory cash crop agriculture on the system of land use. First, although land was plentiful, the practice of fallowing land guaranteed the usufructuary land right that cut the frequency of land clearing and made farming in the rainforests a less strenuous way of eking out a living. Second, *Atila Okondo* was a satire long before colonialism to ridicule any husband whose wife traveled back and forth between the virilocal residence and her kinship group to bring foodstuffs to feed the husband and children. Former Mbole cash crop producers I interviewed in the 1980s frequently associated the absence of agricultural officers in farming and their easy access to food with extortion of foodstuffs and thus with colonial exploitation. This became apparent when Asomba Letoko wondered, "How could someone who has no field feed himself better than the producer?"[34] When Sombo used the proverb "Helping someone build a house does not give you ownership,"[35] he was criticizing the supposed altruism of colonial officials who went around villages telling villagers that they had come to stave off poverty by having people farm their land, but who took more than the producers did. The name was thus a criticism of easy access to foodstuffs by colonial officials though they were not the direct producers.

One can draw two important conclusions from these illustrations. First, the accusations of the villainy of colonial officials underlined the negative effects of colonialism on the village world and the lives of its residents. Second, references to historical memories and specific past events, large and small, showed that such names of colonial officials, by expressing concerns and grievances, were strategies of everyday life.

Names and the Violence of Belgian Colonialism

Colonialism and violence were nearly synonymous and informed the structure of everyday life in the Belgian Congo. Every major colonial economic project, from rubber collection, cash crop cultivation, and labor recruitments to the collection of taxes, caused violence. From the Congo Free State years until 1953, the whip imposed a reign of terror and subordination and inspired various names of brutal colonial officials. Despite the shift from the Congo Free State to the Belgian Congo in 1908 and the end of rubber collection in 1912, Congolese villagers continued to indentify colonialism with ruthless methods of tax collection and labor recruiting, forced village relocation, and sexual exploitation, which were all themes of daily talks that villagers wove into the meanings of names given colonial officials. These collective memories are still remembered today.[36]

There are many accounts to illustrate the relations of situations of actual violence to the names of colonial officials. As a point of entry into the discussion, I use the following exchange that took place in 1906 during a community meeting between a group of Mbole and M. Conti, the colonial agent who laid down the foundations of colonial relations when he created the *chefferies*, the lowest territorial divisions.[37] A typical paternalistic discourse, the exchange stressed the benefits Congolese villagers could gain from their cooperation with and submission to the colonial authorities. As routinely happened during the earlier colonial encounters, the meeting took place under the *owala* tree, and local leaders kept their people away from the official. After a long conversation with the leaders, the official delivered a message he had prepared to ease the integration of the group into the local administration he was building. In a stern tone he stated: "The Arabs, who ravaged your country for years are now defeated; you ever will be free. Now, I like you to gather rubber, copal, kernel, and palm oil, and deliver these goods to your leaders who would forward them to me. If you do this work, I will give you wonderful things."[38]

The speech generated among the meeting attendees reactions that ranged from laughter, lukewarm acceptance, and skepticism to defiance and the murmured rejection of the misrepresentation of anticipated economic rewards of colonialism.[39] The subversive response to the speech was recorded in a surreptitious signifying practice. The Mbole started a tradition of naming traders, colonial state officials, and Congolese auxiliaries appointed to their country *Atama-Atama*, a local variation of the *Matamba-tamba*, the slave raiders from the Indian Ocean whom the Belgian officials referred to as Arabs. From this time onward, the term *Atama-Atama*, first meaning "Enslavers" among the Mbole, became synonymous of *Bula Matari*, which was the typical collective name for all colonial officeholders, and which means, as discussed elsewhere, "Break rocks," or the colonial state, its power, and violence.

Naming European officials after the *Matamba-tamba* and similar names is important for three reasons. First, it shows in a concrete way that the meanings of names described actual colonial situations, and that they were local responses to colonialism and its practices. Second, the explicit reference to memories of the *Matamba-tamba* who had ravaged the Mbole country where they were portrayed invariably in negative roles gives the connotation of protest to accusations of violence, hardships, and meanness. Because the Mbole had openly resisted the *Matamba-tamba*, naming colonial officials after the *Matamba-tamba* suggests that the Mbole were contesting political, economic, and social conditions created by Belgian colonialism. It also shows that the Mbole found the new colonial world they were entering as oppressive and odious as the *Matamba-tamba* trading networks they were leaving behind.[40] Third, the naming of colonial officials means that cultural rationalities that structured the common techniques of protest, specifically gossip, rumors, songs, and subversive dance, were active.[41]

Although vividly explicit in expressing local concerns to early European officials, the Mbole use of historical memories through the naming of colonizers was not unique. Rather it illustrates the dynamics of a naming pattern that was at work everywhere. The naming of the agents of King Leopold II and concessionary companies and Belgian colonial rulers after the names of the *Matamba-tamba,* deeply rooted in the history of the area, was widespread in Eastern Congo until the 1930s. Until Leopold's conquest of Central Africa, trade in slaves and ivory was going on from the Indian Ocean to the entire eastern part of what was to become successively the Congo Free State and Belgian Congo. From Kasongo, a major slave market in Central Africa since 1868, the *Matamba-tamba* extended by the 1880s their trading networks as far west as the Lower Aruwimi, Congo, and Tshuapa rivers, and as far north as Uele and Ituri. From Lake Tanganyika, the *Matamba-tamba* traders reached Southern Katanga. Wherever commercial interests took them and whenever the Congolese refused to trade ivory or to supply porters to carry it, the *Matamba-tamba* burned villages, destroyed crops and herds of goats, killed men, and took women hostages.[42] After the Belgian military campaigns against the *Matamba-tamba* that started in 1892 and that ended two years later with the defeat of Tippo Tib, the Congo Free State established an occupation that continued to use violence that reminded people of the *Matamba-tamba* era. This historical context shaped the naming pattern that generated not only the collective name *Matamba-tamba* but also individual names drawn from personal names of individual *Matamba-tamba* and their powerful local allies, particularly Ngongo Leteta and Lumpungu.[43]

Of the names of the *Matamba-tamba* that became names of colonial officials and social memories of violence, *Angwandima,* "Terror,"

Rumaliza, "Destroyer," and *Bwana Nzige,* "Mister locust," were wide-spread.[44] Eastern Congolese assigned meanings to this category of names that depicted the actions for which each individual *Matamba-tamba* earned his reputation while making comparisons between the two eras. Stories told in the Uele, Aruwimi, Tshuapa, Maniema, Sankuru, and Kisangani areas, regions distant and far away from one another, invariably associated *Angwandima, Rumaliza, Bwana Nzige,* and their parties with the kidnapping of women, cutting off of men's genitals, legs, arms, and hands, piercing of noses and ears, burning of villages, scorching of farms, and killings.[45] Every part of colonial Africa experienced violence, and any comparison seems an exercise in futility. Yet the violence of everyday life during the Congo Free State period was rarely matched or surpassed. To compel Congolese men to gather rubber and supply labor, the builders of the Congo Free State flogged and killed men who resisted orders, and took as hostages the wives of those who fled into the bush. The ruthlessness displayed during recruitment of labor disrupted everyday life and depleted the population of the Congo.[46] By drawing names of colonial officials from the names of cruel *Matamba-tamba,* eastern Congolese villagers accused colonial officials of continuing brutality, exactions, and destruction and conveyed to the colonial rulers a message of protest identical to the one graphically expressed by the title of Ayi Kwei Armah's novel: *The Beautyful Ones Are Not Yet Born.*[47]

Congolese villagers gave Europeans names suggesting violence throughout the entire colonial period. But drawing names of colonial officials from those of the *Matamba-tamba* and comparing the experiences of rubber collectors to the harsh conditions of the *Matamba-tamba*'s occupation expressed the accusations of atrocities and protest more unambiguously than any others they later coined. Such names of the *Matamba-tamba* as *Angwandima, Rumaliza,* and *Bwana Nzige* embodied the collective memories of the ravages of Congolese villages well supported by stories, songs, anthroponyms, and place-names. The testimonies of Eastern Congolese of the 1980s show that whenever these memories were recalled, they still stimulated as much fear and resentment as they did toward the *Matamba-tamba* and colonial officials several decades earlier. The stories of *Matamba-tamba* told by Risasi's father are a case in point. In telling the stories in 1988, Risasi remembered, "Where these names recalled victory, they empowered the community, and where they evoked defeats and massacres, they caused anger that the passing of time has not yet erased."[48] Risasi shared Mariama Bâ's view in *So Long a Letter* that "Pain, when even it's past, leaves the same marks on the individual when recalled."[49] Such names were thus accusations of sufferings and colonial violence.

Naming colonial officials after the *Matamba-tamba* shows that memories of earlier experiences of violence were at work and shaped perceptions of colonialism. Whether they gave colonial officials generic and collective names as the Mbole did with the term *Matamba-tamba* or individual names as many Eastern Congolese did with those drawn from individual names of the *Matamba-tamba*, Congolese underscored the similarities of experiences during the two eras. The power of historical memories to remind people of the stories of brutality transformed this naming pattern in a cultural vehicle through which Congolese expressed their resentment for colonial violence.

Contrasting the meanings of names of colonial officials derived from the reputation and practices of the *Matamba-tamba* with school songs and colonial mottoes propagated during colonization illustrate further the resentment of Congolese villagers for violence. It was plain in the contrast between the images of terror, destruction, and predatory practices that *Angwandima*, *Rumaliza*, and *Bwana Nzige* embodied and conveyed the message of the following song intended by colonial rulers to rally Congolese villagers against the *Matamba-tamba*. The song shows that the names derived from the experiences of *Matamba-tamba* were the accusations of violence and expressions of protest. By celebrating the end of the slave trade, the song vilified all colonial officials because the Mbole called them *Matamba-tamba* and all those whose names were drawn from the personal names of individual *Matamba-tamba* because their personal names meant terror and devastation:

> Bula Matari,
> Our Lord,
> Bula Matari,
> Our Lord,
> Who saved us from slavery (Matamba-tamba)!
> Let us salute,
> Let us salute the Savior.[50]

As an instrument of colonial propaganda designed to change local negative views of colonialism, the song indoctrinated Congolese children in allegiance to the colonial state by deriding the *Matamba-tamba*. The composers of the song apparently manipulated memories of violence to establish hegemonic political relations and were aware of the subversion Congolese villagers conveyed through such names. The liberation by the Europeans was an antithesis to enslavement, of which the Mbole accused state agents in the generic name *Matamba-tamba*.

A second song sung by the Boy Scouts in the late 1950s and 1960s vilified *Ngongo Leteta*, a powerful local ally of the *Matamba-tamba* who later served the Congo State and was executed on 14 September 1893.[51] Like the preceding song, the second shows how the colonial government reminded people of the brutality of the *Matamba-tamba*'s occupation and its violent practices to win over their hearts and minds:

> Ngongo Leteta destroys villages,
> Ah Ngongo Leteta,
> Ngongo Leteta seizes women,
> Ah Ngongo Leteta,
> Ngongo Leteta smashes children's heads,
> Ah! Ngongo Leteta.[52]

Intended to rally Congolese against the *Matamba-tamba* and their local allies, the song shows that casting colonial officials in the role of *Matamba-tamba* was an accusation of violence and an expression of protest against Belgian colonialism. It underscores subversion in the images of violence associated with *Ngongo Leteta*, *Rumaliza*, and *Angwandima*, which have survived until today, especially in the Eastern Congo. The inhabitants of Kisangani, the center of the *Matamba-tamba* commercial empire in Orientale Province, named wicked colonial officials and Congolese policemen after *Angwandima* during the brutal Belgian colonial rule and throughout Mobutu's dictatorship. Today, mothers use it as a teaching tool. They tell their children to behave, or else they will face the wrath of *Angwandima*.[53] A mother of three boys who lives in Kabondo in Kisangani, thirty-eight-year-old Mateso Mungeni tells a vivid story of the power of *Angwandima*'s memory: "I have three little boys who spend time after school playing soccer in a narrow field near the ditch; it is dangerous there and the water is dirty. They are passionate playing and refuse to come to help with small household chores or to eat. Whenever I need them, I have one powerful weapon. I tell them that *Angwandima* is coming and before I finish saying the name, they are inside the house scared to death."[54]

Mateso Mungeni's evocation of *Angwandima* and the obedience of her children testify to its mythical reputation as a symbol of terror and is indicative of the hatred that Congolese villagers directed at the *Matamba-tamba* and their local allies.

Flogging under the watchful eyes of an official, oil on fabric, 1884 (A 770, collection MRAC Tervuren; photo J.-M. Vandyck, MRAC Tervuren ©)

To carry out their mandate, military officers, territorial administrators, agronomists, tax collectors, and crop supervisors relied heavily on the whip. Because of the central role the whip played in their suffering, Congolese named the perpetrators of these abuses after their favored instrument of domination and repression. Between the 1890s and the 1950s, Congolese gave to ruthless colonial officials and private company agents the names *Basikoti* or *Sikoti*, two loanwords from the French word *chicotte*, a widely used hippopotamus-hide whip, and *Fimbo Mingi*, all meaning "Much whipping." Georges Dineur, an ABIR agent at Baringa, received the name *Chicotte* because he loved beating rubber defaulters by ordering up to two hundred lashes in one single session.[55] Commandant Francis Dhanis, a cruel tyrant and colonial warlord who fought the *Matamba-tamba*, earned the name *Fimbo Mingi* from Congolese troops because he preferred whipping to other methods of punishment. From the 1890s until 1910, the Mongo called such colonial officials and agents *Mpimbo Mingi*, which means "Much whipping."[56]

The morphological variety of the name attests to the ubiquity and the commonality of whipping in many language communities, which is well corroborated by oral testimonies, written texts, and transcripts of native courts. In 2003, sixty-year-old Kumingi Yuma told a story of a crop supervisor named *Kabuakiatunge* in Maniema because he wounded Rega cotton cultivators who failed to do their work, lashing them until they bled. A seventy-two-year-old man, Ali Musa, recounted the same year a similar story about *Alinga Tumba,* "Fight lover," who lashed those Lengola who refused to pay taxes and disobeyed chiefs and village elders.[57]

Congolese still criticized the central role of the whip in their relations with colonial state officials by giving them names that kept a tally of lashes they ordered to punish defiant villagers. In telling a story of cash crop production in 1950 in Basoko, Matata Moelealongo spoke of cash crop producers who named ⸱ crop supervisor *Mwambe,* meaning "Eight," "because he always ordered eight lashes to punish rebellious producers by 'lying them prone.'"[58] The story re-created the image of powerlessness in the 1950s, but the image was widespread in the early years of colonialism and was expressed through such names as *Panzi,* "Lying side," and *Alali na Se,* "He who is lying down." Congolese minted *Panzi* during the atrocities of the rubber economy (1891–1912), while the syntagm *Alali na Se* was born out of the hardship of the mandatory cash crop production (1917–60). The Barambo in the Lower-Uele District gave the name *Alali na Se* to an official who, through the late 1940s and early 1950s, ordered insubordinate cotton producers to lie prone before policemen lashed them.[59] Drawn from experiences of whipping, physical and corporeal punishment that Congolese interpreted as the epitome of political repression, domination, and powerlessness, these names were strong accusations of indignities caused by Belgian colonial rule.[60]

Besides the whip, colonial officials deployed verbal threats when situations did not merit physical violence. Broadly, verbal threats came as warnings, orders, and threats of death. As verbal as they were, these forms of violence terrified Congolese as much as the blows of lashes. This punishment stemmed from colonial officials' belief that menaces created less disruption, prevented the erosion of colonial authority, and above all cost less compared to imprisonment that withdrew labor from production and incurred financial expenses. Second, it also derived from an erroneous interpretation and blind acceptance of pictures of docile Congolese staged at the trading posts, public meetings, censuses taking, and clinics. Moreover, work performance and willingness to pay taxes and daily rituals of obedience finish the picture of submissive Congolese the colonial officials sought to create. To be sure, colonial officials expected Congolese to join their feet, take off their hats, bow their heads, and kneel while greeting officials. Most Congolese performed these rituals well, which contributed to the picture of obedience. Yet most colonial officials failed to recognize that rituals of obedience performed by Congolese had multidimensional meanings and many origins. Congolese villagers' unfamiliarity with new realities in a rapidly changing society created confusion, as did changes in numerals and in systems of weights and measures, the monetization of the economy in 1910, and the imposition of lingua franca as the languages of local administrations. The images of obedience lured colonial officials to the use of threats, punishments that Congolese villagers turned into names of their oppressors. This dynamic showed conflicts and tensions in the political relations between the two groups. The naming of colonial officials after the threats aimed at asserting colonial authority negated the relations of domination that colonial officials tried to consolidate.[61]

The name "He who yells at people"[62] is an excellent illustration of how Congolese, when naming colonial officials after verbal threats that the colonial officials regularly used to discipline them, expressed their concerns about colonial interactions, particularly the way colonial officials addressed Congolese villagers. Cotton cultivators in Buta gave the name "He who yells at people" to an agricultural officer in the 1940s because he shouted at them and always raised the pitch of voice when addressing them. For the givers of this and similar names, such behaviors imposed status domination, which was the reason Congolese strongly resented them. To be sure, yelling and elevating the voice reduced men to the status of women and social juniors while they degraded women to the status of children, treatments men and women considered condescending. Names derived from threats such as "He who yells at people" and *Sukuma*, "Push," discussed in chapter 3, were accusations of violence and strong expressions of popular protest against words and acts of humiliation that Congolese villagers endured besides corporeal punishments.[63]

Names drawn from threats were accusations of sufferings and violence. But they were also part of a broader discourse of protests that defied the aggressive colonial propaganda that colonial officials deployed across the countryside through such catchphrases as the "Congo Free State" and the colonial motto, "Work and Progress." They challenged the ideology propagated by the colonial government through its ubiquitous symbol of colonial political domination, the blue flag with a golden

star in its center. Congolese villagers did not read the texts explaining
the meanings of the blue color and golden star of the flag. But they
learned about all these meanings because the colonial government asserted in many ways that the blue color symbolized the darkness of the
Congolese world while the golden star shone the light of European civilization. Congolese consumed the ideology as they listened to such rosy
slogans and stereotypes as "ending intergroup warfare," "lucrative
trade," "liberation from slavery," and the like. In reality, early colonial
propaganda campaigns of freedom produced a kind of irony because
they radicalized the consciousness of Congolese villagers who already
in the 1900s told colonial officials, "Bula Matari no longer allows slavery."[64] They still struck a similar chord in the 1930s through the 1940s
when they told colonial officials, "There are no more worthless people
these days."[65] Colonial officials satirized these aspirations to freedom
and equality of status, and one commented, "For the blacks, not to be a
slave means no longer to be under a chief, not even under a European;
it means no longer to owe anything to anybody, and to live as one
wishes. . . . It means idleness and confusion of liberty with anarchy."[66]
Aspirations of Congolese to freedom and equality of status were reinforced by the loss of power to make decisions and to start productive
undertakings independently. And these concerns surfaced in names as
powerful voices against physical and verbal abuses, autocratic behaviors,
indignities, and claims by colonial officials to cultural chauvinism.[67]

Congolese villagers convey these ideas and concerns in the names
depicting conditions of transporting colonial officials on hammocks
and trade goods on their backs and heads along the colonial roads, scenes
that characterized colonialism before automobiles were introduced.
Congolese cash crop producers, especially those who lived along the
roads, should have welcomed the building of the infrastructure because
it freed them of porterage. Yet even this group of Congolese villagers did
not look at the colonial roads as the windfall of modernity. They believed
that the roads opened the village world to brutal tax collectors and abusive labor recruiters, destroyed indigenous ways of life, caused village relocations, and shifted the financial costs of their construction to local
households. For most rural dwellers, the roads brought instead suffering
and hardships eloquently expressed in the meanings of names of colonial officials and corroborated by many stories of local reactions to the
roads.

Kiswahili, Ciluba, and Lingala speakers who named territorial administrators, agronomists, and tax collectors *Bala-Bala* and *Mala-Mala*

expressed the most pervasive accusations of road-generated sufferings and hardships.[68] In the three languages, the terms mean "Main roads," similar to the river cut through the forests and which Lingala speakers called *ebale*.[69] As they became powerful symbols and images of road-generated sufferings, the names referred to peripatetic officials who moved so frequently, and who presumably never got anything done because of their unending travels, which, until the 1930s, subjected Congolese men to carrying heavy pieces of luggage and roving colonial officials on hammocks.

Bala-Bala and *Mala-Mala* share with *Ndeke* and its reduplication *Ndeke-Ndeke* the meaning "Officials on the move" that transformed them into synonyms. The term *Ndeke* means "Bird." Under colonial rule, it described colonial officials who moved frequently to collect taxes, carry out punitive expeditions, and monitor production of households forced into the cash crop cultivation. Through the name *Ndeke*, Congolese villagers bemoaned the unending travels of itinerate officials because they associated such travels with the burden of carrying loads, the wasting of time, and the lack of noteworthy achievements, aspects of colonialism that swelled their hearts with anger, hostility, and resentment.[70]

A few illustrations prove the point. Emile Torday, the first Kuba ethnographer who also studied many other peoples of southern Congo in the 1890s, received the name *Ndeke* because of his frequent travels. Congolese troops were the first Congolese people to join the most repressive colonial institution and to observe closely the most brutal colonial rulers and give them names. In 1897, for example, Congolese soldiers gave Commandant Henry, a Belgian officer who stumbled on an eighty-seven-kilogram piece of gold in Moto goldfields, the name *Ndeke* because he moved fast as he roamed the region.[71] In all cases, *Ndeke* described what Torday and Henry were doing on the ground. *Ndeke*, however, conveyed a great deal more. It was also a criticism of a roving way of life that Congolese villagers associated with tax collectors, who were perceived as ever wandering across villages to confiscate cash, a role that gave *Ndeke* layers of ugly connotations. A source associates *Ndeke* with unflattering meaning. To be sure, tax collectors wielded coercive power over Congolese villagers, but they enjoyed no respect, particularly those who received the name *Ndeke*. A high-ranking colonial official reported this predicament in the 1930s, noting: "I have heard several times many reflections of Congolese; I have heard and still hear Congolese saying that after looking at how *Bula Matari*'s officials roamed villages to collect taxes, they regarded them a little bit like beggars."[72]

The name *Ndeke* also depicted officials who never finished the projects they started and thus dissipated energies that Congolese villagers
thought could be better spent on productive undertakings and leisure
time. So *Ndeke, Ndeke-Ndeke, Bala-Bala, Mala-Mala*, and similar names
were accusations of wasting time and energies caused by the unending
travels of the colonial officials. Because roving officials disrupted the village world and became a burden for households, these accusations expressed powerful voices of protest against Belgian colonial rule.[73]

Accusations of road-generated sufferings and degrading practices
became the quintessential expressions of resentment of the white men
when *Bala-Bala, Mala-Mala, Ndeke*, and *Ndeke-Ndeke* referred to transporting colonial officials on *Tipoyi*, the hammocks. Throughout colonization, Congolese villagers associated the widespread practice of carrying
Europeans on hammocks with the loss of manhood and the perfect scene
of domination and humiliation of Congolese men. For Congolese villagers, to carry a colonial official on a hammock meant, to borrow a title
from Norman Hodge, *To Kill a Man's Pride*.[74]

The syntagms *Bala-Bala, Mala-Mala, Ndeke*, and *Ndeke-Ndeke* embodied negative views of the role the colonial roads played in integrating
the village world into the oppressive colonial world and its exploitative
economy. Nobody articulated the view better than Matungi, an Eastern
Congo villager who, angry at his colonial world of the 1950s, pondered:
"What happiness have they brought us? They have given us a road we
did not need, a road that brings more and more foreigners and enemies
into our midst, causing trouble, making our women unclean, forcing us
to a way of life that is not ours, planting crops that we do not want,
doing slave's work."[75] Perceiving the colonial road as the cause of enslavement of the village communities, the erosion of indigenous ways of
life, and the defiling of women was a voice of protest against social disruptions. Yet defiling women was not the grievance that caused the most
anger and resentment. The sexual and economic abuse of women became the major concern and source of protest attested to by the meanings of names that depicted the plight of women and their relations
with colonial officials and agents.

At first glace, having an affair or a sexual relation with a colonial
official did not seem exploitative in the peasant economy of the Congo
in which women were the backbone of production. Long-term relationships shielded women from the hardships of mandatory farming
and provided them with material and financial resources unavailable to

Congolese carrying on a *Tipoyi* Reverend Sister Anselma, of the Congregation of Franciscans of Herenthals, at the arrival of the congregation in Ubangi, 1923 (HP.1956.56.484, collection MRAC Tervuren ; photo anonyme, 1923)

women in local communities. By colonial standards, these women were impeccably dressed and well fed, material conditions that enhanced their social standing. These relations, by delaying the marriage of Congolese women to Congolese men, diminished the specter of being taken hostage for the actions of rebellious husbands who refused to collect required quotas of rubber, particularly at the beginning of the colonial intrusion.[76] Escaping agricultural labor and securing material rewards in a colonial world of fewer choices and opportunities enticed women into sexual relations with European officials. In a tale of a premarital affair in the 1950s, Matata Moelealongo talked about the enormous power of seduction that colonial officials drew from these inducements. As she described the barriers her mother confronted in the colonial world, she recalled what her mother considered a spectacular opportunity and achievement: "I may not be the prettiest woman of the village, but I have slept with a white man."[77]

Despite this public acknowledgment of an affair with a white man by Moelealongo's mother, most men and women my research assistants and I interviewed in the 1980s and 1990s thought that the relations between local women and colonial government officials were casual and clandestine and therefore hard to detect because of stringent restrictions that separated the two groups. Atsidri Nyelegodi, like many rural dwell-ers, categorically denied such relations in Ituri, claiming, "sexual rela-tions between Congolese women and white men did not exist at all."[78] Nyelengodi was not alone in his inability to remember sexual relations between local women and colonial officials. Bakonzi Ngilinga, a sixty-three-year-old retired Logo man in 2003, denied these relations, saying, "Before independence, no sexual relations between white men and black women in the rural areas took place. The colonizers considered their civilization superior to ours."[79] Although he experienced colonialism as an adult only in the 1950s in Beni, Jean Paluku struck a similar chord, emphatically stating, "The white men had no sexual relation with black women; the white men did everything they could to avoid the leak of secrets."[80]

The denial of sexual relations by the interviewees does not indicate the absence of affairs between colonial officials and local women in the Congolese countryside. Besides the existence of offspring, colonial offi-cials and Congolese witnesses confirm the relations. According to Frank L. Lambrecht, a health officer, the relations took place and "started with the acquisition of what was commonly called a 'ménagère,' a native girl who supposedly ran the house but whose services were expected to ex-tend beyond the call of such duties. Considered immoral by the Church and the 'landlubbers' back home [Belgium], the custom was an institu-tion as old as colonialism, and served in some instances the purpose of providing a kind of stable household, probably better managed than if passion and impulses had run unchecked. Anyway, the custom was there, and it was followed by most bachelors."[81]

Despite the rewards that sexual relations with colonial officials brought to Congolese women, the manner in which the officials selected the women before they entered the "ménage" made the relations ex-ploitative. In many instances, this manner was similar to the everyday degrading treatment that Congolese men and women suffered any-where under colonial rule. Congolese women suffered yaws (infections), leprosy, sleeping sickness, and venereal diseases, and the prevalence of these diseases made colonial officials wary of sexual relations without medical examinations. But the following description of an ad hoc medi-cal examination for safe sex gives a glimpse into the kinds of treatment Congolese women endured before they entered sexual relations with European officials. Again, Lambrecht tells us:

One of the stories was about a wild party that presumably took place at the Baron's house, during which Doc disappeared with a Budu girl in the direction of the cotton shed. Those who had observed the maneuver guessed what was going on. They were somewhat surprised when a moment later a servant came running, asking the host for a lantern requested, he said, by the munganga (doctor). Willing hands prepared a storm lamp, but also followed the servant to observe, through the gaps in the reed walls, what the doc's game was. . . . What he was doing while his amazed friends looked clandestinely, was to submit the girl to a detailed medical examination, by the light of the lantern. The whole scene may have been highly grotesque and, no doubt, extremely annoying and offensive to the girl. The peeping Toms were discrete enough to retire from the scene after their first curiosity was satisfied, and Doc's diagnosis was never revealed.[82]

Congolese women in the colonial village started relationships with white officials in a different way, which originated in a widespread local tradition. In the nineteenth century, important guests and travelers in Central Africa enjoyed the hospitality of a local leader who provided shelter, food, and female companionship. The practice withstood waves of Christian moral campaigns until the 1930s and still influenced local politics after decrees enacted to fight polygyny and local political competition by cutting the number of small *chefferies* created between 1892 and 1933. Following the custom, local leaders offered female companions, including their own wives, to white officials in response to local political competition enhanced by administrative reforms after the Great Depression. Designed to cut administrative costs during the Great Depression, the administrative reforms of 1933 ended the careers of many local leaders in the local administration and compelled them to manipulate the tradition to save their positions. The situation of the Topoke leaders in the 1930s is a case in point. Colonial officials once described the Topoke chief Boula before the 1930s as brave and loyal, especially after he had saved two European agents during a riot in 1906. Evidence shows that he ruled with an iron fist to the satisfaction of his colonial bosses. Based on his years of service in recruiting workers for the *Huilleries du Congo Belge* (a concessionary company specializing in palm oil production), his report card made him a first-rank colonial chief. Yet he lost his job "because he refused to give his favorite wife to a state agent."[83] His successor, Chief Bolema, learned quickly from the dismissal of his predecessor. Soon after his investiture, he gave his wife Nuka to the tax collector Charles Van de Lanoitte, who called him "my brother." Regardless of his second-rate job performance and polygynous status, Chief Bolema received excellent evaluations and salary raises and maintained his post although his performance in collecting taxes, recruiting labor, and maintaining roads was mediocre.[84]

A public figure, Chief Bolema shrewdly used his wife to promote his political career. But this behavior was not universal. Abuses against women angered local leaders and ordinary men who spoke out by giving unlikable names to those officials who abused local women physically and sexually. During the Congo Free State period when violence was the most common means of dominating local communities, Chief Elua of Mampoko, also a public figure, defended women against the violence of the Lulonga Company. On 5 January 1905, he denounced the atrocities committed by the company agents against women to the Commission of Inquiry:

> I have asked to talk to the Commission because I have a complaint against the white man at Mampoko, *Likwama* (M. Spelier, the Director of Lulonga Company) who is mistreating us. He demands every day and even Sunday twenty women and five men of my village to work at the post. The sentries are always behind to beat them because they think that they are not working much quickly. The sentries abuse especially women. One day they stripped Mongali and introduced mud into her vagina. Many women have died because of the beating. About a month ago, Donanvo, another woman, was flogged by the sentries and died three days later; Mongonde and Mongali brought dead bodies to *Likwama* to complain, but he became angry and chased them without hearing their complaints.[85]

In 1933, Lele men in the Sankuru District tried to poison the territorial administrator Dossogne because he had killed three women during a punitive expedition that took eight lives.[86] During the same period, Chief Bolembe of Topoke in the Aruwimi District far away from the Lele sought unsuccessfully to poison a territorial administrator for the mistreatment of women who "complained to their husbands about being sexually abused by agents of the Lomami Company when husbands were at work."[87]

These illustrations underline two realities. First, whatever the illusions of prestige that casual and short-term relations with colonial officials instilled into the minds of Congolese women, they suffered as much humiliation and exploitation as men.[88] Second, despite the adaptation of select traditions for political purposes, Congolese men, leaders and ordinary men alike, defended women against the abuses of colonialism. Longstanding ideologies of masculinity, which prescribed to men the protection and defense of women, informed this defense of women. The ideologies of masculinity influenced also local interpretations of relations of women with colonial officials, including sexual relations.[89] The reactions of leaders and ordinary men show that any abuse committed by colonial officials against women meant an assault on their masculinity. Attempts by the Lele and Topoke men to poison colonial officials were expected reprisals.

The economic undertakings of women are important entry points into the discussion of naming to understand the extent to which naming captured local comments about the plight of women under colonial rule. To be sure, Congolese perceived low prices of agricultural commodities and the subsequent meager cash flow into the households as an assault on the village world. Let us consider an example to illustrate this point. To supplement their revenue and earnings in the village economy, women often brewed beer. Such economic pursuit was outlawed by local administrations partly because of women's pivotal role in mandatory cash agriculture that required a close control of their labor, and partly because of moralizing campaigns against drunkenness, which colonial officials believed had cut production outputs. To circumvent the highly organized system of control set up by territorial administrators and supervised by state-appointed chiefs at the village level, beer brewing went underground. Despite tactics to hide from officials, women were caught and severely punished. This struggle gave rise to a tradition of naming colonial officials after symbols and metaphors drawn from literary genres. Luba women at Luiza captured the struggle in the name *Nyimi-Nyimi*, meaning "Red ant." Meya Katoto, a female former cotton producer, recalled in 1986: "we used to brew beer in the bush; *Nyimi-Nyimi* followed us, surprised us and punished us. We used the name in songs and conversations as we talked about clandestine beer brewing."[90] In the Luba cultural universe, the red ant was a symbol of fearlessness, while red means "uncivilized." The two meanings contradicted each other and generated a duplicitous message. Reference to the courage of colonial officials by Luba women who experienced harassment conveyed no praise.[91] It rather expressed grievances. But the reference to the lack of civilization (red) was an accusation against prohibiting beer brewing, which was an attempt to take away one source of income. Briefly, the name protested colonial policies to wean female beer brewers away from their means of financial independence in the household.[92]

In their scorn for the abusive relations colonial officials had with
local women, Congolese villagers stressed predatory sexual conduct as
much as economic exploitation. Lingala speakers used the widespread
euphemism *Alinga Mama,* which means "He who loves mother."[93] Congolese villagers gave this generic and collective name to any colonial official accused of womanizing. And the generic and seemingly neutral
name connoted disdain for predatory sexual behavior, which oral testimonies abundantly corroborated. Amisi perceived such officials as
"eagles stealing chicken in one's own backyard."[94] This powerful image
shows the power struggle between Congolese and European men over
access to Congolese women, which Kabuji Bualu highlighted when he
told the tale of a colonial official named *Tshibaka* who liked light-skinned
Lulua women. Ilunga Luboza remembered the white man *Mutombo* who
sexually exploited women in Ngandajika among the Luanga Bena Pebu.
A colonial officeholder earned the names *Munamia* and *Kiranzi* because
he sexually abused women, and Kumingi Yuma believed the abuse was
common between 1945 and 1957 in Kindu. In Bumba Congolese villagers gave a white man the collective name *Beleli,* which means "Lover of
women."[95]

Congolese villagers sometimes used crude names to identify colonial
officials they believed were sexually abusing women. Lonyoyo Louise
Tamile, a Logo woman, told the story of white men who earned the
generic collective name *Agomiriya* between 1920 and 1945 because they
never controlled their sexual impulses. This meaning of *Agomiriya* shifted
and became an insult for an unfaithful husband. A Lokele man, Lotika
Lwa Botende, recalled the story of white men who loved local women in
the 1950s at Yanonge and who received the generic name *Ewa-Olefe,*
"Womanizer." Matata Moelealongo remembered a similar situation in
the story of the colonial official *Makpatu,* "Chaser of women," who had
a similar reputation in the 1950s in Boumane, Basoko.[96]

Briefly, these cases show that whether Congolese men used euphe-
misms or crude names to scorn predatory sexual conduct or employed
metaphors to refer to physical mistreatment of local women, they expressed anger and in many cases protest at violating local norms of sexual behavior.

6

Talking under One's Breath

Praise Names as
Strategic Ambiguities

Praise naming was a longstanding tradition in the Congo designed to celebrate events, families, communities, and corporate groups, and to mark achievements of leaders and ordinary individuals. Praise naming was also surreptitiously duplicitous because speakers paired flattering remarks with negative messages to create strategic ambiguity and convey grievances, which, if crudely expressed, generated tensions and confrontations.[1] Congolese villagers started naming Europeans after praises starting in the early years of colonization and continued the practice throughout the colonial era as they gave praise names to colonial officials and cast them in positive roles for real or perceived resourceful schemes, the reputation of fairness, exceptional work, conviviality, high moral qualities, and the lessening of exploitation. The tradition evolved under colonial rule as Congolese villagers gave likeable colonial officials genuine praise and surreptitious names to express anger at colonial practices and policies that disrupted the daily life in the village world.

The analysis first centers on stories of true celebration of colonial officials and their actions. Second it looks at how Congolese villagers wove grievances of colonial practices into multidimensional meanings of names of praise to create strategic ambiguities, useful in their experiences with colonialism and its agents. In all cases, the analysis highlights the geographical distribution of the name, contexts, events, and situations that informed the meanings of names and that explain the relation of praise to the character and actions of the colonial officials.

Of the names of colonial officials and agents that genuinely praised the colonizers, *Bwana Lubuku* was exemplary. Van Malderen ruled Kasongo in 1902–3 and received the name *Bwana Lubuku*, which painted him as the "Master builder." The residents of Kasongo appreciated the actions of the officer and spoke highly of him: "Bwana Lubuku was a supernatural human being and a famous builder only teaching us how to produce bricks."[2]

Producing bricks was not the decisive factor in shaping how people perceived the official and the choice of the name. The way he went about doing it was. First, he created a good reputation that he cultivated and backed by patiently teaching people the new skill. This skill changed the quality of life and molded local attitude toward him and the work he carried out. A time-consuming and backbreaking work, manufacturing bricks was the same as other economic projects that pitted people here and elsewhere against colonial officials. The tasks required to produce bricks included breaking the ground, pressing the soil, drying the bricks in rows, building kilns, cutting wood, firing the bricks, and transporting them to the construction sites. Kasongo was in a district that pioneered cotton production, and Congolese could resent these tasks as much as they resented cash crop cultivation and porterage. The change from the *Matamba-tamba* regime to the rule of the Congo Free State was not qualitative. The Belgian colonial regime still used violent tactics similar to the practices once used by the *Matamba-tamba*. The continuity of violence in everyday life shaped the way people saw how *Bwana Lubuku* did his job. As people continued to face violence and social disruption caused by protracted wars of conquest and Belgian military campaigns against the *Matamba-tamba*, manufacturing bricks to build houses resonated with the aspirations of local people and thus took on a positive connotation.

Away from Eastern Congo, the Tio in Western Congo named Janssen after a widespread metonym for beauty and good internal disposition, *Soso Mombi*, a short phrase that means "White feathered-chicken." Janssen earned the name because he built a house at the settlement of an important Tio chief who interpreted the building as a display of true friendship.[3] Lingala speakers used the synonymous expression *Soso Mpembe* to name friendly colonial officials. Kikongo speakers in Western Congo celebrated any colonial official they named *Mondele Ngolo*, which means "Strong white man." Extolling the power and the masculinity of colonial officials, *Mondele Ngolo* had synonyms everywhere in the Congo.[4] Kiswahili speakers in Eastern Congo called such colonial officials *Mbavu Nguvu*, "Strong chest," *Aduyi*, "Lion," and *Simba Bulaya*, "Europe's lion," while Lingala speakers named them *Makasi*, "Strong." Colonial officials earned these generic names of praise when they did projects that Congolese thought were feasible only if performed by strong and powerful men who had exceptional physical and moral strengths associated with manhood, masculinity, and virility.[5]

Besides an emphasis on manhood and masculinity, perceptions and a sense of protection and friendship were the foci of praise. For example, colonial officials who received from the Kuba the name *Makupkup,* "Of the old village," the people who defended the Kuba kingdom, were undeniably celebrated. To be sure, any official was named *Makupkup* because his job was to be advisor to the king and thus the Kuba spokesman in the colonial administration. Another telling example comes from Ituri. Because what she did was perceived as an expression of love toward local people, Yolande Lammerat, the wife of Pierre Decuypere, who was prosecutor in the 1950s at Irumu, Bunia, and Kisangani and who became judge in Mbandaka in June 1960, earned the name of praise *Mupenda Batu,* "She who loves people."[6]

These illustrations show that for all the atrocities of colonialism and the ruthless brutality of its agents, village people appreciated friendship, learning, and new technical skills that improved the quality of their lives and conditions of work. Excessive violence characteristic of Belgian colonialism was therefore unnecessarily oppressive. And this is why any name that voiced a critique of violence even slightly, as many did, was an expression of protest. The contexts of genesis and stories re-created from other names suggest that not all the names of praise were expressions of true praise. Indeed, if resourceful schemes generated praise of colonial officials, and maltreatment of Congolese by cruel officials produced negative perceptions of colonialism, the praise of execrable colonial officials was ironic. The inconsistencies between referents and meanings show the duplicity embedded in various messages conveyed by names of praise.

Besides genuine admiration of aspects of colonialism and its officials and agents, praise names appeared to extol colonial officials while criticizing, ridiculing, and insulting them. Although praise names ostensibly praised colonial officials, they bemoaned colonial assaults on the village world. Specific examples show that what appeared to be praise of achievements, affluence, power, elegance, and good looks was ironically the mockery of the power and masculinity or manhood of colonial officials, and at times a strong accusation of economic exploitation and political repression. The ambiguities of praise naming were the ironic meanings that many praise names conveyed and that Congolese villagers gave to both brutal and friendly colonial officials. Congolese villagers expressed praise and protests simultaneously, first by using signifiers that referred to or depicted colonial officials' facial expressions, bodily language, physical appearance, bodily shape and size, cultural assumptions about the body or parts of the body, and local symbols of peace. These depictions and cultural assumptions of the body contained both praise and protest. Second, they drew names from moral qualities that expressed flattering messages at the literal level but criticized, at the cultural and thus deeper level, the ways in which the colonial officials behaved in carrying out colonial policies.

Why did Congolese use praise naming to convey surreptitious messages to colonial officials? Subaltern and peasant studies of Southeast Asia and Africa have shown that under conditions of political domination and economic exploitation, the simultaneous use of praise of authorities and insults to them, seemingly a contradictory and paradoxical political behavior, was a position often motivated by the need for safety.[7] This was true for Congolese villagers living in a colonial world where speaking openly against colonialism in front of a subaltern colonial agent amounted to a crime that was severely punished. Still, Congolese villagers did not shy away from open resistance; nor were they petrified by fears of harsh punishment that accompanied confrontations when they cloaked grievances in names of praise. Congolese people rebelled whenever they could no longer tolerate aspects of colonial exploitation.[8] First, they gave colonial officials names of praise because talking through images, symbols, and literary genres was an effective way to communicate differing and multidimensional messages, one to themselves and another to European colonial officials. Second, Congolese used praise naming as an instrument of protest when they realized that confrontation was no longer a way of coping with colonialism in daily life. This became true as the loss of power denied Congolese the right to speak freely, and they realized that names aptly conveyed differing messages to differing audiences. All these contexts mean that praise naming was part of a broader discourse of protest similar to hidden forms of resistance such as the boiling of seeds before planting them, the cutting of plant roots, and the growing of cash crops on exhausted lands, forms of rural resistance well documented in the Congolese literature.[9]

Praise and protest formed often symmetrical pairs observable in Congolese verbal arts and literary genres. The dichotomy was expressed by the Ngbaka of northern Congo in their saying, "If a man speaks under his breath, there is something evil in his heart."[10] Far away from the north in the inner Congo Basin, the Mbole warning explains the idea much better. In unstable situations, they would say, "Keep a smile

on the lips and war in the heart."[11] The Ngbaka and Mbole sayings
were part of a widespread way of thinking and help formulate the argument that praise of colonial officials was duplicitous. The duplicity of
praise naming can be seen in the reaction of the Azande leader Mopoi,
who still hoped in 1908 that cloaking criticisms of Europeans with praise
"could chip away at the evils of the white man."[12] Congolese villagers
shared this view, and when they succumbed to colonialism, they teased
cultural meanings out of local symbols and literary genres to cloak the
anger and hostility they had toward colonial officials.[13] So the names of
praise extolled colonial officials while they denounced grievances and
the structural constraints that Congolese faced in daily life.

Descriptions and cultural assumptions about the body were the
most common generic and collective names of praise, and most held ambiguous and paradoxical meanings. The sample used in this study en-
compasses a diverse repertoire of depictions of physical strength, good
looks, elegance, gestures, gaits, and stereotypes of gender given to colonial officials playing similar roles. The stereotypes of gender were laudatory feminine gender-derived names given to supposedly handsome
colonial officials. Yet feminine gender-derived names carried an enormous symbolic load and connoted insults and ridicule of the masculinity or the manhood of colonial officials. Others were accusations of extortions of foodstuffs and low prices for cash crops.[14] For illustrations,
I analyze *Libumu*, "Belly," the Kiswahili *Bwana Mzuri*, "Mister handsome," *Mafuta Mingi*, "A lot of fat," *Maina*, "Fat," *Lipumbu*, "Elegant,"
and *Mondele Madami*, "Man who is always with his wife."[15]

In the 1890s, Congolese had already named many Europeans *Mafuta
Mingi* in Lingala and *Bwana Mzuri* in Kiswahili.[16] This naming pattern
was observed in places and regions as far away from one another as Ituri
in the north of the Congo, Yambinga and Aruwimi in the center, Tanganyika in the southeast, and Kasai in the southwest.[17] A few of these
traveling names were translated into local languages. The Kiswahili
term *Bwana Mukubwa*, "Mister tall" or "Big boss," had its synonym in the
Ciluba compound name *Kasongo Mule*, "Tall and lean," the opposite of
the Kikongo *Mundele Kikufi*, "Short white man."[18] Many officials who received these generic individual names were plump, handsome, tall, or
short, and the names meant what officials looked like. But names derived
from looks and physical descriptions of the body had multidimensional
meanings ranging from praise of colonial officials to criticisms of greed,
abuse of power, mockery, and insults. Besides describing the body, names
ascribing feminine gender to male officials conveyed criticisms of sexual

debauchery and a shortcoming in manhood or inappropriate male conduct and behavior. At a deeper level of meaning, such names show surreptitious interpretations of the harsh realities of colonialism and the
ways in which each individual official carried out colonial policies.

From the outset of colonization, colonial officials earned such generic and collective names as *Lipumbu*, "Elegant," *Bwana Kitoko* and its
Kiswahili synonym *Bwana Mzuri*, "Mister handsome," all derived from
the pleasing physical appearance and good looks of colonial officials.
Convinced that they were elegant, cleaner, and tidier than Congolese
villagers were, the receivers of these names accepted their image of
magnificence and never suspected the dissent and mockery such terms
often carried. Despite the apparent admiration of colonial officials conveyed by names derived from social stereotypes of gender, they accused
colonial officials of deficiencies in masculinity and manhood and criticized their greed when the actions of colonial officials failed to match
the flattering discourse about generosity, prosperity, and altruism.

Verbal testimonies and transcripts of native courts provide a body
of evidence showing that "Mister handsome," the primary meaning of
Bwana Mzuri, carries many subtexts that were disdainful critiques of the
lack of power and the deficiency of masculinity and manhood of colonial officials. A 1927 trial transcript taken from a native court of the Bazela Chiefdom in Katanga reads, "The wife wants to leave her husband;
she tells the court that although the husband is good looking, he is not a
man because he does not fulfill his marital obligation that was sexual."
Another trial transcript equally attributing a condescending meaning to
names states: "A husband catches his wife in an adulterous situation and
beats her. The wife calls the husband a 'rooster' and everybody laughs
because the rooster signifies premature ejaculations; she refuses to return with the man because she says that he is only another woman.
These claims are many and make up many divorces we try to stop."[19]

A strong critique of Western gender relations and sex roles was
Mondele Madami, another stereotype of feminine gender that means
"Man who is always with his wife."[20] A colonial official who ruled Bulungu Territory in the 1930s earned the name *Mondele Madami* because he
toured villages always accompanied by his wife. White women in the village were, throughout colonization, an event that generated many interpretations of Western gender and sexuality and that had far-reaching
implications on indigenous cultural practices and local colonial politics.
This was true until the Second World War, when many colonial officials

remained bachelors or left their wives in Belgium while working in the Congo.[21]

While raising questions and curiosity about Western sexuality and gender relations, white women generated admiration. This was evidenced in the tradition of naming light-skinned Congolese girls *Madami, Mwandami, Adami,* and *Atamu,* loanwords from the French word *madame,* a term of address that was becoming a local honorific.[22] Because all these terms were honorifics, this naming pattern showed a strong idealization of white women across the village world. The admiration of white women was also apparent in the behaviors of members of local associations created in the 1940s to restore social harmony. Because of the prestige that white women enjoyed in local communities, female members of *saura,* an anti-colonial association that sprang up in Uele in the 1940s through the 1950s, identified as *madame.*[23]

Despite the admiration Congolese had for white wives, *Mondele Madami* was a subversive accusation that the official was but "a man who behaves like a woman." Because colonial officials relied on Congolese male servants, known in condescending colonial language as *boys*— emasculating the Congolese men—to perform domestic chores, rural dwellers learned quite a lot about what was going on inside the households of colonial officials, including intra-household disputes, menstruation and the accompanying pollution, infidelity, and looseness of colonial officials' wives.[24] Making details of the intimate life and misconduct of officials' wives public created rumors and diminished the prestige and admiration for Europeans. And the relations between the spouses ran counter to local ideologies of masculinity and enhanced the resistance of Congolese men against anti-polygyny policies and the politics of gender equality advocated by colonial state officials who enforced changes in divisions of labor in peasant production.[25] First, in the villages where the public and domestic spheres were gendered and husbands still walked behind wives with arrows and spears to ensure safety and protection, the side-by-side walk violated local norms of proper gender relations and challenged tenets of local sex roles. Second, because of colonial anti-polygyny policies and waves of colonial campaigns for gender equality in the 1920s and 1930s, Congolese men interpreted the couple as a showcase of the ideal monogamous marriage and exemplary expression of gender relations the colonial authorities were wittingly promoting across the village world. The well-documented resistance of Congolese men to monogamy shows that the name *Mondele*

Madami expressed local reactions ranging from a strong popular condemnation of colonial anti-polygyny policies and gender equality to
astonishment toward such policies.[26] Finally and equally important,
husbands saw the official as setting a bad example for their wives. So
gender assumptions captured in a name like "Man who behaves like a
woman" and similar names expressed voices of protest against European sexuality and gender relations because of their perceived corrupt-
ing effects on local gender relations and roles.

Lipumbu, a Lingala word that translates as "Elegant," is the last illustration of names of praise in this group. This was a widespread generic name of praise that Congolese villagers gave to early colonial government officials and those they encountered throughout colonization
until the 1950s. Lieutenant Lefebvre earned the name *Lipumbu* from the
Azande leader Mopoi during the Congo Free State period at the time of
ivory and rubber trade because "l̶. spoke flattering words without paying handsome prices like his predecessor who used to offer guns and
ammunitions to local leaders."[27] A shrewd politician and seasoned
trader, Mopoi had counted guns given in exchange and found that they
were not worth the value of his rubber and ivory. As the officer paid
low prices, the Azande leader held back sales of his goods to negotiate
better prices. Frustrated and angered by the official's stubborn refusal
to raise the prices, which he perceived as an unequal exchange caused
by the official's greed, Mopoi refused to barter his products in 1908 and
called all colonial agents stationed across the Azande country *Batu
Pamba*, a terse phrase that means "Straw men." As face-to-face communication broke down, the Azande leader voiced his frustration and
anger in his message to Lieutenant Lefebvre through a local messenger,
telling him, "The white men ought to know that I am smart."[28] Although this anger does not explain why the official received the name, it
shows that the interactions between Mopoi and the group of colonial
agents caused tensions, which the expression of praise *Lipumbu* belies.
Chief Mopoi and ordinary sellers of rubber and ivory realized that the
agent was greedy despite many promises of lucrative trade.

Briefly, names drawn from gender stereotypes had significations that
are different from the meanings the words "man" and "woman" carry in
Bantu languages of Central Africa because they did not refer to human
anatomy. They were cultural assumptions about colonial conditions and
about male behavior and actions. Besides their denotations, *Mondele Madami, Bwana Mzuri*, and *Bwana Kitoko* were insults to the masculinity and
manhood of colonial officials. These deeper meanings were informed

by local ideas about manhood that only initiation, the single most important ritual of a man's life cycle, could grant to men in Central Africa, where boys were not inducted into manhood until they were initiated.[29] In Central Africa, uninitiated men were considered women, and conversely, women who showed masculine aggressiveness were contemptuously regarded as men. Initiations of colonial officials into initiation schools such as *Lilwa* and *Mambela* were partly genuine wishes to understand local societies for administrative efficacy, and partly deliberate maneuvers to diminish the destructive effects of such negative perceptions of colonial officials on the attitudes of Congolese villagers toward colonial authorities and policies. Despite their variations in meanings and an association with female qualities, names as gender metaphors expressed relations of economic exploitation and political domination.

The most pervasive body metaphors that praised colonial officials and simultaneously scorned the confiscating of food were the names *Maina, Libumu, Mafuta,* and its superlative *Mafuta Mingi.* Aside from *Libumu,* a Lingala word for "Belly," all the other terms signify vegetable oil or animal fat in many Bantu languages, including Kikongo, Lingala, and Kiswahili, which became the languages of command and important instruments of the colonial government for administrating local communities and organizing labor in the industrial sector of the colonial economy.[30] The terms *Mafuta Mingi, Mafuta, Maina,* and *Libumu* were widespread metonyms of power, affluence, and high social status in the Congo and elsewhere in Central Africa before colonization. Some like *Mafuta* were already in use in factories established in the nineteenth century along the Atlantic coast and in the interior of Central Africa, where they meant, along with the Lozi practice of keeping long fingernails, wealth and high social status.[31] Some European receivers of these names were plump, and their names described their physical being and genuinely celebrated likable colonial officials as discussed earlier. But many state officials were given the names *Mafuta Mingi, Mafuta, Maina,* and *Libumu* because they lavishly requisitioned game, goats, chickens, plantains, pineapples, and especially eggs, which became regarded everywhere as "the white man food."[32]

Requisitioning food was only a part of the social relations of production that explains why these names received ugly connotations. Since 1891, villages were required to provide foodstuffs that officials purchased at the *prix d'état,* prices set by the colonial administration and always forced below the value of labor.[33] The system allowed state officials to pay low prices to households and accumulate livestock and large flocks beyond their food needs.[34] So any name whose implicit meaning was an insinuation of the good health colonial officials enjoyed was a critique of the twisted means colonial officials used to get foodstuffs. As colonial officials extracted more than they gave back, Congolese villagers regarded them with disdain as spongers. If calling plump colonial officials *Mafuta Mingi, Maina,* and *Libumu* made sense in everyday language, giving the names to slim ones was ironic. This paradox shows that neither large girth nor a wish to flatter alone explained their choice. In the village world where food producers received low prices, *Mafuta Mingi, Maina,* and *Libumu* were oblique criticisms of low prices of foodstuffs, perceived often as outright extortions.[35] Besides the ostensible admiration of the supposedly "good look" of "well-fed" colonial officials, names depicting the body and looks expressed resentment for onerous food requisitions, which strained the relations between officials and Congolese villagers and sometimes escalated into wars. The war between an official and the Mbesa and the humiliation suffered by Bamanga chiefs illustrate the idea that descriptions of elegance can convey criticisms of exploitation and low prices.

The Mbesa live between the Congo and Lopori rivers, where they encountered Lieutenant Bell and twenty-five unnamed African troops for the first time in 1898, and, on their arrival, sent off emissaries to local leaders to secure fresh foodstuffs. Village leaders agreed to supply foodstuffs but sent none, and this refusal forced the officer and his troops to return to Barumbu, where they found food supplies.[36] A few days later, the officer and his twenty-five troops returned to Modimbi, where they established a military post to speed up the integration of the Mbesa into the administration of the Congo Free State. This second encounter started bringing the Mbesa into the colonial administration and the concession of the Anglo-Belgian India Rubber Company (ABIR) where they became collectors of rubber and suppliers of foodstuffs to the troops and military officer. As happened elsewhere, the refusal to provide foodstuffs was short-lived because the creation of the outpost soon started a compulsory supplying of food. This mandatory supplying of food lasted the entire life of the Belgian Congo and allowed colonial officials to always pay the *prix d'état* to food-producing households. The system was so exploitative it allowed its users to have large herds of goats and poultry yards beyond their personal food needs. These excesses exposed the system to criticisms by higher-ranking officials and caused localized wars, as the story of the Mbesa shows. Indeed, when the Mbesa learned about the officer and his troops who had moved to the post at Yandumba, they sent their leader to supply chickens to Bell, the officer, who angrily asked why they had not offered chickens and eggs previously. Unsatisfied with the Mbesa leader's answer, Lieutenant Bell ordered him to return home, and when the leader turned, Bell shot him in the back. The angered Mbesa attacked, killing Bell and his twenty-five troops.[37]

The name the Mbesa gave the officer tells the story of extortion of foodstuffs. During the administrative inquiry to determine the cause of the war after the punitive expedition, the administration discovered that the Mbesa identified Bell as *Mafuta Mingi*, which means "A lot of fat" although he was hardly plump. Inconsistency between the signifier and the signified suggests that the Mbesa were not referring to the body size of the officer when they named him. Rather, they used the name as a local metonym for greed and named the officer to criticize the demand for foodstuffs that cost their leader his life.[38]

The Mbesa example was not exceptional. Records of native courts and oral testimonies provided by local leaders in Bengamisa area, Uele, and Kasai show many conflicts between colonial officials and Congolese villagers over the supply of foodstuffs, situations that show that *Mafuta Mingi* was an expression of anger at the confiscation of foodstuffs. After their creation in 1926, native courts, mainly designed to settle conflicts between Congolese, became repressive institutions that greedy agronomists, census takers, health officers, tax collectors, and Congolese auxiliaries used to extract lavish quantities of food from the village resources.[39]

Although food requisitions affected households' food security unevenly, they generated everywhere grievances, resentments, and protests well documented by the Commission of Inquiry in 1904–5. The transcripts of native courts detailed how the colonial authorities wanted food supply to be the primary role of Congolese leaders. Chiefs and headmen were the privileged local segment of the colonial social aggregate.[40] Still, like ordinary villagers, they suffered humiliation, violence, and deprivation of salaries when they failed to supply food to colonial officials. The situation the Bamanga chiefs faced in 1929 in Bengamisa highlights the aggressiveness of colonial officials in prosecuting them for failure to bring foodstuffs. Chiefs Gingoru and Adakoli, for example, were fined 100 and 175 francs, respectively, for supplying bad rations, while Chief Zangamo was jailed for fifteen days because of bad rations, and the same reason had Chief Zolu sentenced to ten days in prison.[41]

Bengamisa was a microcosm of the whole Congo. Local leaders in Uele bemoaned their role as suppliers of foodstuffs and lamented, "We are only the *Bula Matari* slaves." In Kasai, a region far from Uele and Bengamisa, a Luba headman equated the arrival of officials in his village with requisitions of chickens, eggs, and goats and complained bitterly that his role in collecting foodstuffs pitted him against his own people. To criticize the greed of gluttonous colonial officials when burdened with excessive food demands, Kiswahili speakers across Eastern Congo blatantly named them *Bapenda Kula*. The phrase, which means "They who love to eat,"[42] expressed strong resentment to the widespread practice of food confiscation. Because of this practice of food extortion, for example, a colonial official posted at Yanonge in the 1950s was named *Mupenda Kula*, which means "He who likes to eat."[43]

In brief, names suggesting praise and admiration of the look of colonial officials carried subtexts, most of which criticized the confiscation of foodstuffs, making the praise of colonial officials subversive expressions that were mostly insults.

Significantly, Congolese gave colonial officials body-depicting generic names that described aspects of the body of colonial officials—shortness, tallness, uncleanness, baldness, gait, and the roundness of the head. Unlike the flattering descriptions of the body associated with power, affluence, ideals of beauty, and social status, these were insults, which still highlighted the themes of ambiguity and the multidimensionality of messages of names. In the 1890s, the first explorers and colonial officials earned such names as *Tshienda Bitekete*, "Lazy walker," in Ciluba, *Moke-Moke*, "Small, small" or "Very small," in Lingala, and *Bwana Kidogo*, "Mister small," in Kiswahili.[44] *Bwana Kidogo* meant in almost every case "Little boss" opposed to *Bwana Mukubwa*, which means "Superior" or "Big boss," irrespective of the body size. This naming of colonial officials and agents after physical descriptions continued in the 1920s until the 1950s. Many were literal renderings of the natural attributes of the body of the name-bearers and were therefore empirical descriptions. Many such physical descriptions were also cultural assumptions and insults to colonial officials. The Ekonda and Kiswahili speakers named "a bearded white man" *Ndjole-Ndjole* and *Ndevu*, respectively.[45] Although the Kiswahili reduplication *Pole-Pole* and its Ciluba synonym, *Tshienda Bitekete*, were representations of the physical bodies of colonial officials and referred to colonial officials who were "Very calm," they also meant "Slow, slow" or "Lazy walker." They were metonyms for slowness and therefore carried a derogatory connotation.[46] When greedy colonial officials remained lean though they confiscated food-stuffs, Lingala speakers named them *Moke-Moke,* a reduplication that means "Very small" or "Small, small" and that had a semantic equivalent in Kiswahili *Bwana Kidogo,* which means "Mister small." Interpreted against the contexts of food confiscation, the names were satires and cynical ironies, which sent a loud message: despite generous food rations that colonial officials received, they were still emaciated as if they suffered malnutrition, a social marker of poverty.[47] By naming colonial officials after such situations, Congolese villagers were telling colonial officials to end the extortions of food because they had not become plump and wealthy.

The theme of ambiguity unfolds in the multidimensionality of meanings of the name of Commandant Middage. The story of the name shows how names depicting the body carried several meanings that expressed simultaneously admiration and concerns about colonial repression. Commandant Middage was appointed to Kasongo in 1897 and built a military camp there, work that earned him the name *Miti,* a Kiswahili term for "trees." *Miti* (sing: *muti*) was not just a botanical term; it was also a cultural category with many meanings, but two were nearly ubiquitous in the societies of the rainforests of Central Africa. First, the term referred to trees that were planted when the village was founded and that symbolized community protection and strength. Second, a tree connoted a person who was skinny and yet strong. Middage earned the name *Miti* because "he was straight like a stick . . . and always wore his belt and military uniforms tightly."[48] The references to the stick (tree), belt, military uniform and camp, posture, and gait of Middage changed the name into a multidimensional identity that expressed praise and criticism of colonialism simultaneously. The connotation of strength associated with *Miti* implied praise of the officer. Even so, the unenviable parts of the description of his gait and posture such as "straight like a stick" and "dressed . . . tightly" were offensive, assigning to the name the meanings of mockery and insult. The military camp, the stick, and the belt were the place, objects, and symbols of colonial violence. The open reference to these instruments of colonial domination was an accusation of violence and stealthily voiced resentments for the state's brutal methods of punishments.[49]

Appropriating local symbols and memories for administrative and economic purposes started as soon as colonialism. The collective name

Pete ya Mai ya Sombe, which means "Stars colored the color of the cassava leaves" or "Green stars," epitomized the stealthy mix of local and colonial symbols in creating powerful composite symbols of colonial authority unfolding diverse and shared perceptions of colonialism. *Pete ya Mai ya Sombe* was given to territorial administrators, officials who ruled *territoires,* administrative divisions created in 1912. They earned the name in the late 1940s through the 1950s in Eastern Congo because they wore "green stars" on the epaulettes of their khaki uniforms, which deliberately set them apart from Congolese villagers.[50] The stars represented the ranks in the hierarchy of colonial administrative power structure, and the green color was a local symbol of peace, which produced multidimensional messages.

Good examples were the green color and first-fruit ceremony found in colonial propaganda written to stimulate mandatory cash crop cultivation in the 1930s and onward Colonial officials appropriated the symbolism of the green color and the ritual of first-fruit when they distributed "green satin flags" to local leaders whose people produced the largest numbers of baskets of cotton during the annual agricultural festivals.[51]

Because it was created out of a local symbol of peace, *Pete ya Mai ya Sombe* evoked at first glance an image of friendly territorial administrators and presupposed the improvement of social relations between these officials and Congolese villagers. But *Pete ya Mai ya Sombe* was not always glorifying the territorial administrators, who were well aware that distributing "green satin flags" during cotton festivals provided no real economic gains to Congolese producers. Only a few believed loftily that the association of economic success with the green color would change the producers' perception of mandatory cash cultivation. Most manifested their frustrations when Congolese discovered the manipulation of local symbols and rituals and transformed the color green into a "weapon of the weak." They then recognized that although Congolese villagers praised them, the villagers despised their policies and repressive practices. This realization transpired not only in localized acts of defiance but also in the meanings of individual names given to colonial state officials.

A close examination of the individual names of territorial administrators shows multiple images of these officials, a few flattering while most were not. Some territorial administrators earned generic names of praise because of their personal qualities and actions and because of the politics of ethnicity that created *territoires ethniques* in 1927 and that men and women of various ethnic groups interpreted as the recognition of their ethnic groups. By promoting the politics of ethnic pride in the 1930s, the policy encouraged Congolese to look favorably at individual territorial administrators. In many places and under many circumstances, *Pete ya Mai ya Sombe* expressed this reality.

The job description of these colonial officials explains the diversity of their perceptions by Congolese villagers. In theory and practice, territorial administrators were responsible for organizing *chefferies*, the building of roads and bridges, and the expansion of agricultural production. Although a few groups of Congolese peoples in Western Congo had been brought into a rudimentary colonial administration after a series of decrees enacted between 1892 and 1912, the integration into these new territorial subdivisions brought colonialism into village communities, and accelerated the end of local political autonomy.[52] The administrative reforms carried out by these officials were regarded mainly as political destabilization and social disruptions, perceptions captured between 1913 and the 1940s in names such as *Kulu-Kulu*, "Violence triggers" or "Troublemaker," *Kituanga*, "He who smashes people" in Kiswahili, and *Mayala*, "Oppressors" in Kikongo.[53] Even as rural conditions improved in the 1950s, village leaders, members of independence movements and African Independent Churches, and ordinary rural dwellers still questioned Belgian political control and colonial violence. These conditions could hardly woo Congolese villagers to name colonial officials after a symbol of peace without such a naming pattern raising suspicions. Arayabu's choice of the name *Pete ya Mai ya Sombe* in 1956 to address the territorial administrator R. Philippart seemed strategic and shows one way Congolese used this category of praise names.

Jean Arayabu was a store clerk in Kindu, the headquarters of Maniema District. In the mid-1950s, colonial officials suspected him of membership in *Kitawala*, an offshoot of watchtower, a religious movement that spread from Zambia to Katanga in the 1920s and from there to the Orientale Province, where it transmuted into a powerful politico-religious movement after the Second World War.[54] The colonial administration unwittingly spread the *Kitawala* movement in Maniema and Orientale Province by relegating its members who were considered dangerous agitators. Following a long trial in Stanleyville, today Kisangani, the court sentenced Arayabu to hard agricultural labor in Kasaji, a penal agricultural settlement in Southern Katanga where the colonial government settled Congolese who challenged its policies of political hegemony.[55] The use of the color green, a local symbol of peace, to address R. Philippart, the territorial administrator who harshly cracked down

on members of *Kitawala*, was ironic. It shows that Arayabu was manipulating the official to avert his deportation from his homeland to Kasaji.
This example provides a glimpse into this group of names with many
meanings.

Conclusion: Names, Protests, and Resistance

Several conclusions emerge from this analysis. The names of colonial
officials that expressed criticisms of colonialism, particularly those expressing accusations of colonial assaults on the village world, tell stories
of the suffering of villagers. As they named the colonizers, Congolese
villagers wove their complaints of social disruptions, political destabilization, and injustice into the connotations of meanness attributed to
the meanings of names of state officials. The accusation that colonial
officials were evil underlined the harmful impact of colonialism on the
village world and the lives of its residents. References to historical memories and specific past events, particularly those pointing to violence,
stressed the similarities between Belgian colonialism and the previous
system of *Matamba-tamba* oppression that Congolese had contested.
Thus, suffering was not the only focus of the accusations in the names.
The association of names with memories of contested events meant that
these complaints expressed protest. The meanings of individual and collective names of praise showed that such names expressed protest, woven
in the cultural assumptions of the body. Some shades of the meanings of
names drawn from stereotypes of gender were criticisms of masculine
deficiencies, emasculated manhood, greed, and food extortion, which
were all part of colonial rule and nurtured a broader anti-colonial discourse. The stealth of double naming and the multidimensionality of
meanings of body-depicting names of colonial officials strongly support
this view.

Astute colonial officials, the targets of the messages, were always
aware of subtle forms of protest, and recorded a body of evidence that
shows that names of praise articulated anti-colonial sentiments against
forms of domination and economic exploitation. The stereotypical
statements by a colonial state official in the 1930s that "Blacks are very
artful and use flatteries to get whatever they want" and that "We must
always remember that what they say is not what they think and how
they feel" are an excellent illustration.[56] The appropriation of names of
praise by colonial officials to mediate paternalistic dominance is another

evidence of praise as protest. And the officials learned the meanings of their names in detailed ethnographies from which they learned the psychology and collective attitudes of Congolese. Although colonial ethnographies produced stereotypes of Congolese, they also yielded informed judgments and local assumptions about legitimate authority, justice, and standards of behavior. This inside information helped colonial officials understand names of praise as the protest against the abuses of colonialism. The practice of giving to a colonial official two names, one flattering and intended for the ears of the official and the other contemptuous and spoken behind his back, gives the names of colonial officials revolutionary content deeply rooted in everyday life.

7

Confronting African Voices

Negotiations and Instrumentalization of Names

M̲ost colonial officials recognized that their local names were voices of village communities and expressed protests, wishes for negotiation, accusations of suffering, and even praise. Based on my own research, this chapter documents various ways colonial officials confronted these voices. The first part of the chapter is a brief discussion of the inevitability of negotiations. It sets the contexts that help us understand why colonial government officials deployed their local identities to construct a discourse of domination. It elucidates the idea that although Belgian colonialism was brutal, it could hardly work without some segments of the village world participating. The second part explores ways in which colonial officials used messages they decoded from their names. It investigates how colonial officials translated messages of praise names into paternalist discourse to woo residents of the villages into colonial economic and political projects and stave off perceptions of colonialism that belied colonialism's civilizing mission. It explores ways officials and agents retooled messages of violence to terrorize Congolese without using the corporal violence suggested by the explicit meanings of their names.

Colonialism and the Inevitability of Negotiations

The exclusion of Congolese from political participation characterized Belgian colonization of the Congo as it did in other parts of Africa. The Congolese had no voice in advisory institutions such as the Commission Permanente pour la Protection des Indigènes and Conseil de

Gouvernement. Missionaries and high-level government officials spoke for them. Even when Congolese were co-opted in the Conseil de Province in the 1950s, they did not carry great weight in the debates to determine their destiny because of their lack of democratic experience and because of their inadequate command of French, the official language of debates.[1] But most officials in the colonial administration, particularly those who carried out policies among the Congolese, acknowledged that such an exclusion harmed colonial purposes. By highlighting the experiences of seasoned officials, the training of the European newcomers shows that the government was aware of the danger of the policy and that it had not always relied on force and threats of force as instruments of state policies. From the outset, colonial officials acknowledged the public meetings, the important role of chiefs' councils (1910–60), and native courts (1926–60), which were the formal avenues for negotiations.[2] Outside these bodies, colonial officials paid attention to the views of colonialism held by Congolese villagers and which Congolese expressed through work songs, the performance of rituals, dances, and other forms of body language.[3]

Several economic, political, and military conditions made negotiations inevitable. First, to lower the financial cost of fighting, the autonomy of local leaders longing for power to make decisions on local affairs required administrative decentralization and some local participation, not just intimidation and violence.[4] Second, the fear of misrepresentation of colonialism and revolts and its impact on long-term political interactions showed to colonial planners the relevance of negotiations with the village world. From the outset, violence showed its limits as an effective and workable long-term instrument of social control. The dispersion of villagers across a huge country, the small size of the police force in each *chefferie* and *secteur,* and the costs of military expeditions diminished the power of the colonial authorities to monitor people and communities.[5] Still, violence generated many responses that worried colonial state officials.[6]

During colonization, Congolese villagers not only rebelled, rioted, and attacked and beat tax collectors and agricultural officers, but they also showed their feelings during public meetings, with their frowning faces and disdainful looks. Frowning was the most common contemptuous bodily language that exemplified the everyday forms of protest during village meetings with colonial officials and caused officials to complain, to imprison arbitrarily, and on occasion to almost shoot Congolese.[7] The frustrations of colonial officials convinced many, especially the proponents of force, of the enormous difficulty of imposing domination solely by violence. Even the most ruthless officials slowly came to recognize the usefulness of incentives and inducements and started combining force with tactics of humiliation. To punish individual resisters, colonial officials used public whipping, stripping, and chaining from the outset. While the need to prevent "agitators" from running away justified chaining, the stripping and flogging of resisters was intended to inflict intense pain on their naked bodies and to humiliate and undermine their standing and prestige. The simultaneous use of violence and tactics of humiliation and inducements was an implicit recognition by colonial officials that no one single method of punishment produced total domination. And the acknowledgment by colonial officials of the limitations of every instrument of social control to generate submission showed that negotiations were inevitable. Gaston-Joseph, an official who ruled the Topoke in the 1920s, illustrates the point.

Quoting *Koffi* in "Le territoire de Ligasa," J. Pirson provides an excerpt, which serves as an entry point into the discussion of the inescapability of negotiations between villagers and the colonial officials. The excerpt depicts colonial situations that set Congolese villagers against colonial officials. It highlights the ambiguities local leaders faced in the 1920s and devises negotiations as the solution to the paradoxes they confronted. The text was a dialogue between village elders, whose views were articulated by their spokesman, and a state-appointed chief whose views mirrored the concerns and responses of the colonial authorities to the demands of Congolese villagers. It shows the many ways the colonial officials turned exploitation and domination into illusions of self-interest, social progress, and economic development:

> SPOKESMAN: Head tax rises each year. Who benefits from the money produced by our labor? Because you are in charge of our interests, you who know well the white man, why do you not get a cut on taxes?
>
> KOFFI: You benefit from taxes you pay; they benefit the community, but you just do not know it. To maintain and arm soldiers, who secure the peace we all enjoy, the white men use tax monies. Besides, the monies you pay are used to purchase medicines to treat you.
>
> SPOKESMAN: White men are taking our guns and refusing to sell us gunpowder. We can no longer kill game and keep off our fields many predators, which destroy our crops.
>
> KOFFI: White men are taking away the guns because of those of you who use them to wage war or to rebel.[8]

Written for the "seasoning" of officials, the text informed the new-comers to the Congo of common grievances that set any colonial official against Congolese villagers. First, it underlines the role of the public meeting—community meetings and councils of elders—as an arena of negotiations.[9] Second, it shows tax hikes, exploitation of labor, confiscation of weapons, and refusal to sell ammunitions as the foci of the debates between colonial officials and Congolese. To be sure, the text prepared the colonial officials to anticipate rural radicalism against unpopular policies and to prevent it by misrepresenting colonialism as a system that only dispensed such desirable goods as health care, peace, and security. When the voices of Congolese villagers denounced ugly aspects of Belgian colonialism, the colonial discourse strived to stifle and thwart rural opposition and to mimic the representations of colonialism that were consistent with the slogans of civilizing mission.

The concerns raised in the text were sharply debated in native courts, the best colonial avenue for negotiations. The debates helped colonial officials figure out the attitudes and intentions of Congolese villagers toward colonial practices. Not all Congolese villagers' views of colonialism were expressed at the chiefs' councils and native courts. During the entire colonial period, native courts competed with local systems of conflict resolution for primacy. The duality of institutions prevented the colonial administration and local allies from monitoring all the information inside the local communities. For instance, conflicts over theft, larceny, bridewealth, and domestic abuses were brought to native courts. Families, kinship groups, and closed associations also settled the same conflicts to restore social harmony. Because of the role of the closed associations as alternate and independent courts, and because of the secrecy in the ways in which closed associations settled community and household conflicts, some key information about the communities and the households escaped the control of local administrations. The gap in the control of inside information about the household, considered the most important unit of production for the mandatory cash crop and the most important unit of reproduction of the labor force for colonial businesses, worried the colonial state officials and private employers.[10] The need for relevant feedback turned negotiations into the prerequisites to screen out subversion and maintain colonialism.[11]

To conclude this discussion on the inevitability of negotiations between Congolese and colonial officials, I return to the excerpt from Gaston-Joseph's *Koffi*. The way of appropriating the Congolese's concerns as described in the excerpt was strikingly similar to the ways in which colonial officials appropriated the messages of names to promote or to change local perceptions of colonialism. The description shows how Congolese and colonial officials constantly negotiated the real and symbolic boundaries of the colonial world during the public meetings and chiefs councils.[12] Through the culturally grounded naming of colonial officials, Congolese produced local representations of colonialism that colonial officials negotiated to either instill fears (messages of violence) or mediate paternalistic dominance (messages of praise), approaches that exemplified the retooling of local voices, creating dynamics that affected the interactions between the Congolese and colonial officials.

Making Voices of Praise into "Iron Hand in a Velvet Glove"

Congolese villagers gave praise names to colonial officials to avoid confrontations, improve public relations, carve concessions, and genuinely extol colonial officials who did their duties with less brutality than other officials. But Congolese villagers had no monopoly over the flattering messages they assigned to colonial anthroponyms as colonial officials also appropriated the messages of praise to organize propaganda campaigns to win over the hearts and minds of the name-givers.

Why colonial officials negotiated praise names and deployed them to maintain colonialism varied greatly depending on short-term objectives. Besides a series of factors that promoted negotiations between colonial officials and Congolese villagers, the appropriation of praise names responded to the preoccupation among colonial officials with discovering the best methods of ruling local communities by adding into their programs those local views of colonialism that reinforced paternalism, the official Belgian policy that mediated relations of domination and exploitation. For most advocates of persuasion as the underlying philosophy of administration, positive local voices helped make the case that the Congolese willingly embraced the colonial project and its economic practices. Although praise names expressed the willingness of Congolese villagers to adhere to colonial "development plans," colonial officials appropriated those names in order to suggest to Congolese that this flattering view of colonialism exemplified the politically cooperative behavior desired of them. Praise names thus provided the inside messages that colonial officials needed not only to mediate paternalism and seduce Congolese villagers but also to convince the colonial government to renounce violence. The messages of praise thus helped the advocates of persuasion in their campaigns for a method of social control that they depicted in the 1950s as "the iron hand in a velvet glove."[13]

The loneliness suffered by colonial officials, especially those who lived in remote outposts, also explains the politics of praise naming. Lonely officials interpreted naming and praise naming as a ritual of adoption into local communities, and most found praise names similar to attending nighttime dances during the full moon, initiation into closed associations, and some social mixing with villagers. The widespread practice of blood brotherhood in the early years when colonial officials exchanged gifts with local leaders and received local titles and names also explains why colonial officials appropriated praise names. Take, for example, the excellent relations between Harry Bombeeck, named *Bombeki,* and a local leader, Mafuta Mingi, at Yambinga, and the gift of a woman by a Topoke leader, Bolima, to Charles Van de Lanoitte, named *Tshoma-Tshoma.*[14] Receiving flattering local identities created a sense of belonging, which was useful in securing personal safety and reaching administrative objectives. To be sure, even fictive membership in the village community allowed colonial power holders to build patronage and attract loyalists and to shape the village leadership to their liking, although creating the new colonial administrative structure always generated internal tensions. And the taking of names of praise was a part of colonial interactions, which helped negotiations over the choice of land to be allocated to cash crop cultivation, village relocations, and the timing of rituals and major events of life cycles, issues that pitted the colonial administration against villagers.[15] Appropriating praise names was therefore a method of subtle control of the minds of villagers, which, in the village world of the 1930s, featured distributing material incentives, showing films and plays, and organizing agricultural shows and festivals.[16] By blurring the gap between colonial propaganda, which promised altruism and prosperity, and the harsh conditions of work and life, manipulating names of praise tried to camouflage the contexts that could have made domination and exploitation easily understandable and in the end stimulate local resistance.

The colonial officials used names suggesting praise in many ways, which served various short-term purposes, and subtly changed the village-level power relations. But two forms remained conspicuous. Elaborate and collective, the first strategy merged into cultural expressions of local worldviews and statements celebrating aspects of European culture, items of behavior, and trade goods. Pragmatic, widespread, and individual, the second strategy consisted of building a usable and unblemished personal reputation out of ideas, symbols, and images drawn from the messages of names of praise. The staged cultural expressions and the individual reputations were designed to disseminate colonial propaganda to root out subversive ideas from the villagers.

As previously stated, violence was not the only instrument of colonial state policy for overcoming local opposition to mandatory cash crop production, labor recruitment, and taxation. A small minority of colonial officials and missionaries adhered to nonviolent methods of administration and incorporated praise of anything European by Congolese villagers into their writings and speeches. Because proponents of nonviolence interpreted messages of praise as the wish of Congolese to participate in colonial economic, cultural, and social programs, they collected flattering local views of colonialism to paint glowing images of colonialism in pamphlets, films, plays, and speeches. Started before the imposition of mandatory cash crop production in 1917, these propaganda programs became common in the 1930s when colonial officials appropriated first-fruit ceremonies to create social environments and cultural décor to encourage cash crop producers to raise production. Local administrations appropriated such local cultural forms to create new forms of collective consciousness compatible with the colonial ideologies of obedience and servility.[17] Indeed, the proponents of less violence teased out of the names of praise positive local voices about colonial officials and colonial rule and then staged them into cultural expressions to entice peasants to embrace the colonial work ethic, European lifestyle, and taste for new imports.[18] Written by Gérôme, a Catholic Marist Brother of the Buta Congregation, and performed in 1938 by cotton cultivators in Buta, *Cultivons du coton* is a play in which the missionary mixed colonial propaganda with local voices and commentaries about colonial rule to change everyday Congolese perceptions of cash crop production and colonialism. It uses subtle ways to wean subversive and ugly representations of the colonial state and cotton companies away from local ways of thinking.[19]

The play was a well-crafted response to the resistance of Congolese peasants who suffered the brutality of the cotton economy from 1919, when it was imposed in Buta, to 1959, when rural mass movements for independence halted cash crop cultivation. As in other important cotton-producing areas of the colonial Congo, cotton cultivation in Buta intruded into everyday life and minimally rewarded cotton growers. As elsewhere, peasants in Buta gave to colonial government officials and agents of *Compagnie Cotonnière Congolaise* names such as "Lightning," "He who checks if the seeds had not been negligently thrown away," and "He who yells at people."[20] Accusations of suffering and expressions of protest, these voices produced the intended results: they worried colonial officials because they jeopardized maintaining and expanding cotton cultivation. It should not surprise anyone that the first act of the play discussed tax payments and the ways in which cotton and the entire rural economy transformed the rhythms of rural life. Still less surprising, the text highlighted the hardships of cotton cultivation and political repression, concerns that cotton growers echoed in songs and names. The play then turned the harsh realities of the cotton economy into an acceptable predicament and growing cotton into the most important colonial economic initiative to generate the household's prosperity. A scene featuring poor villagers articulated the ways in which colonial officials merged local voices into cultural expressions to persuade Congolese of the economic gains of cotton production. When a poor Congolese peasant asked, "Aren't we vulgar taxpayers?" and "Isn't a taxpayer's lot to bewail?" the voice of the colonial administration, speaking through a prosperous cotton producer and owner of a bicycle, replied, "Why is the taxpayer plight to be bewailed?" Passages of the play such as "the white man of cotton . . . taught us how to be smart," and many scenes of dance and music performances in the play, which exemplified the enjoyable and lucrative side of the cash crop economy, echoed the topics of praise names. Like wild rubber that produced "the white man of rubber vine,"[21] the most despicable representation of the early colonial economy, cotton, produced "the white man of cotton," which remained a symbol of exploitation and repression until the 1950s. A villain in Congolese peasants' eyes and collective imagination, "the white man of cotton" teaches people "how to be so smart" in the play, an action that humanizes cash crop overseers and turns them into selfless benefactors. Viewed by most producers as a symbol of exploitation, here cotton now generated not only money left over after payment of taxes, but it also brought prestige, wealth, and increased social status to individuals and families. The possession of prestigious imports such as bicycles and colorful clothes changed the cultivation of cotton into the most lucrative of colonial economic initiatives in Buta and the whole district of Upper Uele. The merging of messages and ideas suggestive of praise of colonizers into cultural expressions thus shows "how perceptions, experiences, and problems are being 'worked out' in an open, never-ending process."[22]

The praise naming of King Baudouin as *Bwana Kitoko* epitomized the intersection of praise and colonial propaganda. Given to the king during his visit to the colony in 1955, it shows how the messages of praise were used as propaganda campaigns by colonial officials to manipulate Congolese sentiments to delay the rise of nationalism. Congolese had named colonial officials *Kitoko, Bwana Kitoko, Kitoko Mingi,* and *Citoko* when they encountered the Europeans who conquered their land and established Belgian rule.[23] The term *Kitoko* means "Handsome," "Beautiful," and "Delicious taste" in many Bantu languages. The manipulation of the term for propaganda purposes is shown first in the irregular morphology of the expression. In a conventional Kiswahili pattern, *Bwana* was used as an honorific before a personal name to distinguish superiors from subaltern agents. It means thus "master" and "mister," as explained in chapter 3. Van Berghe, the director of the Institut pour la recherche scientifique en Afrique centrale (IRSAC) in Lwiro, received the name *Bwana Mukubwa* because he was "Master tall" and "Big boss," meanings that accurately describe his rank and height. He was the director of the research center and a tall man. Unlike *Bwana,* the term *Kitoko* is Kiswahili, Kikongo, and Lingala and means "handsome" in all languages. The name *Bwana Kitoko* became at once a Kiswahili, Lingala, and Kikongo expression. Besides the praise of the physical attributes of the king—he was young and handsome—the syntagm was coined by the colonial officials to win over speakers of the three languages.[24]

Besides staging messages and ideas gleaned from names of praise into cultural expressions for Congolese consumption, individual officials used their names of praise by adapting their individual behavior to their meanings, which were, according to colonial officials, local positive interpretations of colonialism. This strategy, like the collective cultural expressions, was designed to influence local perceptions of colonialism and wean Congolese peasants away from the ever-growing awareness of the gap between the hard conditions of work and their low standards of living, and the colonial ideology that promised "wonderful things."[25]

Despite differences in the familiarity with local customs and the misinterpretation of specific colonial situations by the colonial officials, the practice was uniform. Colonial officials built a good reputation and backed it up with paternalistic behaviors and policies that showed the image propagated by their praise name. Of these policies, exemptions

from taxation and corvée labor for a few years were notable and resonated well with Congolese villagers because it relieved the households of
extreme stresses. Equally important was the display of friendly interactions of colonial officials with Congolese children through godfatherhood, games and play, fictive preferential marriage with girls, and the
distribution of small cash and cigarettes; all shed a positive light on the
reputation of the official and colonial rule.[26] As the "manufactured"
reputation grew stronger and spread across villages, colonial officials
further subsumed a personality reflective of the reputation drawn from
the name. The officials then performed actions that reinforced the
reputation, creating expectations of better colonial relations, and influenced local perceptions of colonialism. Colonial officials whose personality matched their good reputation carried out the most arduous projects, including those that affected negatively the nutritional status and
health of villagers. Even when praise names were not staged into elaborate and public cultural expressions, they still gave officials the means
to circulate selected messages that showed their personality and embel-
lished the ways they carried out colonial policies.

Briefly, this discussion shows that praise names first generated in colonial officials a sense of belonging to local communities, a sense that affected the ways they carried out colonial policies. A part of the strategy
to shape local memories of colonial experiences, the appropriation of
praise by colonial officials shows the dynamism of colonial relations and
the complexities and subtleties in the ways in which they struggled with
the limits of their power. It explains how colonial officials negotiated the
boundaries of the colonial world at the village level rather than unilater-
ally imposing them. Exploring names of praise also shows unwitting participation of villagers in the formation of Belgian paternalism.

The advocates of violence rejected praise names as an effective
means of controlling Congolese minds. They claimed that the practice
eroded the foundations of the colonial authority. They shared the observation of Pecheur, an official who claimed, "Our humanitarian and
compassionate reaction was noticeable in the eyes of Blacks, and gave
them the impression that we were weak. We ought always to remember
that Blacks rarely appreciate good will without force."[27] The advocates
of violence used instead names suggesting violence even when, after the
Second World War, the central administration in Brussels had begun to
discourage the excessive use of violence against Congolese cash crop
producers and workers.

Appropriation and Instrumentalization
of Images of Violence and Repression

The commitment to end killings and excessive beatings was one of the stated motives for the takeover of the Congo Free State by the Belgian government in 1908.[28] And if the economic and political situations under Belgian rule still justified the production of names suggesting the brutality of colonial officials, their dissemination by the officials was paradoxical because such names reminded Congolese villagers of the horrors of colonialism. Contextualized, this ambivalence shows that the advocates of violence deployed messages of violence to keep Congolese villagers in fear and perpetuate colonial domination.

As shown earlier, names drawn from experiences of violence were accusations of suffering and criticisms of the abuses of colonialism. To be sure, these accusations satisfied brutal colonial officials who expected Congolese villagers to be fearful and docile. Because the accusations of violence showed fears and concerns about colonial relations, they persuaded brutal colonial officials that Congolese understood the colonial logic that underlay "the policy of the iron fist" the colonial state pursued during and after the Congo Free State. The policy of force as an instrument of state policy and the widespread practice of stereotyping Congolese as "lazy" and "indolent" justified the central role of violence and appropriation of names to propagate messages of violence. So colonial officials employed such names suggesting violence to instill fear and root out subtle and open forms of insubordination from the village communities.[29]

The prime example of colonial propaganda to promote images of violence embedded in the meanings of names of colonial officials to control Congolese by fear was *Bula Matari,* which even today reminds people of violence as the salient feature of the colonial state and Belgian colonialism.

All colonial office holders used *Bula Matari* supposedly to celebrate European material power and technical superiority, and the reputation of violence that *Bula Matari* embodied always preceded colonial officials wherever they moved across villages.[30] Each official created, however, his personal reputation when he took on an individual name that suggested violence and to which he sometimes added personal commentaries. The addition of personal commentaries to an individual name was the best evidence of appropriation of names by colonial officials who longed for images of violence that would keep villagers in fear or change local perceptions of colonialism. As the bearers of names received the names and adjusted personal behaviors to the ways they put policies into effect, they confirmed the reputation and propagated the image of violence.

A telling illustration of how colonial officials appropriated Congolese voices was *Kitatshindja*, a name that Kiswahili speakers in Kasongo gave Moltedo in the 1890s. The name originated in his use of excessive violence and means "slaughter" or "He who cuts people in pieces," a menacing image that he transformed into a powerful weapon of terror. Indeed, once Moltedo appropriated *Kitatshindja* as his local identity, he added his own commentaries and presented the message in a powerful tercet, threatening Congolese he suspected of contesting his power, "Mungu djulu, Bula Matari Tchini, Kitatshindja katikati,"[31] a phrase that translates as "God in the Heavens, Bula Matari on Earth, and Kitatshindja in the middle." In 1930, long after the official had left his post in Kasongo, A. Dallons and V. Cornet highlighted the impact of *Kitatshindja*'s tyranny, stressing that "these words [tercet] left no doubt on the value and the power of his orders, and no doubt lingered in the mind of anyone who listened to them." The report shows that this assessment hardly seemed an exaggeration because the words of Moltedo still had tremendous power nearly four decades later: "The officer left a strong mark on people because they talked about him terrorized. People asserted that *Kitatshindja* conducted his entire world with extreme perfection and firmness, and told people that in making decisions, he followed only his own mind and will. When on tour, the official was always preceded by a team of slit gong beaters to announce his arrival."[32]

These tactics of intimidation and brutality greatly scared off Congolese villagers to such an extent that "on his passage across a village, many people always fled to the bush."[33] This reaction of Congolese villagers to *Kitatshindja* means that the image of Belgian officials across the village world as despots, known in colonial parlance as *roi de brousse*, "king of the bush," was firmly established.

Congolese villagers were not, however, voiceless, frightened, or incapable of any response against the official's madness. The naming of Moltedo that recorded the experience was the first evidence of their voice, while the second lies in the morphology of the name. The ugliness of the message was conveyed by the meaning of the prefix *ki*. A diminutive, the prefix *ki* denoted anything of little importance, contempt, and condescension. All these meanings show that *Kitatshindja* was an insult that Moltedo, without knowledge of the language, unknowingly addressed to himself. Indeed, every time he pronounced his name to scare people, he was saying, "I am a despicable little man."[34]

The syntagm *Lumandemulu* was another name that shows how colonial agents and officials used names as an instrument of state policy to terrorize rubber collectors. After the appointment of Philibert-Joseph Van de Moere as district commissioner of Leopold District on 26 July 1906, Congolese villagers named him *Lumandemulu*, which derived from Van de Moere and comprised two local mispronunciations. The first, *Lumande*, was a mispronunciation of "Van de" that was also a congruency derived from the French word *amande*, which generated the loanword *Lumande*, meaning "fine," and *Mulu*, which derives from "Moere." As a loanword, *Lumandemulu* means "Van de Moere, the fine collector." The official received the name because his administration focused on the collection of fines and taxes. Until the colonial government monetized the economy in 1910, colonial officials employed brutal methods to collect taxes and fines in labor and goods that the Commission of Inquiry in 1904–5 documented in detail.[35] The themes of exploitation and repression were still recorded when Congolese named him *Bandungu*, a word that means "Pepper." The meaning of this second name reinforces the message of the first name and means, given the atrocities and abuses caused by the collection of rubber, the harsh conditions of life. The message was that colonial situations were still as oppressive as they were at the beginning of the colonial encounter when the official earned the first name. Every time Captain-commander Philibert-Joseph Van de Moere signed either name on the official correspondence and administrative papers, he spread the reputation of toughness and disseminated the local perception of the attribute of the colonial state as a predator and violent ruler.[36]

It is hard to measure the impact of individual insults and mockery and the accusations of violence on the decline of the Belgian political control and economic exploitation. The examples show that prefixation, like the suffixation analyzed in chapter 4, was an important tool in the linguistic arsenals deployed by Congolese villagers to ridicule colonial officials and protest against the violence of colonialism, political domination, and economic exploitation, defeating colonial political hegemony.

Unlike the foregoing names that spread the reputation of terror drawn from the acts and experiences of violence, Charles Van de Lanoitte's use of his name illustrates a different method of appropriation of local cultural forms, which started in the mid-1930s and became established in the 1940s and 1950s. It consisted in teasing out of names the messages of violence to "manufacture" obedience without physical violence against Congolese.[37]

A tax collector, Charles Van de Lanoitte spent the first part of his colonial career in the southern part of the Aruwimi District of the Lower Lomami and Middle Congo rivers, where he built a strong reputation of terror explicit in his name *Tshoma-Tshoma*, a reduplication that means "He who burns people." As he faced the resistance of Congolese tax defaulters dispersed in the rainforests that remained a safe heaven until the 1940s, he exploited his long-established reputation of terror to ease the collection of taxes. His outburst of pride and excitement offers a glimpse into the success of his method: "I have thus in an innocent way convinced for ever the Bangelima that the white man *Tshoma-Tshoma* ('He who burns [people]') was truly an incarnated devil or at least one of his closest kinfolks." This excerpt attests to the skillful use of the reputation of terror that the names of colonial officials propagated. Another excerpt illustrates the impact of the reputation of violence on local response as it points to witchcraft, a widespread metaphor for the annihilation of a person's essence: "Everywhere I go my reputation as a sorcerer will pave the way, and I will be feared."[38] Although the passage seems to exaggerate the coercive power of the tax collector, it connects the reputation of the colonial official to the behaviors and reactions of the Congolese villagers.

The story deserves further quotation at length to illustrate the complexity of the ways in which colonial officials transformed their names into instruments of terror without violence. This maneuver becomes evident in parts of the story that talk about his experience in the northern area of the Aruwimi District where Van de Lanoitte still used his reputation of ruthless tax collector to terrify the Bangelima taxpayers. The story is told as a dialogue between Charles de Lanoitte and a seasoned colleague who offered him hospitality and advice about the Bangelima country:

> Do you know how to swim?
> I swim like an otter! Why are you asking the question?
> Do you have life insurance?
> My God yes . . . What is the relation?
> You need one more because you have the happiness to retire soon and walk next year in Debrouckere Place or elsewhere, your body.
> Damn! What do you mean?

I simply mean that you go to the part of the district that is a dumping ground among the Bangelima, who are the nastiest people. They have not, in three years, paid taxes; bushes invade roads; you will cross all the rivers by swimming; the region is further infected with malaria and mosquitoes; most people have not paid their taxes in years; if you dare to use force, I am afraid you will be brought back dead.

Why should I be dead?

I mean you will be brought back in an advanced stage of decomposition after having received a sword or a poisoned arrow in your belly.

From the first contact, I feel that I am facing a stiff passive resistance. Chiefs answer me, with hypocrite smiles, that all the men have gone to hunt far in the forest and that they will not be back before eight days . . . With a calm but firm tone, I repeat my orders, and add that if they do not obey them, I will announce the measures I will take. Then I let them go. As I remain alone, I think for a long time and wonder, if tomorrow the war is declared, I will ever lose my prestige in the whole region. For this reason, I will not be able to collect taxes, and my security will be compromised. Never have I been in such a situation.

To calm my nerves, I walk to the nearby river. When I come back to the Post, the night has fallen . . . and my boy Narcisse asked me.

Are you not afraid of Monama, the water spirit? I do not give him an answer. An incredible and crazy idea in my mind becomes clear. If I succeed this night, slit gongs will spread the news that I have occult and fearsome powers in the entire country, and I will reach my goals. Superstition will then achieve what threats and persuasion did not do, even if it means that the conversion of the Congolese . . . into Christianity is delayed by one more century. Narcisse is perfectly a pagan . . . He has no fear of God and devil, and he ridicules Spirits . . . healers and sorcerers. He also has some rare talents, particularly the capacity to imitate the squeals of animals. This falls well, and I explain to him what I expect of him and a few moments later, he goes carrying a sheet in his hand in the middle of the night without being seen by anybody. Meanwhile I call village leaders and the chief to come back for the second time asking the chief to bring the leopard-teeth collar that I saw him wearing a while ago: I want to buy it from him. According to the custom, I need a piece of cloth or an object that belongs to him to execute the type of spell I plan.

These brave men arrive later, vaguely worried why they are called on later. Faking to ignore that each carried a sword around the belt, I welcome them friendly and after long discussions, I get the famous collar. I ask them later to come with me to the river though the tornado was imminent. The place looked as sinister as it could be with many bamboo trees bending under the wind, and further, the river was rolling its waters black like the ink. Suddenly, and to the surprise of the crowd, I shout for a long time and this cry echoed, "Water spirit, Water spirit!"

The chief has guessed my intention, but it was too late: with all my energies, I threw the collar toward dense reeds along the river. Nobody would dare go to find it because he would be driven away by the current and eaten by the awesome spirit. By throwing an object belonging to the chief, and I point him as the target of my public condemnation, and from now onward, I will be the only one to unleash angry spirits . . . A terrible silence hangs over: frogs are quiet everywhere. Suddenly, a hyena cry comes from the river so lugubrious that I started having fears. The water spirit that does not seem to be in a good mood . . . Around me, old village leaders are afraid and beg the aquatic spirits for mercy; the chief gnashes his teeth like a Maxim gun. They are all afraid and I dare to tell the water spirit to ravage all the villages where my orders will not be obeyed!

A hideous ghost slowly stands in the middle of reeds and seems to come to us. Suddenly, an irresistible panic arouses and there is a rush for running to the village . . . Ten seconds later, tom-tom, xylophones, balafons, and hunting trumpets produce big noises . . .

In a few minutes, all the Bangelima in a circle of one hundred kilometers radius learn that the white man has an evil power . . . I can now sleep. Everywhere I go my reputation as a sorcerer will pave the way, and I will be feared.

I was not wrong on the results of my subterfuge: I get from natives all what I want because I showed them the water spirit. Tax collection has become easy: twenty thousand francs in three days; my colleagues in Basoko will not believe it.

I returned three months later to Basoko in good health with two hundred and fifty thousand francs of tax money; my *boys* [emphasis added] were not beaten and my belly was not opened.[39]

Unique in its detail, this conversation shows that like most tax collectors, Charles Van de Lanoitte encountered resistance from taxpayers, and like most tax collectors, he relied on violence to break the opposition of Congolese taxes defaulters. Once his reputation of cruelty was established, he no longer used violence to get most villagers pay taxes. The official then pursued the official policy of paternalism, which stood

in sharp contrast to the image of terror the meaning of his name pro-
jected. For all his reputation of burning people alive, he was godfather
to many boys and preferential husband to many girls among Lokele,
Mbole, Ngandu, and Topoke peoples. This subterfuge shows that although colonial officials became godfathers, the practice was not intended to help religious conversion. Instead, it was a clever handling of
a new Christian institution for political purposes. Written and oral
sources show that colonial officials and missionaries in the Aruwimi District knew in the 1930s that godfatherhood among local peoples carried
little religious meaning and significance outside a small group of Congolese schoolteachers, nurses, and catechists. The mission station was
still a cultural and economic enclave of colonial modernity, and Christianity still had little or no impact on the lives of most villagers. The local
administration and missions still bitterly complained about polygyny,
preferential marriage, poison ordeals, and accusations of witchcraft, situations that showed a failure of Christianity in shaping the social out-
look and daily life of villagers.

Like Charles Van de Lanoitte, Congolese manipulated godfatherhood and delayed marriage. Although it appeared a Western institution
in form, godfatherhood was not in essence a new institution because it resembled the local institution of blood brotherhood that had established
alliances in the ancestral time. Village-level interactions such as the
mingling of the official with Congolese, the sharing of cigarettes, the gift
of small amounts of money, and shared leisure time during the full moon
likened godfatherhood to blood brotherhood and created strong expectations of friendship and alliance. In a colonial social aggregate divided
by race, class, and power, these interactions appeared close to diminish-
ing the social distance and inadvertently led Congolese to liken godfatherhood to blood brotherhood. More important, though Congolese
villagers could not entirely escape taxes, the intimate interactions suggest
that the methods of tax collection became less brutal than the name still
suggested they were, and that the official purposefully maintained the
reputation of violence to reinforce his power, which already proved useful in easing the collection of taxes. The appreciation of the official's service by a local leader supported the idea that there was a gap between the
reputation and the deployment of violence. At the end of his term, the
Congolese leader told him, "White man, you were good to us. Do we
know what kind of person your successor will be?" The maneuvers and
appreciation of the official's work by the village leader contradict the
meaning of *Tshoma-Tshoma*, "He who burns people." They show that the

tax collector used the reputation of terror to frighten taxpayers without using the corporal punishments the reputation purported he did.

Coined in the 1930s, *Tshoma-Tshoma* shows that the Congolese of the 1890s and 1900s were not alone in recording the violence of everyday life in the names that were appropriated by the colonizers to intimidate the village peoples. The subsequent generations recorded their experiences of the two world wars, the Great Depression, mandatory cash crop cultivation, compulsory village relocations, conscription, ruthless labor recruitments, and whipping that lasted until 1959, the year when the colonial government outlawed it. And the successive generations of colonial officials appropriated the accusations of violence to intimidate the name-givers who defied the colonial social order. Like Van de Lanoitte, the territorial administrator of the Stanleyville Five Jean earned in the 1930s the name *Kituanga*, which means "He who smashes people" or "Grinder." Congolese derived the name from the Kiswahili verb *kutuanga*, which means "to grind." The name conveyed a great deal more. Like most identities given to colonial officials, *Kituanga* was first the accusation of violence and suffering, and second the expression of anger and contempt. The negative meaning was conveyed by the prefix *ki*, a diminutive that denotes insignificance and refers to things rather than humans. Every time he sensed any resistance to his policies, the official brandished his name to reminded people of his firmness and the violence and suffering they would endure, all intended to keep people in fear.[40]

Despite the success of staged violence, even the most unyielding proponents of force found images of violence counterproductive because they reminded Congolese villagers of the devastating effects of colonialism on everyday life. During the rubber economy, for example, Jean Fievez earned the name *Tange*, a local word for "bed." The officer received the name because he lined up people to kill them with one bullet, a practice designed to save ammunition. Rubber atrocities blamed on *Tange* gave the name the double meaning of "He who can strangulate me" and "Lying face down," the latter seen as the position of the dead. As long as the name served the interests of rubber collection, Fievez used it as a powerful instrument of repression against villagers. But when rubber collection came under attack, prompting a Commission of Inquiry in 1904–5, any name of an agent that suggested atrocity and terror turned into a powerful weapon against King Leopold's regime of terror. Indeed, personal names of the oppressors yielded comments on the experiences of rubber collectors, provided shocking testimonies of abuses to the campaigns against King Leopold II, and compelled Fievez to ask Congolese rubber collectors to call him *Tata,* a name that means "Father" in Lingala and other Bantu languages.

The term "father" also means "leader" in the ideologies of the "house" and "village" in Central Africa.[41] Unlike *Tange,* which referred to dying, *Tata* celebrated leadership and fatherhood, two convenient notions well suited to propagate Belgian ideology of paternalism. This change of name was an effort by Fievez to negotiate a laudatory identity that still legitimized his leadership, to hope loftily for a change of local perceptions of his relations with rubber collectors, and to ward off external campaigns against rubber atrocities. It also highlights the interplay between changes of names, colonial economic practices, and the personal interests of subaltern agents who constantly feared delay in promotion and sometimes loss of job. Indeed, from the beginning of local administrations in 1889 to their collapse in 1959, high-ranking officials punished subordinates and denied them promotion because of unauthorized use of excessive violence. Despite differences of personality among the name-bearers and the complexity of colonial situations, the example suggests the impact of messages of names on the ways colonial agents interacted with villagers and carried out colonial policies.

Names as accusations of violence created a sense of guilt among colonial officials who opposed exploitative economic schemes. This was especially true among colonial officials who, already in the early 1920s, had opposed exploitative policies in peasant production. These colonial officials had first believed in rural development through commodity production and accepted government explanations of mandatory cultivation of cash crops. They believed that cash crop cultivation would steer cash flows into the households and ease the collection of taxes and allow them leisure time. Like their counterparts, these officials resorted to force and threats of force and received names that propagated the fears of violence and expressed concerns about abuses. Until the Second World War, the names spread different representations of violence. The image of *Tshoma-Tshoma,* "He who burns people," for example, spread an ugly message that Van de Lanoitte was "the incarnation of the devil," which allowed him to collect in three months as much as 250,000 francs of tax money from the Bangelima who had the reputation of opposition to taxation. Nonetheless, for all his success in collecting cash, he candidly confessed, "I am confronting resistance and the future is not promising . . . After all, all these brave blacks are right; I have come to harass and have them pay taxes in their forests where they live free and happy; if I were in their place, I would do the same."[42]

Besides forging a sense of guilt, any message of names interpreted by colonial officials as protest worried them. Many acknowledged that negative perceptions of colonialism eroded the foundations of the colonial authority and endangered their personal safety. To disguise such fears, colonial officials accepted the images of horror as late as the Second World War when the colonial government was cutting its reliance on brutality. Appropriating a reputation of violence such as "Europe's lion," "Leopard," "Water spirit," and "Serpent," to mention only a few, removed any humanity from the face of a labor recruiter, a cash crop overseer, or a tax collector. The images of horror eased the recruitment of workers, the expansion of cash crop cultivation, the transfer of cash from households, the plunder, and destruction of religious and ritual objects and of cultural forms that colonial officials deemed morally repulsive. But any practice that helped colonialism look horrendous radicalized Congolese consciousness, thwarted colonialism, and caused fears and worries about personal safety of colonial officials.[43]

J. Pirson provides the first vivid example that illustrates these points. Territorial administrator of Ligasa Territory in the 1920s, he confronted the hostility of the Topoke to colonialism, which dated back to the wars of colonial conquest and culminated in 1907 in the killing of Lorh and Ruette, two agents of the Anglo-Belgian India Rubber Company (ABIR) at Yabohila.[44] Because of this rebellion and other acts of defiance, colonial officials labeled the Topoke "austere people," a hostile stereotype that strained relations between successive generations of colonial officials and the Topoke. As time passed and violence proved unworkable, colonial officials slowly took into account the Topoke's voices, particularly the concerns of the elders. This policy reversal appears in Pirson's advice of 1928 to his counterparts and successors: "It is important for a territorial administrator to know profoundly the ways of thinking and seeing of these middlemen. Their ideas for our own interests are priceless." Another colonial official expressed fears over personal safety in the mid-1930s when he warned Charles Van de Lanoitte, "You go . . . among the Bangelima who are among the nastiest people . . . most have not paid their taxes in years; if you dare to use force, I am afraid you will be brought back dead."[45] Standing against the policy of crushing open resistance during the Second World War, an official refused to enlist in the colonial army: "I won't be part of the killing squad. I hear what they say." So, as colonial officials learned more about local attitudes toward colonialism from messages that were accusations of violence, they used the knowledge to crack the codes of messages embedded in their local identities. The common outcome was a shift from a total reliance on violence to some negotiation, which resulted in the change of administrative style.

The messages drawn from names grew radical once they trickled down into village rumors, nighttime dances, different rituals of life cycles, and work songs. The radicalism of these voices was tied to the predicaments and cultural assumptions according to which a Congolese singer or listener interpreted the messages. As powerful voices of protest, names denounced abuses of colonialism and evils of colonial officials, ugly aspects of colonial everyday life, which resulted in cumulative transformation of the consciousness of oppressed Congolese and colonial officials. Based on years of minute observations, a territorial administrator wrote in 1936 to express the situation forcefully: "listen to the songs that accompany their rituals, they have no direct relationship to the rituals, and to these words the black attributes a sense and magic virtue."[46] Although divided by age, gender, status, and class, each villager who consistently learned of abuses of colonialism developed an understanding of the system, which reinforced rebellious attitudes toward colonial rulers. Because colonial officials had no control over the production, dissemination, and usages of messages, the spread of colonial anthroponyms engendered new subversive rumors and stories about colonialism. The expression of accusations of suffering through cultural forms not only sapped the authority and prestige of tax collectors, agricultural officers, and territorial administrators but also tormented their consciences.

Briefly, giving colonial officials names suggesting violence was an accusation of the suffering and the hardship of colonial situations. These accusations spread a shared understanding of various aspects of colonialism as depicted by the names. Once colonial officials appropriated them as feedback and periodically backed them with brutality, their messages became powerful weapons at the hands of colonial officials to intimidate Congolese villagers and perpetuate fears of repression. As colonial officials appropriated names suggesting violence, they wore the mask of terrorists, which allowed them to carry out tasks without resorting to violence. Although names reminiscent of violence kept many Congolese villagers submissive, they conversely created fear, guilt, and a sense of insecurity among brutal colonial officials and affected the ways these officials carried out colonial policies and interacted with Congolese villagers.

Conclusions

This book pursues two basic objectives, one methodological, the other epistemological or conceptual. Methodologically, I show that the meanings of names given to explorers, missionaries, state officials, and agents of companies conveyed substantial information about colonial rule, local situations, and colonial material conditions created by colonialism. The hundreds of illustrations of names show that whether one interprets the meanings of colonial anthroponyms as objective observations or perceptions of colonialism, they provide unparalleled access to local ideas about the effects of colonial situations on the lives of Congolese. Although such conditions changed according to colonial projects and local response, colonial anthroponyms everywhere discussed the punishments, the repressive colonial intrusion into personal and collective life, the disruption of local economies and culture, and the ways in which colonialism set the rhythms of daily life in the village world. Many were explicit criticisms of practices of domination, oppression, and exploitation. They were commentaries about the effects of colonialism on the experiences of Congolese villagers from the time of European explorations in the 1870s to the end of colonization of the Congo on 30 June 1960. The seemingly disparate bits of testimonies woven into the meanings of names of colonial officials turned into collective memories and valuable local commentaries on colonial rule and the daily life of village people. This study shows that by adapting Central African naming conventions to colonial situations, Congolese recorded their concerns about colonialism and their everyday life and therefore transformed the names of Europeans into sources of their colonial experiences. Briefly, the meanings of names of colonial officials are important sources of history of Congolese colonial experiences once contextualized and subjected to the rules of evidence.

Congolese villagers named colonial officials collectively and individually. Although collective names described mainly colonial situations that dominated an era and overwhelmed the totality of experiences of the community, individual names recorded the routines of colonial interactions that characterized colonialism at the village level, including the ways in which individual Europeans behaved and carried out colonial policies. Congolese villagers did not record every experience of daily life when naming explorers and colonial state officials, nor did the names narrate all the happenings in the village, the fields, and the workplaces. Still, the naming of colonial officials encompassed a variety of events, scenes, circumstances, conditions of work and everyday life, and mindsets, all of which formed the basic social structure shaping interactions between Congolese villagers and colonial officials. The names of colonial officials were therefore a repository of observations and perceptions of colonialism, stories, and memories of Belgian colonialism.

An enormous advantage of names, among many, was the recording of the everyday happenings from which one can deduce an understanding of the conditions and structures that caused the events being observed and described. As a result, exploring names allowed centering the analysis on the interactions of concrete people with structures that shaped their lives. This is important for the writing of the histories of ordinary villagers who did not leave written records of their own and who recorded and expressed their concerns about colonial rule through names. By listening to the voices of Congolese, the book highlights the complexity in the ways Congolese thought of the colonial world of political and economic limitations, violence, and fewer opportunities. The inside information shows that Congolese were more than just victims of European processes and turns the exploration of names into a way into the collective memories, ideologies, mindsets, and historical consciousness to show how Congolese understood large processes that affected and changed their everyday lives. In this regard, the book proves its claim to methodological innovation.

The ability to name colonial officials testifies to the cultural autonomy against which Congolese evaluated their experiences of colonialism. Congolese agency was apparent in the messages of praise, protest, and satire against colonial officials, which yield ideas about Congolese minds. Because of the violence they faced daily, Congolese villagers' free social space shrank, and many did not find in open resistance the best option to negotiate local matters. Since the 1870s, King Leopold II transformed what became successively the Congo Free State and Belgian Congo into a colonial space filled with increasing constraints, limitations, and lack of autonomy through the creation and use of the colonial army, the local police force, whipping, and prisons.[1] Although colonial power holders could never control everyday life in the colonial social aggregate, Congolese villagers were not heroic warriors fighting day and night.[2] The lack of freedom also affected state-appointed chiefs whose resistance led to their exile, removal from office, and deprivation of salaries. The naming of colonial officials became instrumental in constructing a political language to express dissatisfaction and negotiate aspects of colonialism villagers regarded as intolerable.[3] This way, Congolese kept some measure of cultural autonomy that accurately identified and gave a face to their oppressors and exploiters.

Themes and topics that emerge from the names open up new areas of research as they enrich old ones. To be sure, the meanings of names show that names captured Congolese thoughts and perceptions of unfolding colonial events, colonial structural constraints, and ideologies, and all shaped the village world where, while Congolese experienced violence and few economic outlets, colonial officials constantly struggled to expand their challenged power.[4] Based on these data, the book argues that approaching histories of Congolese experiences of colonialism through names allowed the re-creation of everyday life in the village world under colonial rule. Many illustrations show that the history of naming explained the politics of negotiations in which Congolese and colonial officials were engaged as they endlessly adopted meanings and messages as weapons and as they struggled over the real and symbolic boundaries of power, domination, and exploitation. By focusing on the intersection of colonial rule and naming practices, the book captures the dynamics of power relations and illuminates the interconnections among colonialism, cultural forms and expressions, and social experiences.

Congolese villagers wove into individual and collective names the accusations of injustice, exploitation, violence, sexual exploitation, and confiscation of cash, foodstuffs, and labor into symbols and metaphors of praise.[5] These accusations show the workings of local cultural forces and mindsets—the ability of Congolese to create and disseminate forms of social consciousness under the watchful eyes of the state-appointed chiefs, elders, policemen, agricultural monitors, and messengers, the segment of Congolese included in the colonial administrative structure. The coding of local voices challenges the passivity of Congolese villagers and buries once and for all the old imaginary view of Africa, which the notion of the invention of Africa has unwittingly resurrected.

A seemingly contradictory political behavior motivated by the need to skirt retaliation and ensure safety, praise naming of the oppressors was a widespread response to colonial political domination and economic exploitation.[6] It represents the coding of messages and challenges the notion of the invention of Africa. The multidimensional messages of the meanings of names show that through praise naming, villagers cloaked ugly meanings and hostile messages in local symbols of authority, attributes of power, and colonial uniforms, most of which suggested kindness, peace, and beauty but which equally criticized colonial rule. It also shows the complexities and sophistication of Congolese in understanding broader processes that transformed their everyday lives and communities. Unlike some previous analyses that stressed the confiscation and transfer of resources to the colonial state and various sectors of capital to comprehend the political behavior of exploited peasants and workers, this study shows that cultural interpretations of unequal colonial relations shaped Congolese understandings of their plight as much as the confiscation of resources.[7] A history of colonialism based on the meanings of names thus expands prevailing paradigms as it shifts the exclusive focus from material exploitation once posited by historical materialism and those paradigms that either focused only on local notions of fairness or stressed only the pursuit of individual economic gains to explain African responses to colonialism.[8]

Although physical confrontations played a vital role in the struggles of Congolese against colonialism, Congolese villagers were not "heroic tribal warriors" engaged day and night in rebellions. Open rebellions were rare, but when they did break out, colonial troops killed rebels, burned houses, destroyed standing crops, and confiscated herds of goats and cattle and poultry yards. By undermining long-term social reproduction of the village world, scorched earth policies and harsh punishments compelled Congolese to realize the limits of confrontation and choose subtler forms of protest. Because colonial officials dismissed cultural messages as meaningless, praise naming generated duplicitous messages through which Congolese villagers talked about colonialism subversively without fear. In the broader local responses to colonialism, praise naming was the same as singing surreptitious songs, spreading sarcastic rumors, dancing obscene dances, and making wicked innuendoes about the colonizers, forms of protest colonial officials could hardly censor.[9] So this study amplifies the literature on the surreptitious forms of protest, shifting from an earlier focus in the 1960s and 1970s on rebellions, social banditry, and social movements.[10]

Despite the struggle of Congolese villagers to hide some categories of messages, the colonizers understood most messages embedded in their names. First, I quote excerpts and lists of names collected in the colonial archives. The accuracy of translations from local languages into French shows colonial officials' comprehensive knowledge of naming and a deep understanding of the loaded messages of names.[11] Second, many names, even those that infuriated colonial officials and provoked retaliation, were in Lingala, Kiswahili, Kikongo, and Ciluba, the languages the colonial officials spoke and appropriated to run local administrations. With varying individual ability, colonial officials became competent in these languages and decoded some layers of deeper meanings of messages. Third, Congolese villagers who worked for local administrations informed European officials about village life and provided information that enabled them to decipher much in the messages of names. Archives, oral testimonies, historical novels, and memoirs of former colonial officials show that Congolese house workers, agricultural monitors, interpreters, and messengers were valuable informants who sometimes played the role of spies. They revealed the village gossips who allowed officials to figure out shades of meaning in the names. The access to inside information allowed agronomists to arrest preventively Congolese villagers they suspected of making trouble—even for minor disorderly conduct and verbal exchanges with officials during village community meetings and for referring to officials by derogatory names.[12]

Colonial officials appropriated local representations of colonialism embedded in their names to either instill fear or mediate paternalistic dominance. When villagers named officials after experiences of violence, they wittingly or unwittingly gave to the proponents of violence the evidence that violence caused fear and submission—two foundations of colonial authority. By masking their faces into menacing representations of colonialism, colonial officials sometimes transformed Congolese villagers into fearful commodity producers and tax payers. Names suggesting violence thus turned into weapons of terror. And although terror did not suppress opposition, it affected its forms and influenced its timing and frequency. The taking over of laudatory representations of colonialism tells a different story. Although colonial officials used it to hide the hardships of colonialism, it simultaneously showed that the actual power of individual colonial officials was thin. So the names of colonial officials as the voices of the community tell much about the workings of colonialism. The layers and shades of meaning of names show the many ways in which colonial officials carried out their mandate, the ways in which they negotiated micro-level concerns, and the contradictions created by their policies. This transpired in the ways they appropriated and tried to change their names. In reality, the search for laudatory identities by colonial officials seemed at odds with the acts and threats of violence, the twin instruments of colonial power in colonial Congo. The change of names by colonial officials was designed to alter the negative perceptions of colonialism held by the villagers.[13]

In summary, the understanding of colonialism through the names of colonial officials is a strategic approach to re-create the ways Congolese and colonial officials constructed and negotiated the boundaries of power, collaboration, and powerlessness. It shows the complexity in the ways Congolese dealt with a perplexing world of uncertainty, limitations, violence, and fewer opportunities, as well as the attempts by colonial officials to frustrate the autonomy suggested by Congolese naming. And the study of names provides insights into Congolese mindsets and the historical consciousness and expands our knowledge of Congolese villagers' understanding of large processes that shaped everyday lives in the village world.

SAMPLE OF NAMES USED IN THIS WORK

Local names	Translation	Location	Real names
Abombo	———	Kisangani	Dupont
Adami	Madam	Opala	generic
Adamisu (Adamiso)	Knowing eyes, control, anger	Basoko	———
Aduyi	Lion	———	———
Aginu	Kneeling	Kisangani	Genot
Agomiriya	Abuser of women; Unfaithful husband	Moto	generic
Alali na Se	He who is lying down	Équateur	———
Alinga Mama	He who loves mother; Womanizer	Aruwimi	generic
Alangwi Likaya	Drunken smoker	———	———
Alinga Tumba	Fight lover	———	———
Alube	King Albert	Kasai	King Albert
Angbalima	Terror	Basoko, Eastern Congo	———
Angbotalikume	———	Basoko	———
Angwandima	Terror	Eastern Congo	———
Asali Monkanda	He has written a letter	Kisangani	D'Hondt
Atama-Atama	Enslavers	Opala	any whites
Atamu	Madam	Opala	generic
Ataso	Attention	everywhere	generic
Atila Okondo	He who does not let land lie fallow	Opala	any crops supervisor
Awaya-Awaya	Lack of direction	Kasai	generic
Bajunu	Kneeling	Kisangani	generic
Bakola	Generation	Inongo	Cloetens et al.
Bala-Bala	Main road; Officials on the move	everywhere	any itinerate agent
Balikpe	Leaves eater	Uele	G. Schweinfurth
Balikuhe	He was eating raw and bland food	Uele	G. Miani
Bambenga	Red pepper	Équateur	———
Bana Munama	Water spirit	Kisangani	Wouters

163

Local names	Translation	Location	Real names
Bandungu	Pepper	Lac Leopold II	P.-J. Van de Moere
Bapenda Kula	They who love to eat	Ituri	generic
Basikoti	Much whipping; Hippopotamus-hide whip	everywhere	generic
Batu Pamba	Straw men	Uele	generic
Beleli	Lover of women	Bumba	generic
Bikengakenga	——	Katanga	——
Bola-Bola	Beat, beat; Ruthless beater	Équateur	——
Bolemba	Stupefying vine for killing fish	Équateur, Opala	——
Bombeki	——	Équateur	H. Bombeeck
Bosolo	——	Équateur	——
Bula Matari	Break rocks	——	any agent
Bula Matende	Dynamiter; Break rocks	Vivi, Basoko	Van Kerkhoven
Bumba	Who comes from Bumba	Kisangani	Luthy
Bwana Kapia	Second-born of twins	Katanga	Delvaux
Bwana Kaseya	——	Kasongo	Verditch
Bwana Kenengene	——	Katanga	——
Bwana Kidogo	Mister small; Little boss	Eastern Congo	——
Bwana Kioseni	——	——	——
Bwana Kitoko	Mister handsome	everywhere	King Baudouin
Bwana Leke	Mister Leke	Kasai	Legat
Bwana Lubuku	Master builder	Kasongo	Van Malderen
Bwana Lutshina	——	Katanga	——
Bwana Maibwe	Mister stone	Katanga	R. Ramelot
Bwana Mukubwa	Big boss; Superior; Mister tall	Eastern Congo	——
Bwana Mzuri	Mister handsome	Katanga	——
Bwana Ndeke	Mister bird	Kilo	Henry
Bwana Ndeke	Mister bird	Kisangani	L. Oswald, L. Adhémar, C. de Leuze
Bwana Nioka	Mister snake	Katanga	Gilson
Bwana Nzige	Mister locust	——	any violent agent
Bwana Pangabisoto	——	Katanga	——
Bwana Tomasi	Mister Thomas	Katanga	——
Bwana Tumbaku	——	Kisangani	T. Nicolas
Chakundia	He who can eat me	Katanga	——
Chicotte	Whipping	Baringa	G. Dineur
Cibalabala	Wild cat	Kasai	F. Van Nimmen, J. Van Uden
Cibutama	To hide small scar	Kasai	R. Bearts
Cimpanga	Bull	Kasai	A. Demunster
Ciswa-bantu	He who loves people	Kasai	A. Lippens
Citoko	Handsome	Kasai	——
Djeke	——	Katanga	——

Local names	Translation	Location	Real names
Djoko Deli	——	Kasai	——
Ebeni	——	Katanga	——
Ebuka-Buka	Breaker of things into pieces	Ekonda, Équateur	——
Efanja	He who disperses people	Ekonda, Équateur	
Ekanda	——	Bolobo	Grenfell
Ekanga-kanga	He who arrests people arbitrarily and indiscriminately	Équateur	——
Ekatankoi	——	Tomba	Steinbeck
Ekuma	He who destroys things	Équateur	——
Eminimbi	Emin, the wicked	Uele	E. Schnitzer (Emin Pacha)
Engalala	Palm leaf	Lac Leopold II	Lemaire
Etumba Mbilo	Office that resembles a battlefield	——	——
Ewa-Olefe	Womanizer	Yanonge	generic
Fasa ou Nkosa Nkosa	——	Inongo	
Fazzari	——	Basoko, Mbesa	——
Fimbo Mingi	Much whipping; Hippopotamus-hide whip	Kasongo	Baron Dhanis
Genda genda	——	——	——
Guruguru	Pierced ear lobes	Uele	Ibrahim
Hela	onomatopoea	Isangi	Harens
Hoy na Gola	——	Kisangani	Butticaz
Iboko	——	Tomba	Lieventhal
Ikeleso		——	——
Ikoka	He who shoots people	——	——
Ikuka	Bitter shrub	——	——
Ilanga	Enmity	Équateur	
Ipanga Ngunda	He who destroys the country	Upper Congo	the Congo Free State
Ipipola	Copulation	Opala	——
Itumba Mbilu	War-like office	Tomba	——
Kabalo	Horse	Kasai	Gillain
Kabangu	Small scar; Device of torture	Kasai	L. De Brandt
Kabesa Babo	——	Lulubourg	Wissman
Kabuakiatunge	Whipping	Maniema	——
Kakese	Small, junior	Katanga	——
Kamuziki	Little music	Lac Leopold II	A. J. G. Bolle
Kangipipe	——	Katanga	
Kapiteni	Captain	Province Orientale	generic
Kaputi	——	Inongo	J. de Dixmude
Kaseya	——	Katanga	
Kashabala	——	Kasai	Gaspar
Kasiama Nkoi	——	——	——

Local names	Translation	Location	Real names
Kasongo Bushila	Tall and lean	Kasai	Bugschlag
Kasongo Mule	Tall and lean	Kasai	Gillain
Kelekele	———	Katanga	———
Kelelo	Bugle	Lac Leopold II	A. J. G. Bolle
Kilupula	———	Katanga	———
Kimbwi	Hyena	Katanga	———
Kiomba Musinga	———	Katanga	———
Kitatshindja	He who cuts people in pieces	Kasongo	Moltedo
Kitoko (Kitoko Mingi)	Handsome; Beautiful; Delicious taste	everywhere	any handsome agent
Kituanga	He who smashes people; Grinder	Kisangani	Five Jean
Kobinda	———	———	Sergers
Koja	———	Uele	G. Junker
Kolongo	———	Kisangani	Lauwers Atay
Koma-Koma	He who can strangle me	Équateur	———
Komanda	Commander	———	generic
Konga	———	Katanga	Crawford
Kulu-Kulu	Violence trigger; Troublemaker	Katanga	———
Kuta Bongo	———	Basoko	Purnode
Lambo	———	Katanga	———
Lamu	———	Katanga	———
Liamamba	Millipede	Ekonda, Opala	———
Liboma	He who kills	Équateur	———
Libumbu	Elegance	———	Lefevre
Libumu	Belly	Province Orientale	———
Likoka	Shooter	Tumba	———
Likoke	Prickly tree	Ekonda	———
Likwama	———	Mampoko	M. Spelier
Lilanga'atumbe	Garden destructor	Équateur	———
Limende	———	Yahisuli	———
Liombo	Broom; Flywhisk	Opala	Wautier
Lipumbu	Elegant	Province Orientale	———
Lokesa	———	Basoko	Dekeyzer
Lokonga	Venomous snake	Ekonda, Opala	———
Lombolembo	———	Kisangani	Jamsin
Longo-Longo	Tall, tall	Kilo, Moto	———
Longwango	———	Lac Leopold II	G. O. Schioz
Longwani	———	Katanga	———
Loponge	onomatopoea	Basoko	P. Ponthier
Luanda	Predatory trade	Kazembe	M. Caetano Pereira
Lubuku	Builder	Kasongo	Van Malderen
Lukwako	Go back where you came from	Zimba	———

Local names	Translation	Location	Real names
Lumandemulu	Fine collector	Lac Léopold II	P.-J. Van de Moere
Madami	Madam	Opala	generic
Mafuta	Fat	Katanga	——
Mafuta Mingi	A lot of fat	Mbesa, Bengamisa, Kilo, Moto, Bakumu	Bell, M. Poils
Maiene mingi	A lot of fat	Ba	——
Maina	Fat	——	——
Makasi	Force, power, strong	Aruwimi	——
Makisi	——	Katanga	——
Makpatu	Chaser of women	Basoko	——
Makupkup	Of the old village	Kuba	——
Malakolo	——	Zimba	——
Mala-Mala	Main roads; Officials on the move	Kasai	——
Malanda (Molanda)	Follower	Uele	Van Hende
Malenge	——	Ubangi	——
Malonga Longa	——	Katanga	——
Malu-Malu	Rush, rush	Lac Léopold II	——
Mandevu Mingi	Beard	Province Orientale	——
Mangbe	Lightning; Scrapers of the heaps; White cannibals	Buta	——
Mangema	——	Zimba	——
Matala-Tala (Tala-Tala)	Mirror, eyeglasses, scrutiny; Witchcraft	Buta	——
Matamba-Tamba	Enslavers	Opala	any agent
Matcho Kali	Angry eyes; Harshness	Opala	——
Matuba	Words	Territoire des cataractes	——
Mayala	Oppressor	Territoire des cataractes	——
Mbavu Munene	Big chest	everywhere	——
Mbavu Nguvu	Strong chest	everywhere	——
Mfumu Mantese	Prince who has things to say	——	A. De Meulemeester
Miere-Miere	Many knives; Ferocious and wild warrior	Kazembe	Mayo-Monteiro
Miso Minei	Four eyes; Thief	Aruwimi	——
Miso Nkoyi	Leopard's eyes; Anger	——	——
Miti	Trees	Kasongo	Middage
Moke	Small, short	Aruwimi	generic
Moke-Moke	Small, small; Very small	Uele-Itimbiri	Verstracten
Molanda	Follower	Uele	Hinde
Mondele Madami	Man who is always with his wife	Bandundu, Bulungu	——

Local names	Translation	Location	Real names
Mondele Mboka	Village white man; Native son; Head of the post	Aruwimi	———
Mondele na Kawa	White man of coffee	Province Orientale	generic
Mondele na Loso	White man of rice	Province Orientale	generic
Mondele na Mbila	White man of palm oil tree	Province Orientale	generic
Mondele Ngolo	Strong white man	Bas Congo	———
Monganga na Mabele	Earth healer; Mine prospector	Province Orientale	———
Monginda (Bonginda)	———	Tomba	Durieux
Mpimbo Mingi	Much whipping	Équateur	———
Msirikanda	———	Province Orientale	De Meulemeester
Mudiata ou Nyata	———	Katanga	Thiry
Mukalenge Leka	Prince Leka	———	Legat
Mundele Kikufi	Short white man	Territoire des cataractes	———
Mundele Mbisi	———	Bas Congo	———
Mundele Mbwa	———	Bas Congo	———
Mundele Ngolo	Strong white man	Bas Congo	———
Mundele Nioka	White man who is like a snake	Bas Congo	———
Mundele Nzazi	———	Bas Congo	———
Munyololo	Chain, rope	Eastern Congo	———
Mupe	Priest	Eastern Congo	generic
Mupenda Batu	He who loves people	Irumu, Ituri, Eastern Congo	generic
Mupenda Kula	He who likes to eat	Yanonge	———
Muzungu wa Pamba	White man of cotton	Kongolo	———
Mwambe	Eight; Eight lashes	Basoko	———
Mwana Mputu	Child of Europe	Équateur	H. Bombeeck
Mwandami	Madam	———	generic
Mwendo-Mwendo	Travel, travel; Voyage at the foot of the world	Kazembe	M. Caetano Pereira
Nabira	———	Uele	G. Casati
Nafranki	He has white beard and long hair	Uele	G. Miani
Ndeke, Ndeke-Ndeke	Bird; Officials on the move	———	generic
Ndevu	Bearded white man	Eastern Congo	———
Ndjole-Ndjole	Bearded white man	Ekonda	———
Ndoki	Witch	Kasongo	Elter
Ngangabuka	Priest; God's healer	Kasai	———
Nganga Nzambe	Priest; God's healer	Équateur, Province Orientale	———
Ngolo Mingi	Much power	Bas Congo	———

Local names	Translation	Location	Real names
Ngonga na butu	Nightly talking slit gong	Équateur, Province Orientale	———
Ngongo Leteta	Bad official	Eastern Congo	generic
Nialakowombu	———	Lac Leopold II	J. M. F. Tumers
Niangeniange	———	Kisangani	G. Geerearts
Nkake	Lightning; White cannibals	Province Orientale, Équateur	———
Nkangobeko	———	Inongo	Cloetens
Nkoso	Parrot	———	———
Nkoyi (Nkoi)	Leopard	Lac Leopold II	H. Dupuis
Nsoni Mingi	Very shameful	———	Shaw
Ntange	Bed	Lac Leopold II	J. Fievez
Nyimi-Nyimi	Red ant; Lack of civilization	Kasai	———
Nyoka	Snake; Resentment	Katanga	Wilson
Nzoku	Elephant	———	———
Nzokumasi	———	Bas Congo	———
Ondele W'Ekonge	White men of urena lobata	Opala	———
Padiri	Priest	Eastern Congo	———
Paipo	Pipe	Kilo, Moto	———
Pamba	———	Lac Leopold II	J. Fievez
Panzi	Lying side	Tomba	J. Fievez
Pebe	———	Tomba	Clark
Pete ya Mai ya Sombe	Green stars; Stars colored the color of the cassava leaves	Province Orientale	———
Pole-Pole	Very calm; Slow walker; Lazy walker	Eastern Congo	generic
Rumaliza	Destroyer	Eastern Congo	———
Sango	Father	Eastern Congo, Équateur	———
Sato	———	———	G. Casati
Sesa	———	Basoko, Mongeliema	Chaltin
Sikitele	Secretary	Bandundu, Équateur, Province Orientale	generic
Sikoti	Much whipping; Hippopotamus-hide whip	———	generic
Simba Bulaya	Europe's lion	Katanga, Eastern Congo	———
Singa	———	Basoko	Van Wert
Situka	———	Kisangani	Foerch
Sokele (Lokele)	———	Lac Leopold II	L. A. Borms

Local names	Translation	Location	Real names
Soso Aleli	Rooster has crowed	Province Orientale	———
Soso Mombi	White-feathered chicken	Chez Gobila	Janssen
Soso Mpembe	White-feathered chicken	Lac Leopold II	Janssen
Sukuma	Push	Nyangwe	Losange
Tange	Bed	Équateur	J. Fievez
Tata	Father	Équateur	J. Fievez
Tomansangu	Send news; News maker	Bas Congo	———
Tomilali	Court	Opala	———
Tomo	———	Katanga	———
Toro	———	Basoko	Lund
Tshienda Bitekete	Lazy walker	Kasai	———
Tshiwayawaya	Balance in breeze	Kasai	———
Tshoma-Tshoma	He who burns people	Aruwimi	C. Van de Lanoitte
Tshombe Bululu	Bitter cassava leaves	Kasai	Gillain
Tuku-Tuku	Motorcycle	Kongolo	generic
Tuku-Tuku	Motorcycle	Kisangani	V. Rue
Tumbaku	Tobacco; Sticky mouth and stained teeth	Kisangani	N. Tobback
Tumba Lombe	Home burner	Équateur	———
Tupa Mokono	Throw hand	Moto	———
Vandebunduki	Vande, the gunman	Lac Leopold II	L. Van den Broeke
Vandenbuluki	Vande, the witch	Lac Leopold II	L. Van den Broeke
Va-nsina	Sit down	———	J. Vansina
Wai-Wai	Big troublemaker	Kamina	generic
Yamba-Yamba	Defecate, defecate	Kasongo	Bosoni

NOTES

Introduction

1. R. Howard-Malvelde, *Creating Context in Andean Cultures* (New York: Oxford University Press, 1997), 96; J. Vansina, *Oral Tradition as History* (Madison: University of Wisconsin Press, 1985); D. Laya, ed., *La tradition orale: Problématique et méthodologie des sources de l'histoire africaine* (Abbeville: P. Paillart, 1972).

2. O. Likaka, "Working for the Taxman Makes People Thinner: Economy and Demography in the Congo," unpublished manuscript. The title of the paper was derived from the saying "Wando wo limolo," which is common among the Kembe, a group of Mbole people, and which means "Emaciation caused by taxation."

3. Dimandja Luhaka, "Cours d'histoire politique du Zaire moderne et indépendant," Unaza, Lubumbashi. The professor had a tremendous ability to remember and tell stories that were invaluable materials for the writing of the social history of the Congo.

4. B. Crine, *La structure sociale des Foma* (Brussels: CEDAF 4, 1972).

5. B. Jewsiewicki, *Naître et mourir au Zaïre: Un demi-siècle d'histoire au quotidien* (Paris: Karthala, 1993); B. Jewsiewicki, *Musique urbaine au Katanga: De Malaika à Santu Kïmbangu* (Paris: L'Harmattan, 2003); B. Jewsiewicki, *Mami Wata: La peinture urbaine au Congo* (Paris: Gallimard, 2003); B. Jewsiewicki, *A Congo Chronicle: Patrice Lumumba in Urban Art* (New York: Museum for African Art, 1999); J. Fabian, *Remembering the Present: Painting and Popular History in Zaire* (Berkeley: University of California Press, 1993).

6. D. De Lannoy, Mabiala Seda Diangwala, and Bongeli Yeikelo Ya Ato, *Tango ya ba Noko. Le temps des oncles: Recueil des témoignages zairois* (Brussels: CEDAF 5–6, 1986); B. Verhaegen, ed., *Kisangani: Histoire d'une ville* (Kisangani: PUZ, 1976); B. Verhaegen, *Introduction à l'histoire immédiate* (Gembloux, 1974).

7. L. Vail and L. White, *Power and the Praise Poem: Southern African Voices in History* (Charlottesville: University Press of Virginia, 1991); see also their "Forms of Resistance: Songs and Perceptions of Power in Colonial Mozambique," in *Banditry, Rebellion and Social Protest in Africa*, ed. D. Crummey (Portsmouth N.H.: Heinemann, 1986).

8. L. White, *Speaking with Vampires: Rumor and History in Colonial Africa* (Berkeley: University of California Press, 2000); B. Bozzoli, *Women of Phokeng: Consciousness, Life Strategy, and Migrancy in South Africa, 1900–1983* (Portsmouth, N.H.: Heinemann, 1991).

9. A. Isaacman, *Cotton Is the Mother of Poverty, 1938–1961* (Portsmouth, N.H.: Heinemann, 1996); T. Sunseri, *Vilimani: Labor Migration and Rural Change in Early Colonial Tanzania* (Portsmouth, N.H.: Heinemann, 2002).

10. E. Mandala, *Work and Control in a Peasant Economy* (Madison: University of Wisconsin Press, 1990); E. Mandala, *The End of Chidyerano: A History of Food and Everyday Life in Malawi, 1860–2004* (Portsmouth, N.H.: Heinemann, 2005).

11. O. Likaka, "L'impact de l'organisation politique et administrative dans le Territoire d'Opala," MA thesis, Unaza, Lubumbashi, 1981.

12. P. Joyce and R. Lewin, *Les trusts au Congo* (Brussels: Société belge d'Editions, 1961); M. Merlier, *Le Congo de la colonisation belge à l'indépendance* (Paris: Maspero, 1962), 57–185; Likaka, *Rural Society*, 71–107; J. Marchal, *L'état libre du Congo: Paradis perdu*, 2 vols. (Brussels: Editions Paula Bellings, 1996).

13. N. Yelengi, "The PFB Railroad, Society and Culture in Rural Katanga (Colonial Zaire)," *Africa* (Rome) 52, no. 2 (1997); J. Vansina, *Kingdoms of the Savanna* (Madison: University of Wisconsin Press, 1965); Mandala, *End of Chidyerano;* Sunseri, *Vilimani;* Vail and White, "Forms of Resistance"; Isaacman, *Cotton Is the Mother;* Bozzoli, *Women of Phokeng*, 3; Jewsiewicki, *Naître et mourir au Zaire;* M. Vancraenbroeck, *Les médailles de la présence belge en Afrique centrale, 1876–1960* (Brussels: Bibliothèque Royale, 1996); N. Hunt, *A Colonial Lexicon of Birth Ritual, Medicalization, and Mobility in the Congo* (Durham, N.C.: Duke University Press, 1999); D. Crummey, ed., *Banditry, Rebellion and Social Protest in Africa* (Portsmouth N.H.: Heinemann, 1986); Fabian, *Remembering the Present.*

14. J. Vansina, *Living with Africa* (Madison: University of Wisconsin Press, 1994); D. Crummey, "Introduction: 'The Great Beast,'" in Crummey, *Banditry, Rebellion and Social Protest*, 10–11.

15. V. Mudimbe, *The Idea of Africa* (Bloomington: Indiana University Press, 1994); Fabian, *Remembering the Present;* Jewsiewicki, *Naître et mourir au Zaire.*

16. Vancraenbroeck, *Les médailles*, 65. Unless otherwise indicated, all translations are my own.

17. Ibid.

18. A. Gramsci, *Letters from Prison* (New York: Harper and Row, 1973); B. Lincoln, *Discourse and the Construction of Society* (New York: Oxford University Press, 1989); J. Scott, *Domination and the Arts of Resistance: Hidden Transcripts* (New Haven, Conn.: Yale University Press, 1990).

19. V. Y. Mudimbe, *The Invention of Africa: Gnosis, Philosophy, and the Order of Knowledge* (Bloomington: Indiana University Press, 1988). For a critique of postmodernism, see Vansina, *Living with Africa*, 217–220; K. Windschuttle, *The Killing of History: How Literary Critics and Social Theorists Are Murdering Our Past* (New York: Free Press, 1997).

20. S. Schwartz, *Implicit Understandings: Observing, Reporting, and Reflecting on the Encounters between Europeans and Other Peoples in the Early Modern Era* (Cambridge: Cambridge University Press, 1995); T. Asad, *Anthropology and the Colonial Encounter* (New York: Humanities Press, 1973).

21. Windschuttle, *The Killing of History*, 12.

22. A. Portelli, *The Battle of Valle Giulia: Oral History and the Art of Dialogue* (Madison: University of Wisconsin Press, 1997), ix.

23. J. Ki-Zerbo, *Histoire générale de l'Afrique* (Paris: Hatier, 1972), 15. For similar statements, see J. Vansina, *De la tradition orale* (Kinshasa: Editions universitaires du Congo, 1961); Vansina, *Kingdoms;* Vansina, *Oral Tradition.*

24. A. Van Zandycke, "La révolte de Luluabourg (4 juillet 1895)," *Zaïre* 11 (1950): 934; F. Lambrecht, *In the Shade of an Acacia Tree: Memoirs of a Health Officer in Africa, 1945–1959* (Philadelphia: American Philosophical Society, 1991), 237; A. Cauvin, *Bwana Kitoko: Un livre réalisé au cours du voyage du roi des Belges au Congo et dans le Ruanda-Urundi* (Paris: Elsevier, 1956).

25. G. Nzongola-Ntalaza, *The Congo, from Leopold to Kabila: A People's History* (London: Zed Books, 2002); C. Young and T. Turner, *The Rise and Decline of the Zairian State* (Madison: University of Wisconsin Press, 1985); M. Schatzberg, *The Dialectics of Oppression in Zaire* (Bloomington: Indiana University Press, 1988).

26. Interview with Lufundja, Lubumbashi, 14 August 1986.

27. Group interview with Lwamba Bilonda and Mugaza wa Beya, Lubumbashi, 16 August 1986.

28. O. Likaka, "Colonialisme et clichés sociaux au Congo belge," *Africa* (Rome) 52, no. 1 (1997): 1–27.

29. F. Mulambu, "Cultures obligatoires et colonisation dans l'ex-Congo belge," *Cahiers du CEDAF* 6–7 (1974); Likaka, *Rural Society;* M. Merlier, *Le Congo de la colonisation;* E. Morel, *Red Rubber: The Story of the Rubber Slave Trade Flourishing on the Congo in the Year of Grace 1906* (New York: Haskell House, 1906), 43–79; D. Vangroenweghe, *Du sang sur les lianes: Léopold II et son Congo* (Brussels: Didier Hatier, 1985), 113; J. Marchal, *L'état libre du Congo,* 1:283–391.

30. E. M'Bokolo, Introduction to Jewsiewicki, *Naître et mourir au Zaïre,* 28; R. Depoorter, *Stanleyville où le Lualaba devenait Congo* (Brussels: Didier Hatier, 1992), 152; A. Dallons and V. Cornet, "Evolution de poste de Kasongo à travers le temps, 1865–1931," A.I. (1407), A.A., Brussels; Van de Lanoitte, *Sur les rivières glauques,* 128, 169; J. Vellut, "Matériaux pour une image du blanc dans la société coloniale du Congo belge," in *Stéréotypes nationaux et préjugés raciaux au XIXe et XXe siècles: Sources et methods pour une approche historique,* ed. J. Pirotte (Leuven: Editions Nauwelaerts, 1982); J. Vanden Bossche, *Sectes et associations indigènes au Congo belge* (Léopoldville: Editions du Bulletin Militaire, 1954), 11.

31. L. Lotar, "Souveniers de l'Uele," *Congo* 4, no. 2 (1931), 506, 508; Schweinfurth, *Heart of Africa* (London, 1873), 1:514.

32. "Rapport relatif au projet de création du secteur Kazu-Zimba-Kindunga," A.I. (1409), A.A., Brussels.

33. A. Césaire, *Discourse on Colonialism,* trans. Joan Pinkham (New York: Monthly Review, 1972); F. Fanon, *The Wretched of the Earth,* trans. Constance Farrington (New York: Grove Press, 1963); Vangroenweghe, *Du sang.*

34. J. Farber, "Enquête sur les Bazela, district de Tanganyika, territoire des Kibara," 1932, A.I. (1367), A.A., Brussels; Depoorter, *Stanleyville.*

35. Likaka, "Colonisation et clichés sociaux"; interview with Lwamba Bilonda and Mugaza wa Beya, Lubumbashi, 16 August 1986; interview with David Madi, Kisangani, April 2003.

36. A. Ravet, "La fête du coton," *Bulletin du comité cotonnier congolais* 10 (1938): 56; Ravet, "L'exposition agricole de Buta (Uele) 4 et 5 Novembre 1939," *Bulletin du comité cotonnier congolais* 16 (1940): 3–4; Jérôme, "Cultivons du coton," *Bulletin du comité cotonnier congolais* 7 (1937): 72–73; "Rapport annuel sur la culture et le commerce du coton, modèle C, District du Congo-Ubangi," 1938, A.P.O., Kisangani.

37. P. Abrams, *Historical Sociology* (Ithaca, N.Y.: Cornell University Press, 1982), xiii.

38. H. Ward, *Five Years with the Congo Cannibals* (London, 1890); Schweinfurth, *Heart*

of Africa, 1:513–514; H. Johnston, *George Grenfell and the Congo* (New York, 1890), 1:445; J. Monteiro, *Angola and the River Congo*, 2 vols. (London: Frank Cass, 1968).

39. J. Farber, "Enquête sur les Bazela, district de Tanganyika, territoire des Kibara," 1932; Dallons and Cornet, "Evolution de poste de Kasongo"; Van de Lanoitte, *Sur les rivières glauques*, 169.

40. Vellut, "Matériaux pour une image du blanc dans la société coloniale du Congo belge."

41. T. Biaya, "Ethnopsychologie de quelques anthroponymes africains des missionnaires catholiques du Kasai colonial," *Annales Aequatoria* 16 (1995): 184.

42. E. Boelaert, H. Vinck, and C. Lonkama, "Arrivée des Blancs sur les bords des rivières équatoriales (Part II et fin)," *Annales Aequatoria* 17 (1996); E. Boelaert, H. Vinck, and C. Lonkama, "Addenda et Corrigenda: Annales Aequatoria 1980–1999," *Annales Aequatoria* 21 (2000).

43. Isaacman, *Cotton Is the Mother*; L. Vail and L. White, "Forms of Resistance."

44. Sunseri, *Vilimani*, 119; M. Kaniki, ed., *Tanzania under Colonial Rule* (London: Longman, 1980), 159. During the Congo and Visuality Workshop, 11–13 April 2007, at University of Michigan, Ann Arbor, Professor David Cohen mentioned that he collected about seven thousand names given to colonial officials in Uganda.

45. Sembene Ousmane, *God's Bits of Woods* (London: Heinemann, 1970); F. Oyono, *Une vie de boy* (Paris: Julliard, 1956); C. Achebe, *Things Fall Apart* (New York: Anchor Books, 1994); C. Hamidou Kane, *Ambiguous Adventure* (Portsmouth, N.H.: Heinemann, 1972).

46. Merlier, *Le Congo*, 215–275; Sikitele Gize, "Les racines de la révolte Pende de 1931," *Etudes d'histoire africaine* 5 (1973); M. Lovens, "La révolte de Masisi-Lubutu (Congo belge, Janvier–Mai, 1944)," *Cahiers du CEDAF* 3–4 (1974); Likaka, *Rural Society*, 108–134.

47. Vansina, *De la tradition*; Vansina, *Kingdoms*; Vansina, *Oral Tradition*; D. Dibwe dia Mwembu, *Faire de l'histoire orale dans une ville africaine: La methode de Jan Vansina appliquée à Lubumbashi (R-D Congo)* (Paris: L'Harmattan, 2008); Mandala, *Work and Control*; N. Yelengi, "The Impact of the Construction and Development of the Port Francqui-Bukama Railroad on the Rural Population of Katanga, Belgian Congo" (Ph.D. diss., University of Minnesota, 1993); Likaka, *Rural Society*, 26–29; Vail and White, "Forms of Resistance"; Bozzoli, *Women of Phokeng*; Vancraenbroeck, *Les médailles*.

Chapter 1. The Dynamics of Naming in Precolonial Congo

1. G. Liénart, "La signification du nom chez les peuples Bantu," *Le langage et l'homme* 5 (1968): 44; T. Biaya, "Ethnopsychologie de quelques anthroponymes africains des missionnaires catholiques du Kasai colonial," *Annales Aequatoria* 16 (1995):184.

2. These innovations included political ideas, religious practices, trade, crops, hunting, and fishing techniques.

3. In many societies names received during the initiation were known only to the initiates. G. Balandier, *Daily Life in the Kingdom of the Kongo: From the Sixteenth to the Eighteenth Century*, trans. Helen Weaver (New York: Pantheon Books, 1968), 214, 227.

4. "Notes sur les Gwaka," (1411) A.A., Brussels.

5. Missionaries were stunned when they learned that parents could not punish their children who bore the names of their own parents: "Can you beat your father?" Liénart discussed the problem in "La signification du nom."

6. R. Agomatanakahn, *Introduction à l'anthroponymie zairoise* (Lubumbashi: Celta, 1974), 36; J. Vansina, *Paths in the Rainforests* (Madison: University of Wisconsin Press,

1994), 79; J. Vansina, "Noms personnels et structures sociales chez les Tyo (Teke)," *Bulletin des séances de l'Académie royale des sciences d'Outre-Mer*, n.s. 10 (1964): 795.

7. J. Vansina, *How Societies Are Born: Governance in West Central Africa before 1600* (Charlottesville: University of Virginia Press, 2004), 142; A. Ndinga-Mbo, *Onomastique et histoire au Congo-Brazzaville* (Paris: L'Harmattan, 2004), 151.

8. Ndinga-Mbo, *Onomastique*, 167–174.

9. Lilwa was the Mbole male initiation association.

10. G. Hulstaert, "Noms de personnes chez les Nkundo," *Aequatoria* 3 (1956): 92; Agomatanakahn, *Introduction*, 44.

11. O. Tshonga, "Les noms des jumeaux dans la région de l'Equateur (Zaire)," *Annales Aequatoria* 4 (1983): 57; B. Tanghe, *Le culte du serpent chez les Ngbandi* (Bruges: Les Presses Gruuthuuse, 1926), 66.

12. Tanghe, *Le culte*, 48.

13. Interview with Ngoyi Bukonda, DeKalb, Ill., 17 March 2002.

14. Tanghe, *Le culte*, 66.

15. Interview with Nkasa T. Yelengi, Duluth, Minn., 13 February 2006; Tshonga, "Les noms des jumeaux," 57–58.

16. O. Likaka, "Colonisation et construction d'identités: l'administration belge et l'identité Mbole," *Revue Française d'Histoire d'Outre-Mer* 85, no. 321 (1998): 31; G. Liénart, "La signification du nom," 46.

17. J. Vansina, *Kingdoms of the Savanna* (Madison: University of Wisconsin Press, 1965), 9.

18. J. Vansina, *The Children of Woot: A History of the Kuba Peoples* (Madison: University of Wisconsin Press, 1978), 42, 68–69.

19. Vansina, *Kingdoms*, 88.

20. Agomatanakahn, *Introduction*, 36.

21. Interview with Ngandali Dabet, Minneapolis, 14 July 1990; interview with Ngbabu, Kisangani, 11 February 2003; "Notes sur les Gwaka"; Agomatanakahn, *Introduction*, 36.

22. A. Ryckmans, "Etude sur les signaux de 'mondo' (tambour-téléphone) chez les Bayaka du Territoire de Popokabaka," *Zaire* (1956): 496; Lauwers, "Notes sur la peuplade des Bambole," 1932, A.I. (1410), A.A., Brussels.

23. Agomatanakahn, *Introduction*, 39.

24. Interview with Basikaba Tanabanu, Kisangani, 23 May 2003.

25. Interview with Pene wa Pene, Kisangani, 24 April 2003.

26. A. Brenez, "Pourquoi je ne ferai pas parti du corps des volontaires," *Avenir colonial Belge*, 8 Décembre 1932, F.P. (2450), A.A., Brussels; interview with Basikaba Tanabanu, Kisangani, 23 May 2003; interview with Bili, Kisangani, 17 August 1989; interview with Bobwande, Lubumbashi, 16 July 1986.

27. Chiefdom councils were institutions created in 1957 to increase local participation in the governance of chiefdoms. For the story of Mbayo, see Liénart, "La signification du nom," 53.

Chapter 2. Colonialism and the Village World

1. S. Nelson, *Colonialism in the Congo Basin: 1880–1940* (Athens: Ohio University Center for International Studies, 1994), 44.

2. D. Vangroenweghe, *Du sang sur les lianes: Léopold II et son Congo* (Brussels: Didier

Hatier, 1985); P. Joyce and R. Lewin, *Les trusts au Congo* (Brussels: Société belge d'Editions, 1961); J.-L. Vellut, "Mining in the Belgian Congo," in *History of Central Africa*, ed. D. Birmingham and P. Martin (London: Longman, 1983); J. Higginson, *A Working Class in the Making: Belgian Colonial Labor Policy, Private Enterprise, and the African Mineworker, 1907–1951* (Madison: University of Wisconsin Press, 1989), 23–29.

3. M. Merlier, *Le Congo de la colonisation belge à l'indépendance* (Paris: Maspero, 1962), 57–185.

4. D. Cordell, "The Savanna Belt of North-Central Africa," in Birmingham and Martin, *History of Central Africa*, 1:63; O. Likaka, "Le commerce dans l'Uele au 19ième siècle" (graduate thesis, Unaza, Lubumbashi, 1977), 13.

5. L. Lotar, "Souvenirs de l'Uele," *Congo* 2, no. 2 (1930): 152; G. Schweinfurth, *Au Coeur de l'Afrique* (Paris: Hachette et cie, 1875), 1:429.

6. A. Thuriaux-Hennebert, "Les grands chefs Bandia et Zande de la région Uele-Bomu, 1860–1895," *Etudes d'histoire africaine* 3 (1972): 172–173; P. Denis, *Histoire des Mangbetu et Matsaga jusqu'à l'arrivée des Belges* (Tervuren: MRAC, 1961), 84, 107.

7. Vangroenweghe, *Du sang*; E. Morel, *Red Rubber: The Story of the Rubber Slave Trade Flourishing on the Congo in the Year of Grace 1906* (New York: Haskell House, 1906), 77; J. Vansina, *Paths in the Rainforests* (Madison: Univ. sity of Wisconsin Press, 1994); C. Coquery-Vidrovitch, *Le Congo au temps des compagnies concessionnaires, 1893–1930* (Paris, 1972).

8. Equateur Province was the most productive region of copal.

9. J. Crokaert, *Boula Matari* (Brussels: Librairie Albert Dewit, 1929), 193.

10. "Relèvement moral des indigènes, service de la justice," Coquilathville, 14 April 1920, A.A., Brussels.

11. Kasendwe Kibonge, "Les cultures obligatoires dans le Tanganyika" (MA thesis, Unaza,Lubumbashi, 1981), 59–71; F. Mulambu, "Cultures obligatoires et colonisation dans l'ex-Congo belge," *Cahiers du CEDAF* 6–7 (1974).

12. O. Likaka, *Rural Society and Cotton in the Belgian Congo* (Madison: University of Wisconsin Press, 1997), 92; J.-L. Vellut, "Rural Poverty in Western Shaba, ca. 1890–1930," in *The Roots of Rural Poverty in Central and Southern Africa*, ed. R. Palmer and N. Parsons (Berkeley: University of California Press, 1977); Merlier, *Le Congo*, 89–116.

13. J.-L. Vellut, "La violence armée dans l'Etat Indépendant du Congo," *Culture et développement* 16, no. 3–4 (1984): 690; Likaka, *Rural Society*, 71–89; Merlier, *Le Congo*, 119–185; B. Lwamba, "Histoire du mouvement ouvrier au Congo belge (1914–1960): Cas de la Province du Katanga" (PhD diss., Université de Lubumbashi, 1985), 26–29; Palmer and Parsons, *Roots of Rural Poverty*; Vangroenweghe, *Du sang*, 113–115.

14. Sikitele Gize, "Les raciness de la révolte pende de 1931," *Etudes d'histoire africaine* 5 (1973); M. Lovens, "La révolte de Masisi-Lubutu," *Cahiers du CEDAF* 3–4 (1974); O. Likaka, "Rural Protest: The Mbole against the Belgian Colonial Rule, 1893–1959," *International Journal African Historical Studies* 27, no. 3 (1994).

15. Likaka, *Rural Society*, 99.

16. N. Northrop, *Beyond the Bend in the River: Congolese Labor in Eastern Zaire, 1865–1940* (Athens: Ohio University Center for International Studies, 1988), 198–200; Nelson, *Colonialism in the Congo Basin*, 71–72.

17. Likaka, *Rural Society*, 42, 135.

18. L. Yaskold-Gabszewicz, "Rapport annuel sur la campagne cotonnière 1937–1938," Stanleyville, 7 May 1938, A.P.O., Kisangani.

19. G. Depi, "La Caisse de réserve cotonnière," *Bulletin de la Banque Centrale du Congo*

belge et du Ruanda-Urundi (1957): 65; A. Landeghem, "1921–1936: Quinze années de culture de coton au Congo belge," *Bulletin du Comité Cotonnier Congolais* 4 (1936): 3.

20. Landeghem, "1921–1936," 3–4.

21. A. Ruwet, "Panorama industriel du Congo: Le coton (II)," 22 February 1945, A.A. Brussels.

22. Agri (385) 119, "Prix de vente moyen" and Agri (378) H coton, A.A. Brussels; "Monographie du coton congolais," *Bulletin trimestriel du comité cotonnier congolais* 6 (1937): 58.

23. Interview with Ndjadi Vincent, Kisangani, 27 April 2003; "Hygiène des travailleurs occupés à la construction de routes," Boma, 26 May 1926, A.A. Brussels.

24. Nelson, *Colonialism in the Congo Basin*, 44; interviews with the following: Kabuji Bualu, Kisangani, 12 January 2003; Kasala, Lubumbashi, 25 June 1989; Kashi, Lubumbashi, 19 March 1988; Matata Moelealongo, Kisangani, 19 March 2003; Mbala, Lubumbashi, 26 October 1989.

25. "Inspection du Kwango et Bashilele," Léopoldville, 30 September 1933, A.A. Brussels.

26. Vellut, "Rural Poverty in Western Shaba"; Merlier, *Le Congo*, 174; Likaka, *Rural Society*, 75–89.

27. F. Cattier, *Etude sur la situation du Congo* (Brussels, 1905), 329; A. Lejeune-choquet, *Histoire militaire du Congo* (Brussels: Edition Alfred Castaigne, 1906), 42; Merlier, *Le Congo*, 32–34.

28. "Rapport d'inspection judiciaire du premier trimestre de Niangara," 1949, A.P.O., Kisangani.

29. Interview with Mugaza wa Beya, Lubumbashi, 16 August 1986.

30. M. Vancraenbroeck, *Les médailles de la présence belge en Afrique centrale, 1876–1960* (Brussels: Bibliothèque Royale, 1996), 65.

31. "Kultur Schande," *Danziger Zeitung*, 30, A.I. (1407), A.A., Brussels.

32. Higginson, *Working Class;* Bakonzi Agoyo, "The Gold Mines of Kilo-Moto in Northeastern Zaire, 1905–1960" (PhD diss., University of Wisconsin, 1982); Chechu Dyilo, "Recrutement de la main-d'oeuvre aux mines de Kilo-Moto" (MA thesis, Unaza, Lubumbashi, 1981); Vellut, "Mining in the Belgian Congo."

33. Commissaire Général, "Recrutement: Appui a accorder aux entreprises industrielles," June 1917, A.P.O., Kisangani; "Emploi des contraints aux mines," Stanleyville, July 1917, A.I. (1416), A.A., Brussels.

34. R. de Briey, *Congo* 2, no. 5 (1923): 248; A. Bertrand, "Lettre au G. G. à Boma," 18 June 1917, A.A., Brussels; "Dénonciation Siffer par Leplae: Dossier Siffer," Stanleyville, 7 March 1917, A.A., Brussels.

35. Chechu, "Recrutement de la main-d'oeuvre," 54.

36. "Mines-Moto," Arebi, 26 September 1913, A.I. (1416), A.A., Brussels; "Portage route Andulu-Mongbalu," Bula, 6 January 1925, A.A. Brussels; F. Lambrecht, *In the Shade of an Acacia Tree: Memoirs of a Health Officer in Africa, 1945–1959* (Philadelphia: American Philosophical Society, 1991), 108; "Note pour Monsieur le Gouverneur Général," [1917], A.A., Brussels; interview with Avochi, Kisangani, March 1989.

37. "Portage route Andulu-Mongbalu."

38. "Dénonciation Siffer par Leplae, dossier Siffer."

39. G. Malengreau, "Les lotissements agricoles au Congo beige," *Bulletin agricole du Congo beige* 43 (1952): 208; Dossier Z 260, lettre de l'Igr directeur de Kilo à l'AT de Gombari, 17 November 1917, A.P.O., Kisangani; A. de Meulemeester, "L'agriculture dans la

Province Orientale en 1920," *Bulletin agricole du Congo beige* 12, no. 4 (1921): 652; Chechu Dyilo, "Le recrutement."

40. Vanden Broeck, "Abus aux mines de Moto," Léopoldville, 30 October 1925, A.I. (1416), A.A., Brussels; "Ind. no. 121 RIM no. 4457," Irumu, 17 July 1924, notes written by Jules Campill, A.A.,'Brussels.

41. A. de Meulemeester, "Rapport, mines de Moto," Stanleyville, 16 April 1925, A.P.O., Kisangani.

42. Vanden Broeck, "Abus aux mines de Moto."

43. De Meulemeester, "Rapport, mines de Moto"; Aimo/14 B, Boma, 26 May 1926, A.A., Brussels.

44. J. Magotte, *Circonscriptions indigènes* (La Louvière: Imprimerie Louviéroise, 1938).

45. F. Grevisse, *La grande pitié des juridictions indigènes* (Brussels: IRCB, 1949), 65.

46. Ibid. Many documents in A.I. (1367), A.A., Brussels, hold the same views.

47. "Rapport sur l'agriculture," District du Haut-Uele, 1917, 1938, 1951, A.P.O., Kisangani; "Rapport annuel AIMO," Territoire de Paulis, 1957, A.P.O., Kisangani; "Rapport d'inspection du Territoire de Dungu," 1952, 24, A.P.O., Kisangani; "Rapport d'inspection du Territoire de Buta," 1954, 43, A.P.O., Kisangani; "Rapport d'inspection du Territoire d'Angu," 1945, A.P.O., Kisangani.

48. "Rapport d'inspection du territoire d'Ango," 1938, A.P.O., Kisangani.

49. "Rapport d'inspection du Territoire de Dungu," 1952, 24.

50. "Rapport d'inspection du Territoire de Buta," 1954, 43.

51. "Rapport d'inspection du Territoire d'Angu," 1945.

52. "Rapport d'inspection du Territoire d'Ango," 1938.

53. "Rapport d'inspection du Territoire de Dungu," 1952, 24.

54. Grevisse, *La grande pitié*, 65.

55. "A propos des problèmes du milieu rural congolais," *Problèmes sociaux congolais* 36 (1957): 152; E. Leplae, "L'agriculture coloniale dans la discussion du budget du Congo belge pour 1914," *Bulletin agricole du Congo belge* (1914): 17; F. Van der Linden, "Paysans et prolétaires noirs," *Revue de la société belge d'études et d'expansion* 47, no. 31 (1948): 371; Cattier, *Etude sur la situation*; A. Bertrand, *Le problème de la main-d'oeuvre au Congo* (Brussels, 1955).

56. V. Mudimbe, *The Idea of Africa* (Bloomington: Indiana University Press, 1994), 108, 110; J. Vansina, *Kingdoms of the Savanna* (Madison: University of Wisconsin Press, 1965), 221.

57. T. Biaya, "Ethnopsychologie de quelques anthroponymes Africains des missionnaires catholiques du Kasai colonial," *Annales Aequatoria* 16 (1995): 198. The term *Kïnini* in many Congolese languages today is synonymous with "pills"; interview with Katayi Tende, Lubumbashi, July 17, 1986.

58. M. Lyons, *The Colonial Disease: A Social History of Sleeping Sickness in Northern Zaire, 1900–1940* (Cambridge: Cambridge University Press, 1992), 131–135; Françoise-Marie, "Lettre," *Bulletin du comité cotonnier congolais* 15 (1939).

59. V. Roelens, "Les abus du recrutement de la main-d'oeuvre au Congo: Une protestation des chefs religieux catholiques de la Colonies," *Le Flambeau* (1923).

60. A. Engels, "Polygamie: dot," Conquilathville, 15 September 1919, A.I. (1416), A.A., Brussels.

61. Van den Eede, "Lutte contre la polygamie," Libenge, 14 November 1923, A.I. (1416), A.A., Brussels; E. Hertveld, "Lutte contre la polygamie," District de l'Ubangi, Libenge, 14 November 1923, A.I. (1416), A.A., Brussels; Requier, "Note sur la polygamie

dans le territoire de Budjala," Itoko, 10 September 1921, A.A., Brussels; P. Eloi Hertveld au gouverneur de la Province de l'Equateur, Coquilathville sd., A.A., Brussels; *Bulletin du comité cotonnier congolais* (1937), A.P.O., Kisangani.

62. *Recueil mensuel* (1914), 159, 262; (1918), 140; (1920), 60; *Conseil de Province Orientale* (1948), 728, A.P.O., Kisangani.

63. Van den Eede, "Lutte contre la polygamie."

64. Likaka, *Rural Society*, 99–102.

65. R. Harms, *Games against Nature: An Eco-cultural History of the Nunu of Equatorial Africa* (New York: Cambridge University Press, 1987), 125.

66. J. Vansina, *The Children of Woot: A History of the Kuba Peoples* (Madison: University of Wisconsin Press, 1978), 184.

67. Vansina, *Kingdoms*, 80–82.

68. For theoretical discussions of domination and exploitation, see James Scott's two books, *Domination and the Arts of Resistance: Hidden Transcripts* (New Haven, Conn.: Yale University Press, 1990) and *Weapons of the Weak: Day-to-Day Forms of Resistance* (New Haven, Conn.: Yale University Press, 1985).

Chapter 3. Naming, Colonialism, Making History, and Social Memories

1. A. Césaire, *Discourse on Colonialism*, trans. Joan Pinkham (New York: Monthly Review, 1972); A. Memmi, *The Colonizer and the Colonized*, trans. Howard Greenfield (Boston: Beacon Press, 1967).

2. S. Schwartz, ed., *Implicit Understandings: Observing, Reporting, and Reflecting on the Encounters between Europeans and Other Peoples in the Early Modern Era* (New York: Cambridge University Press, 1994), 15; J. Vansina, *Paths in the Rainforests* (Madison: University of Wisconsin Press, 1994), 239–248.

3. O. Likaka, "Colonialisme et clichés sociaux au Congo Belge," *Africa* (Rome) 52, no. 1 (1997); J.-L. Vellut, "Matériaux pour une image du blanc dans la société coloniale du Congo belge," in *Stéréotypes nationaux et préjugés raciaux aux XIXe et XXe siècles: Sources et methods pour une approchehistorique*, ed. J. Pirotte (Leuven: Editions Nauwelaerts, 1982), 109.

4. G. Schweinfurth, *The Heart of Africa* (London, 1873), 1:513–514; Van de Lanoitte, *Sur les rivières glauques de l'Equateur* (Paris: Editions de la revue Iris, 1938), 128.

5. A. Dallons and V. Cornet, "Evolution de poste de Kasongo à travers le temps, 1865–1931," A.I. (1407), A.A., Brussels.

6. Ibid.

7. E. Leplae, "Comment les indigènes du Congo belge sont arrivés à produire annuellement 20.000 tonnes de coton-fibre," *Coton et culture cotonnière*, 3 (1935): 181; "Rapport d'inspection du Territoire d'Ango," 1933, A.P.O., Kisangani; interview with Mugaza wa Beya, Lubumbashi, August 16, 1986.

8. M. Merlier, *Le Congo de la colonisation belge à l'indépendance* (Paris: Maspero, 1962), 27–129.

9. F. Lambrecht, *In the Shade of an Acacia Tree: Memoirs of a Health Officer in Africa, 1945–1959* (Philadelphia: American Philosophical Society, 1991), 237; P. Salmon, *La carrière africaine de Harry Bombeeck, agent commercial (1896–1899)* (Brussels: Institut de sociologie, Université libre de Bruxelles, 1990), 93; J. Farber, "Enquête sur les Bazela, district de Tanganyika, territoire des Kibara," 1932, A.I. (1367), A.A., Brussels; Delanghe, "Principaux événements concernant l'histoire du district du Lac Léopold II depuis la

pénétration européenne (Stanley) (1877–1930)," 1958, A.I. (1407), A.A., Brussels; Achten, "Rapport," Léopoldville, 15 October 1912, A.A., Brussels.

10. In standard Kikongo, *Bula Matari* is grammatically incorrect; the correct form is *Bula Matadi.*

11. F. Bontinck, "Les deux Bula Matari," *Etudes congolaises* 13, no. 3 (1969): 83.

12. The meanings of many names show that other representations of the colonial state were as accurate as *Bula Matari* was in depicting the colonial state and the contexts and ideological currents of the time that underlay its adoption. The choice of *Bula Matari* instead of them was strategic.

13. J. Pirson, "Le territoire de Ligasa," 1923, A.I. (1407), A.A., Brussels; B. Jewsiewicki, "African Peasants in the Totalitarian Colonial Society of the Belgian Congo," in *Peasants in Africa: Historical and Contemporary Perspectives,* ed. M. Klein (Beverly Hills, Calif.: Sage, 1983).

14. Jewsiewicki, "African Peasants"; Vansina, *Paths,* 240.

15. F. Mulambu, "Cultures obligatoires et colonisation dans l'ex-Congo belge," *Cahiers du CEDAF* 6–7 (1974); O. Likaka, *Rural Society and Cotton in the Belgian Congo* (Madison: University of Wisconsin Press, 1997).

16. Pirson, "Le territoire de Ligasa"; · Verbeke, "Etude sur la peuplade des Bombesa," 1927, A.I. (1412), A.A., Brussels; "Rapport annuel sur la campagne cotonnière 1937/38," A.P.O., Kisangani; interview with Lunyasi Tanganyika, 22 March 2003; interview with Louise Lonyoyo Tamile, 25 March 2003; interview with Kidumu, Kisangani, 17 July 1988.

17. T. Biaya, "Ethnopsychologie de quelques anthroponymes africains des missionnaires catholiques du Kasai colonial," *Annales Aequatoria* 16 (1995): 209; R-J. Cornet, *Bwana Muganga: Hommes en blanc en Afrique noire* (Brussels: Académie royale des sciences d'Outre-Mer, 1960).

18. Interview with Aserme Azibolia Mango, Kisangani, 2 April 2003; interview with Kidumu; interview with Risasi, Lubumbashi, 6 September 1988.

19. "Déplacement de villages," 29 April 1938, A.I. (1403), A.A., Brussels; H. L. Keyaser, "Notes synthétiques complétant la documentation des Rapports annuels AIMO 1933 des A. T. du Tanganyika," A.A., Brussels"; Yogolelo wa Kasimba, "Mission du recrutement de la main-d'oeuvre de l'Union Minière du Haut-Katanga au Maniema, 1928" (MA thesis, Unaza, Lubumbashi, 1974); "Rapport de la Commission de la main-d'oeuvre au Cong," 1924–25; "Rapport de la Commission de la main-d'oeuvre indigène," 1924–25, 1928, 1930–31.

20. To decode the political messages of such names, an examination of local status of blacksmiths should be considered. In fact, where the status of metalworkers was traditionally despised, the meanings of the collective names given to European geologists and mine prospectors were often derogatory.

21. Lambrecht, *In the Shade,* 237; Salmon, *La carrière africaine,* 93; Farber, "Enquête sur les Bazela."

22. *Bula Matari* derived from the detonation of a charge of dynamite, a single event, but the conditions of violence in the colony later determined its use as a collective name for all colonial officials.

23. Biaya, "Ethnopsychologie de quelques anthroponymes africains," 184.

24. Agomatanakahn, *Introduction à l'anthroponymie zairoise* (Lubumbashi: Celta, 1974), 21, 39.

25. *Mputu* is a loanword from Portuguese; it referred at first to the Portuguese, who were the first Europeans to arrive in Central Africa, and later came to mean European.

26. Salmon, *La carrière africaine*, 93.

27. A. Van Zandycke, "La révolte de Luluabourg (4 juillet 1895)," *Zaïre* 11 (1950): 934; R. Depoorter, *Stanleyville où le Lualaba devenait Congo* (Brussels: Didier Hatier, 1992), 152; M. Storme, "Konflikt in de Kasai-Missie," *Bulletin d'ARSOM* 33, no. 1 (1965): 328; M. Storme, "La mutinerie militaire au Kasai en 1895," *Bulletin d'ARSOM* 38, no. 4 (1970): 18.

28. Biaya, "Ethnopsychologie de quelques anthroponymes africains," 197.

29. Ibid., 191, 202.

30. Lambrecht, *In the Shade*, 237; Salmon, *La carrière africaine*, 93.

31. Achten, "Rapport."

32. Interview with Victor Asangu, Kisangani, 26 July 1989; interview with Asi Loosa, Kisangani, 24 July 1989; interview with Asomo Wenga, Letutu Yakuma, 12 July 1980.

33. Protestant missionaries are not the focus of the analysis, but they did receive names. The Reverend William Sheppard, who was the first missionary to visit the capital of the Kuba kingdom and co-founder of the American Presbyterian Congo Mission (APCM) in 1891 at Luebo in Kasai with the Reverend Samuel Lapsley, an African American Presbyterian clergyman, was named *Shipat* in Bushong and *Shapit* in Kete. Because of his good work among the Kuba, these loanwords do not convey the figurative meanings that numerous similar names carry.

34. *O* and *u* in Buluki and Boloki are allophones, that is, they can be used interchangeably without changing the meaning of the word.

35. The naming pattern helped Congolese to describe specific actions of individual officials or to differentiate a group of Europeans according to their ranks.

36. G. Nzongola-Ntalaza, *The Congo from Leopold to Kabila: A People's History* (London: Zed Books, 2002), 266; M. Storme, "Het Onstaat van de Kasai Missie," *Bulletin d'ARSOM* 24, no. 3 (1961): 15.

37. Depoorter, *Stanleyville*, 152.

38. D. Biebuyck, *Hero and Chief: Epic Literature from the Banyanga, Zaïre Republic* (Berkeley: University of California Press, 1978), 38; Vansina, *Paths*, 214; interview with Ali Musa, Kisangani, 28 March 2003.

39. Interview with Akandji Masudi, Kisangani March 2003; interview with Umba, Lubumbashi, 16 April 1988; interview with Bobwande, Lubumbashi, 12 July 1986.

40. Interview with Katayi Tende, Lubumbashi, 24 August 1986.

41. Jan Vansina, letter to O. Likaka, 11 May 2007.

42. Farber, "Enquête sur les Bazela"; Tessaroli, "Procès verbal," 29 February 1909, A.I. (1367), A.A., Brussels; Georges Schepers, "Mon père, le commissaire de district Tshitoko," e-mail to author, 25 July 1998; interview with Kumingi Yuma, Kisangani, 12 February 2003; interview with Kongolo, Ilunga, and Kinku, Lubumbashi, 28 May 1988.

43. "Rapport relatif au projet de création du secteur Kazu-Zimba-Kindunga," A.I. (1409), A.A., Brussels.

44. Interview with Bobwande, Lubumbashi, 12 July 1986; interview with Boloko, Kisangani, 16 April 1989; Likaka, *Rural Society*, 45.

45. Van de Lanoitte, *Sur les rivières glauques*, 128; Depoorter, *Stanleyville;* Biaya, "Ethnopsychologie de quelques anthroponymes africains."

46. Among other colonial mechanisms of social control figured handouts, structural reforms, and elaborate propaganda campaigns designed to win over the hearts and minds of the Congolese peasants.

47. The objective of the punishment was to keep the individual housebound. For a full description of the practice among the Mbole, see Lauwers, "Notes sur la peuplade des Bambole," 1932, A.I. (1410), A.A., Brussels; Van den Eede, "Etudes sur la tribu des Bobango," A.I. (1407), A.A., Brussels.

48. Interview with Risasi, Lubumbashi, September 23, 1988; interview with Lufundja, Lubumbashi, 18 August 1986; interview with Louise Lonyoyo Tamile, 25 March 2003.

49. O. Likaka, "Colonisation et construction d'identités: l'administration belge et l'identité Mbole, 1910–1960," *Revue Française d'Histoire d'Outre-mer* 85, no. 321 (1998): 31.

50. Depoorter, *Stanleyville*, 152; interview with Mugaza wa Beya, Lubumbashi, 16 August 1986.

51. Interview with Mugaza wa Beya, Lubumbashi, 16 August 1986.

52. V. Mudimbe, *The Invention of Africa: Gnosis, Philosophy, and the Order of Knowledge* (Bloomington: Indiana University Press, 1988).

53. Vansina, *Paths*, 43; Likaka, *Rural S̲.̲ ̲'ety*, 18–28.

54. "Rapport relatif au projet de création"; E. Boelaert, H. Vinck, and C. Lonkamba, "Arrivée des Blancs sur les bords des rivières équatoriales (Part II et fin)," *Annales Aequatoria* 17 (1996): 452, 480.

55. Nkulu Kalala, "Les réactions africaines aux impositions des cultures: Cas du Territoire de Kamina, 1935–1959" (MA thesis, Université de Lubumbashi, 1983).

56. Interview with Ngoziombo Ngbenzi, Kisangani, 16 March 2003; interview with Ntambwe Mukendi, Kisangani, 29 March 2003.

57. Interview with Lwamba Bilonda, Lubumbashi, 16 August 1986; interview with Tshibanda Nduba Musaka, Lubumbashi, 12 August 1986; interview with Lwaka Mukandja, Lubumbashi, 14 August 1986.

58. M. Mutamba, *Makoko: Roi des Bateke (1880–1892)* (Kinshasa: Edideps, 1987), 33.

59. Interview with Osoko Litale, Lelema, 21 July 1980.

60. Likaka, *Rural Society*, 45–70.

61. Delanghe, "Principaux événements concernant l'histoire."

62. Ibid.

63. A. Ryckmans, "Etude sur les signaux de 'mondo' (tambour-téléphone) chez les Bayaka du Territoire de Popokabaka," *Zaire* 5 (1956): 496.

64. Interview with Lwaka Mukandja, Lubumbashi, 14 August 1986. *Paipo* means "pipe" and identified officials who smoked a pipe.

65. Vanden Broeck, "Abus aux mines de Moto," Léopoldville, 30 October 1925, A.I. (1416), A.A., Brussels; Jules Campill, "Monsieur l'officier de police judiciaire de et à Kilo," Irumu, 17 July 1924, A.I. (1416), A.A., Brussels; interview with Atsidri Nyelegody, Kisangani, 16 February 2003.

66. I discuss this in chapter 6. A. Cauvin, *Bwana Kitoko: Un livre réalisé au cours du voyage du roi des Belges au Congo et dans le Ruanda-Urundi* (Paris: Elsevier, 1956); Depoorter, *Stanleyville;* Dallons and Cornet, "Evolution de poste de Kasongo"; "Rapport relatif au projet de création."

67. Howard-Malvelde, *Creating Context in Andean Cultures* (New York: Oxford University Press, 1997), 96. For a discussion of the methodologies of oral sources, see J. Vansina,

Oral Tradition as History (Madison: University of Wisconsin Press, 1985), and D. Laya, ed., *La tradition orale: Problématique et méthodologie des sources de l'histoire africaine* (Abbeville: P. Paillart, 1972).

Chapter 4. Early Naming, Explorations, Trade, and Rubber Collection

1. L. Lotar, "Souvenirs de l'Uele," *Congo* 4, no. 2 (1931): 513.
2. Ibid., 506.
3. Ibid., 506, 508.
4. A. Thuriaux-Hennebert, "Les grands chefs Bandia et Zande de la région Uele-Bomu, 1860–1895," *Etudes d'histoire africaine* 3 (1972): 172–173; P. Denis, *Histoire des Mangbetu et Matsaga jusqu'à l'arrivée des Belges* (Tervuren: MRAC, 1961), 84, 107.
5. G. Schweinfurth, *The Heart of Africa* (London, 1873), 1:513.
6. D. Cordell, "The Savanna Belt of North-Central Africa," in *History of Central Africa*, ed. D. Birmingham and P. Martin (London: Longman, 1983), 1:63; O. Likaka, "Le commerce dans l'Uele au 19ième siècle" (graduate thesis, Unaza, Lubumbashi, 1977), 13.
7. C. Zagourski, *Lost Africa* (Milano: Skira Editore, 2001), 20–45.
8. Schweinfurth, *Heart of Africa*, 1:513.
9. "Organisation judiciaire et procédure du tribunal coutumier de Kimese," A.I. (1618), A.A., Brussels.
10. L. De Sousberghe, "Noms donnés aux Pygmées et souvenirs laissés par eux chez les Pende et Lunda de la Loange," *Congo-Tervuren* 6, no. 3 (1960): 86.
11. D. Birmingham, *Empire in Africa: Angola and Its Neighbors* (Athens: Ohio University Press, 2006), 66; P. Martin, "The Violence of Empire," in *History of Central Africa*, ed. D. Birmingham and P. Martin (London: Longman, 1983), 2:2.
12. J. Vansina, "Probing the Past of the Lower Kwilu Peoples (Zaire)," *Paideuma* 19–20 (1974): 357.
13. "Organisation judiciaire et procédure."
14. D. Vangroenweghe, *Du sang sur les lianes: Léopold II et son Congo* (Brussels: Didier Hatier, 1986); S. Nelson, *Colonialism in the Congo Basin: 1880–1940* (Athens: Ohio University Center for International Studies, 1994).
15. J.-L. Vellut, "Matériaux pour une image du blanc dans la société coloniale du Congo belge," in *Stéréotypes nationaux et préjugés raciaux au XIXe et XXe siècles: Sources et methods pour une approche historique*, ed. J. Pirotte (Leuven: Nauwelaert, 1982), 109.
16. Vangroenweghe, *Du sang*, 113–115.
17. O. Likaka, "Colonialisme et clichés sociaux au Congo belge," *Africa* (Rome) 52, no. 1 (1997): 1–27.
18. A.I. (1367), A.A., Brussels.
19. B. Jewsiewicki, "African Peasants in the Totalitarian Colonial Society of the Belgian Congo," in *Peasants in Africa: Historical and Contemporary Perspectives*, ed. M. Klein (Beverly Hills, Calif.: Sage, 1982); *Bulletin agricole du Congo belge* (1951), 843.
20. E. Morel, *Red Rubber: The Story of the Rubber Slave Trade Flourishing on the Congo in the Year of Grace 1906* (New York: Haskell House, 1906); F. Cattier, *Etude sur la situation du Congo* (Brussels, 1905); J.-L. Vellut, "Rapport Casement," *Enquêtes et documents d'histoire africaine* 6 (1985); A. Doyle, *The Crime of the Congo* (New York: Doubleday, Page and Company, 1909).

21. "Rapport sur l'inongo," 1911, A.I. (1397), A.A, Brussels; "Quelques notes sur l'inongo recueillies par le sous-lieutenant Grégoire à l'occasion d'une opération de police exécutée dans la région des Lokonge (poste de Mompono)," 1912, A.I. (1397), A.A., Brussels; interview with Lunyasi Tanganyika, 22 March 2003; interview with Aserme Azibolia Mango, Kisangani, 2 April 2003.

22. A.I. (1397), A.A., Brussels.

23. O. Likaka, *Rural Society and Cotton in the Belgian Congo* (Madison: University of Wisconsin Press, 1997), 12–44; F. Mulambu, "Cultures obligatoires et colonisation dans l'ex-Congo belge," *Cahiers du CEDAF* 6–7 (1974).

24. Interview with Katayi Tende, Lubumbashi, 24 August 1986; interview with Lwamba Bilonda and Mugaza wa Beya, Lubumbashi, 16 August 1986; interview with Ujanga, Kisangani, 12 September 1989.

25. Likaka, *Rural Society,* 73–79; interviews with the following: Bakonzi Ngilinga, Kisangani, 23 March 2003; Longange Elenga, Kisangani, 28 March 2003; Ngoziombo Ngbenzi, Kisangani, 9 February 2003; Paul Misite, Kisangani, 24 April 2003; Ntambwe Mukendi, Kisangani, 29 March 2003; Lufundja, Lubumbashi, 18 August 1986.

26. H. Johnston, *George Grenfell and the Congo* (New York, 1890), 1:445; Morel, *Red Rubber,* 32, 43–79.

27. E. Boelaert, H. Vinck, and C. Lonkamba, "Arrivée des Blancs sur les bords des rivières équatoriales (Part II et fin)," *Annales Aequatoria* 17 (1996).

28. Ibid. Putela was an eight-year-old boy native of Bombanda.

29. Ibid.

30. Marchal, *L'état libre du Congo: Paradis perdu* (Brussels: Editions Paula Bellings, 1996), 1:283–391; Vangroenweghe, *Du sang,* 97–119.

31. Interview with Victor Asangu, Kisangani, 26 July 1989.

32. Interview with Wenga Asomo, Letutu Yakuma, 12 July 1980.

33. J. Pirson, "Le territoire de Ligasa," 1923, A.I. (1407), A.A., Brussels.

Chapter 5. Naming and Belgian Colonial Rule

1. M. Merlier, *Le Congo de la colonisation belge à l'indépendance* (Paris: Maspero, 1962), 119–144; O. Likaka, *Rural Society and Cotton in Colonial Zaire* (Madison: University of Wisconsin Press, 1997), 71–89; P. Joyce and R. Lewin, *Les trusts au Congo* (Brussels: Société belge d'Editions, 1961), 74.

2. A. Dallons and V. Cornet, "Evolution de poste de Kasongo à travers le temps, 1865–1931," A.I. (1407), A.A., Brussels.

3. Ibid.

4. J. Vanden Bossche, *Sectes et associations indigènes au Congo belge* (Léopoldville: Editions du Bulletin militaire, 1954), 11; *Chronique du Katanga*, Elisabethville, 7 October 1921; interview with Ntambwe Mukendi, Kisangani, 29 March 2003; interview with Jean Paluku, Kisangani, 11 February 2003.

5. Vanden Bossche, *Sectes,* 12; P. Tempels, *Bantu Philosophy* (Paris: Présence africaine, 1959).

6. E. Boelaert, H. Vinck, and C. Lonkamba, "Arrivée des Blancs sur les bords des rivières équatoriales (Part II et fin)," *Annales Aequatoria* 17 (1996): 371.

7. C. Van de Lanoitte, *Sur les rivières glauques de l'Equateur* (Paris: Editions de la revue Iris, 1938), 169; J. Farber, "Enquête sur les Bazela, district de Tanganyika, territoire des

Kibara," 1932, A.I. (1367), A.A., Brussels; Boelaert, Vinck, and Lonkamba, "Arrivée des Blancs," 476, 494, 679.

8. Françoise-Marie, "Lettre," *Bulletin du comité cotonnier congolais* 15 (1939); Van de Lanoitte, *Sur les rivières glauques,* 169.

9. A. Landeghem, "1921–1936: Quinze années de culture de coton au Congo belge," *Bulletin du Comite Cotonnier Congolais* 4 (1936); interview with Aserme Azibolia, Kisangani, 18 March 2003. The messages conveyed through the nickname "Lightning" were revealed by colonial officials who were the targets of the messages and who learned about local resistance assigned to the term indirectly. Concerned with the high frequency of lightning that burned cotton mills in the Uele District in the 1930s through the 1940s, colonial officials investigated and traced the origin of the problem to the presence of iron ore deposits. In the course of the investigation, they also learned that for all Congolese, "lightning strikes only when enemies sent it."

10. Van de Lanoitte, *Sur les rivières glauques,* 169.

11. Interviews with the following: Kabuji Bualu, Kisangani, 12 January 2003; Kasala, Lubumbashi, 14 June 1989; Kashi, Lubumbashi, 19 March 1988; Katayi Tende, Lubumbashi, 24 August 1986.

12. Likaka, *Rural Society,* 72–78.

13. Interview with Denda, Kisangani, 25 June 1989; interview with Kidumu, Kisangani, 17 July 1988.

14. J.-L. Vellut, "Matériaux pour une image du blanc dans la société coloniale du Congo belge," in *Stéréotypes nationaux et préjugés raciaux aux XIXe et XXe siècles: Sources et methods pour une approche historique,* ed. J. Pirotte (Leuven: Editions Nauwelaerts, 1982), 108.

15. N. Northrop, *Beyond the Bend in the River: Congolese Labor in Eastern Zaire, 1865–1940* (Athens: Ohio University Center for International Studies, 1988), 47–54; R. de Briey, *Congo* 2, no. 5 (1923): 248; A. Bertrand, "Lettre au G. G. à Boma," 18 June 1917, A.A., Brussels; Bakonzi Agoyo, "The Gold Mines of Kilo-Moto in Northeastern Zaire, 1905–1960" (PhD diss., University of Wisconsin–Madison, 1982); Chechu Dyilo, "Recrutement de la main-d'oeuvre aux mines de Kilo-Moto" (MA thesis, Unaza, Lubumbashi, 1981), 47; Commissaire Général, "Recrutement: Appui à accorder aux entreprises industrielles," June 1917, A.P.O., Kisangani.

16. L. Verbeke, "Etude sur la peuplade des Bombesa," 1927, A.I. (1412), A.A., Brussels.

17. Interview with Kongolo, Ilunga, and Kinku, Lubumbashi, 28 May 1988; Boelaert, Vinck, and Lonkamba, "Arrivée des Blancs."

18. G. Brausch, "Origine de la politique indigène belge en Afrique, 1879–1908," *Revue de l'Institut de Sociologie* 3 (1955): 468; R. Anstey, *King Leopold's Legacy: The Congo under Belgian Rule, 1908–1960* (Oxford: Oxford University Press, 1969); O. Likaka, "L'impact de l'organisation politique et administrative dans le Territoire d'Opala" (MA thesis, Unaza, Lubumbashi, 1981), 55–80.

19. Brausch, "Origine de la politique indigène belge," 468; Anstey, *King Leopold's Legacy; Manuel pour le fonctionnaire s'intéressant au coton,* Circulaires, 1922.

20. Northrop, *Beyond the Bend,* 58; Nelson, *Colonialism,* 86–87.

21. "Historique des Bambole," A.T.O., Opala.

22. O. Likaka, "Colonialisme et clichés sociaux au Congo belge," *Africa* (Rome) 52, no. 1 (1997).

23. Farber, "Enquête sur les Bazela."

24. When Father J. Garmyn received the name *Matala-Tala* in 1901, it symbolized his intellectualism. See T. Biaya, "Ethnopsychologie de quelques anthroponymes africains des missionnaires catholiques du Kasai colonial," *Annales Aequatoria* 16 (1995): 204–205.

25. "Historique des Bambole"; "Rapport d'enquête," 30 March 1925, A.T.O., Opala; Van de Lanoitte, *Sur les rivières glauques*, 169; interviews with the following: Kabuji Bualu, Kisangani, 12 January 2003; Kasala, Lubumbashi, 14 June 1989; Kashi, Lubumbashi, 16 March 1988; Katayi Tende, Lubumbashi, 24 August 1986.

26. Interviews with the following: Kabuji Bualu, Kisangani, 12 January 2003; Kasala, Lubumbashi, 14 June 1989; Kashi, Lubumbashi, 16 March 1988; Katayi Tende, Lubumbashi, 24 August 1986.

27. For a theoretical discussion of domination and exploitation, see J. Scott, *Domination and the Arts of Resistance* (New Haven, Conn.: Yale University Press, 1990); J. Scott, *Weapons of the Weak: Day-to-Day Forms of Resistance* (New Haven, Conn.: Yale University Press, 1985).

28. Interviews with the following: Katumbo, Lubumbashi, July, 1986; Akandji Masudi, Kisangani, March 2003; Katayi Tende, Lubumbashi, 24 August 1986; Lola, Lelema, 3 August 1977; Masudi Shabani, Kisangani, 11 January 2003; Ntumba, Likasi, October 1988.

29. "Mines-Moto," Arebi, 26 September 1913, A.I. (1416), A.A., Brussels; "Portage route Andulu-Mongbalu," Bula, 6 January 1925, A.A., Brussels; "Déplacement de villages," 29 April 1938, A.I. (1403), A.A., Brussels.

30. Interview with Mbali Nondolo, Kisangani, 24 April 2003.

31. It was during holy days that poultry was consumed. Interviews with the following: Avochi, Kisangani, March 1989; Mugaza wa Beya, Lubumbashi, 16 August 1986; Katayi Tende, Lubumbashi, 24 August 1986; Lwamba Bilonda, Lubumbashi, 16 August 1986.

32. "Tam-Tam," 28 November 1945, A.I. (1414), A.A., Brussels.

33. Interview with Lola, Lelema, 3 August 1977; interview with Victor Asangu, Kisangani, 26 July 1989; "Historique des Bambole."

34. Interview with Asomba Letoko, Opala, 15 July 1980.

35. Interview with Sombo, Kisangani, 18 September 2003; interview with Asi Loosa, Kisangani, 24 July 1989; interview with Asomo Wenga, Opala, 12 July 1980.

36. Interview with Ujanga, Kisangani, August and September 1989; interview with Matata Moelealongo, Kisangani, 18 February 2003; interview with Tshibanda Nduba Musaka, Lubumbashi, 12 August 1986.

37. O. Likaka, "Rural Protest: The Mbole against the Belgian Colonial Rule, 1893–1959," *International Journal of African Historical Studies* 27, no. 3 (1994). See also O. Likaka, "The Mbole conseil des chefs et notables and the Politics of Negotiations, 1910–1960," *Anthropos* 92 (1997).

38. Likaka, "L'impact de l'organisation," 58–59.

39. Interview with Asomo Wenga, Letutu Yakuma, 12 July 1980; interview with Ofunga, Yanga, 24 July 1980; interview with Lomata, Yaokoko, 24 July 1980.

40. F. Renault, *Lavigérie, l'esclavage africain et l'Europe* (Paris: Editions E. de Boccard, 1982); A. Delcommune, *Vingt années de vie africaine* (Brussels: Ferdinand Larcier, 1922), 1: 301, 308; Likaka, "Rural Protest," 591–594.

41. "Historique des Bambole"; L. Vail and L. White, "Forms of Resistance: Songs and Perceptions of Power in Colonial Mozambique," in *Banditry, Rebellion and Social*

Protest in Africa, ed. D. Crummey (Portsmouth N.H.: Heinemann, 1986); A. Isaacman, *Cotton Is the Mother of Poverty, 1938–1961* (Portsmouth, N.H.: Heinemann, 1996).

42. T. Turner, "Memory, Myth and Ethnicity: A Review of Recent Literature and Some Cases from Zaire," *History in Africa* 19 (1992): 391–393; J. Vansina, *Kingdoms of the Savanna* (Madison: University of Wisconsin Press, 1965), 9; Likaka, "Rural Protest."

43. Biaya, "Ethnopsychologie de quelques anthroponymes," 191.

44. Nzongola-Ntalaza, *The Congo, from Leopold to Kabila: A People's History* (London: Zed Books, 2002), 44.

45. G. Van Der Kerken, *L'ethnie Mongo* (Brussels: IRCB, 1944), 469–473; Delcommune, *Vingt années*, 303; A. Lejeune-choquet, *Histoire militaire du Congo* (Brussels: Edition Alfred Castaigne, 1906), 42.

46. Northrop, *Beyond the Bend*, 15; Nzongola-Ntalaza, *Congo*, 22; N. Yelengi, "Building a Colonial Railroad and the Labor Crisis in the Belgian Congo: Case of the Port Franqui-Bukama, 1923–1928," *Likundoli: Histoire et Devenir* 2 (1999–2000).

47. Ayi Kwei Armah, *The Beautyful Ones Are Not Yet Born* (London: Heinemann, 1968). The novel is a critique of the corrupt postcolonial Ghanaian state and neocolonial Ghanaian society.

48. Interview with Risasi, Lubumbashi, 23 September 1988.

49. Mariama Bâ, *So Long a Letter*, trans. Modupé Bodé-Thomas (Portsmouth, N.H.: Heinemann, 1981), 55.

50. Interview with Victor Asangu, Kisangani, 26 July 1989.

51. A. Van Zandycke, "La révolte de Luluabourg (4 juillet 1895)," *Zaire* 11 (1950): 931.

52. "Dossier politique," A.P.O., Kisangani.

53. This reaction was identical to Bushong mothers who used *Bimbaangl* (Europeans) or the names of slave traders to discipline their children. Jan Vansina, personal communication.

54. Interview with Mungeni Mateso, Kisangani, 23 June 1989.

55. D. Vangroenweghe, *Du sang sur les lianes: Léopold II et son Congo* (Brussels: Didier Hatier, 1985), 115.

56. The Yaka in Western Congo later named Dhanis *Kasongo* because he came to their area from Kasongo, a post he ruled in the early 1890s in Maniema on the bank of the Congo River. See A. Ryckmans, "Etude sur les signaux de 'mondo' (tambour-telephone) chez les Bayaka du Territoire de Popokabaka," *Zaire* (1956): 500; J.-L. Vellut, "La violence armée dans l'Etat Indépendant du Congo," *Culture et développement* 16, no. 3–4 (1984): 690; R. Depoorter, *Stanleyville où le Lualaba devenait Congo* (Brussels: Didier Hatier, 1992), 152; Boelaert, Vinck, and Lonkamba, "Arrivée des Blancs."

57. Interview with Ali Musa, Kisangani, 28 March 2003; interview with Kumingi Yuma, Kisangani, 12 February 2003.

58. Interview with Matata Moelealongo, Kisangani, 18 February 2003.

59. Interview with Midi Abuba, Kisangani, 18 February 2003.

60. Laying down on the side or the stomach was a widespread image of defenselessness in verbal arts of many precolonial societies of the Congo, and attacking someone in this position translated as cowardice.

61. Vellut, "La violence armée," 690; interview with Kumingi Yuma, Kisangani, 22 February 2003; interview with Midi Abuba, Kisangani, 22 February 2003; interview with Matata Moelealongo, Kisangani, 18 March 2003.

188 *Notes to pages 109–116*

62. Françoise-Marie, "Lettre," *Bulletin du comité cotonnier congolais* 15 (1939); Van de Lanoitte, *Sur les rivières glauques,* 169.

63. Dallons and Cornet, "Evolution de poste de Kasongo"; P. Freire, *The Pedagogy of the Oppressed,* trans. Myra Berqman Ramos (New York: Continuum, 2006), 42; interview with Paul Misite, Kisangani, 22 April 2003; interview with Mosolo, Kisangani, 12 February 1989.

64. "Rapport politique sur la situation politique: Rapport mensuel sur la situation générale du district de l'Uele, zone de Bomokandi, 1910," 1910, A.I. (1372), A.A., Brussels.

65. A. Ravet, "L'exposition agricole de Buta," *Bulletin du comité cotonnier congolais* 16 (1940); A. Ravet, "La fête du coton," *Bulletin du comité cotonnier congolais* 10 (1938).

66. "Rapport annuel sur la situation générale du district de l'Uele, Zone de Bomokandi," 1910, A.I. (1372), A.A., Brussels.

67. Interview with Lunyasi Tanganyika, Kisangani, 22 March 2003; interview with Lonyoyo Louise Tamile, Kisangani, 25 March 2003; interview with Aserme Azibolia Mango, Kisangani, 2 April 2003.

68. The name *Bala-Bala* was common in the Aruwimi where Lingala was spoken. Van de Lanoitte, *Sur les rivières glauques,* 169.

69. R. Agomatanakahn, *Introduction ∴ l'anthroponymie zairoise* (Lubumbashi: Celta, 1974), 21.

70. Interviews with the following: Ndjadi Vincent, Kisangani, 27 April 2003; Mosolo, Kisangani, 12 February 1989; Lunyasi Tanganyika, Kisangani, 22 March 2003; Mugaza wa Beya, Lubumbashi, 16 August 1986; Kongolo, Ilunga, and Kinku, Lubumbashi, 28 May 1988.

71. M. Vancraenbroeck, *Les médailles de la présence belge en Afrique centrale, 1876–1960* (Brussels: Bibliothèque Royale de la Belgique, 1996), 65.

72. R. Pecheur, "Observations sur la mentalité des populations du Congo," A.I. (1412), A.A., Brussels; interview with Atsidri Nyelegodi, Kisangani, 16 February 2003.

73. Interview with Katayi Tende, Lubumbashi, 16 August 1986; interview with Masudi Shabani, Kisangani, 11 January 2003.

74. N. Hodge, ed., *To Kill a Man's Pride* (Johannesburg: Ravan Press, 1984).

75. M. Turnbull, *The Lonely African* (New York: Simon and Schuster, 1962), 81.

76. Vangroenweghe, *Du sang,* 114; F. Cattier, *Etude sur la situation du Congo* (Brussels, 1904), 350–351.

77. Interview with Matata Moelealongo, Kisangani, 16 March 2003.

78. Interview with Atsidri Nyelegodi, Kisangani, March, 2003.

79. Interview with Bakonzi Ngilinga, Kisangani, 25 February 2003.

80. Interview with Jean Paluku, Kisangani, March 2003.

81. F. Lambrecht, *In the Shade of an Acacia Tree: Memoirs of a Health Officer in Africa, 1945–1959* (Philadelphia: American Philosophical Society, 1991), 106.

82. Ibid., 108.

83. Van de Lanoitte, *Sur les rivières glauques,* 36–37.

84. Ibid., 38–39; "Inspection du Kwango et Bashilele," Léopoldville, 30 September 1933, A.A., Brussels. The Lele of Kasai reacted the same way against Dossogne.

85. Delanghe, "Principaux événements concernant l'histoire du district du Lac Léopold II depuis la pénétration européenne (Stanley) (1877–1930)," 1958 A.I. (1407), A.A., Brussels.

86. "Inspection du Kwango et Bashilele."

87. Van de Lanoitte, *Sur les rivières glauques*, 38–39; interview with Gesege, Kisangani, February 2003.

88. L. White, *The Comforts of Home: Prostitution in Colonial Nairobi* (Chicago: University of Chicago Press, 1990).

89. Lambrecht, *In the Shade*, 106.

90. Interview with Meya Katoto, Lubumbashi, 24 July 2003.

91. Interview with Dibwe Dia Mwembu, Lubumbashi, 22 August 2003.

92. Interview with Meya Katoto, Lubumbashi, 24 July 2003; interview with Kongolo, Ilunga, and Kinku, Lubumbashi, 28 May 1988.

93. Van de Lanoitte, *Sur les rivières glauques*, 169.

94. Interview with Amisi, Kisangani, 28 May 2003.

95. Interviews with the following: Longange Elenga, Kisangani, 28 March 2003; Kabuji Bualu, Kisangani, 12 January 2003; Ilunga Luboza, Kisangani, February 2003; Kumingi Yuma, Kisangani, 12 February 2003.

96. Interview with Lonyoyo Louise Tamile, Kisangani, 28 March, 2003; Lotika Lwa Botende, Kisangani, 16 March 2003; Matata Moelealongo, Kisangani, March 2003.

Chapter 6. Talking under One's Breath

1. Interviews with the following: Amisi, Kisangani, 28 May 2003; Ntambwe Mukendi, Kisangani, March 2003; Misite Paul, Kisangani, 22 April 2003; Katayi Tende, Lubumbashi, 24 August 1986.

2. A. Dallons and V. Cornet, "Evolution de poste de Kasongo à travers le temps, 1865–1931," A.I (1407), A.A., Brussels; interview with Risasi, Lubumbashi, 23 September 1986.

3. Delanghe, "Principaux événements concernant l'histoire du district du Lac Léopold II depuis la pénétration européenne (Stanley) (1877–1930)," 1958, A.I. (1407), A.A, Brussels.

4. Achten, "Rapport," Léopoldville, 15 October 1912, A.A., Brussels; Delanghe, "Principaux événements concernant l'histoire."

5. "Rapport relatif au projet de création du secteur Kazu-Zimba-Kindunga," A.I. (1409), A.A., Brussels; "Organisation judiciaire et procédure du tribunal coutumier de Kimese," A.I. (1618), A.A., Brussels; C. Van de Lanoitte, *Sur les rivières glauques*, 169. In 1890 the Kongo named H. Ward "hero" because he killed a leopard with a gun. In Kongo culture, like elsewhere in the rainforests, the leopard was a symbol of authority. Killing a leopard and disposing of its spoil were events of extraordinary symbolic and political significance. Despite the surface meaning of heroism embedded in the action of killing a leopard, the name suggested violence because it was associated with guns and a traditional symbol of power.

6. The correct form in standard Kiswahili is *Mupenda Watu*. Kiswahili spoken here was not standard, and Yolande Lamerat was not speaking perfect Kiswahili when I interviewed her. Interview with Yolande Lamerat, Brussels, August 1987.

7. J. Scott, *Domination and the Arts of Resistance: Hidden Transcripts* (New Haven, Conn.: Yale University Press, 1990).

8. O. Likaka, *Rural Society and Cotton in the Belgian Congo* (Madison: University of Wisconsin Press, 1997), 108–139; Sikitele Gize, "Les racines de la révolte pende de 1931," *Etudes d'histoire africaine* 5 (1972); M. Lovens, "La révolte de Masisi-Lubutu (Congo belge,

Janvier–Mai, 1944)," *Cahiers du CEDAF* (1974); B. Lwamba, "Histoire du mouvement ouvrier au Congo belge (1914–1960): Cas de la Province du Katanga" (PhD diss., Université de Lubumbashi, 1985).

9. O. Likaka, "Rural Protest: The Mbole and the Belgian Rule, 1893–1959" *International Journal of African Historical Studies*, 27, no. 3 (1994); Likaka, *Rural Society*, 108–134.

10. "Notes sur les Gwaka," A.I. (1411), A.A., Brussels.

11. "Rapport d'enquête," 30 March 1925, A.T.O., Opala; interview with Asomo Wenga, Letutu Yakuma, 12 July 1980; interview with Osoko Litale, Lelema, 21 July 1980.

12. "Secteur Bwere, Gurba Dungu," Sili, 4 September 1908, A.A., Brussels; interview with Mugaza wa Beya, Lubumbashi 16 August 1986.

13. Interview with Akandji Masudi, Kisangani March 2003; interview with Tebonge Dame, Kisangani March 2003; interview with Aserme Azibolia, Kisangani, 18 March 2003.

14. Analyses of mechanisms of exploitation include M. Merlier, *Le Congo de la colonisation belge à l'indépendance* (Paris: Maspero, 1962); Likaka, *Rural Society*, 71–88; B. Jewsiewicki, "African Peasants in the Totalitarian Colonial Society of the Belgian Congo," in *Peasants in Africa: Historical and Contemporary Perspectives*, ed. M. Klein (Beverley Hills, Calif.: Sage, 1983); J. Peemans, *Diffusion du progrès et convergence des prix: Congo belge, 1900–1960* (Louvain: Nauwelaerts, 1970).

15. "Secteur Bwere, Gurba Dungu"; Van de Lanoitte, *Sur les rivières glauques*, 169; interview with Kashi, Lubumbashi, 19 March 1988; interview with Katayi Tende, Lubumbashi, 24 August 1986.

16. Delanghe, "Principaux événements concernant l'histoire."

17. J. Farber, "Enquête sur les Bazela, district de Tanganyika, territoire des Kibara," 1932, A.I. (1367), A.A., Brussels; Georges Schepers, "Mon père, le commissaire de district Tshitoko," e-mail to author, 25 July 1998; interview with Kongolo, Ilunga, and Kinku, Lubumbashi, 28 May 1988.

18. "Rapport relatif au projet de création."

19. "Organisation judiciaire."

20. R. Smith, "L'administration coloniale belge et les villageois, les Yansi du nord de Bulungu, 1920–1940 (Zaire)," *Cahiers du CEDAF* 3 (1976).

21. F. Lambrecht, *In the Shade of an Acacia Tree: Memoirs of a Health Officer in Africa, 1945–1959* (Philadelphia: American Philosophical Society, 1991), 106.

22. Interviews with the following: Lonyoyo Louise Tamile, Kisangani, 28 March 2003; Lwaka Mukandja, Lubumbashi, 14 August 1986; Kumingi Yuma, Kisangani, 12 February 2003; Katumbo, Lubumbashi, 30 July 1986.

23. Colinet, "Le Sura: Etude sommaire d'une nouvelle secte secrète se développant dans le Territoire de Doruma," 1931, A.I. (1397), A.A., Brussels.

24. Interview with Kabuji Bualu, Kisangani, 12 January 2003; interview with Kumingi Yuma, Kisangani, 14 February 2003; interview with Matata Moelealongo, Kisangani, 19 February 2003.

25. Likaka, *Rural Society*, 102–107.

26. Van den Eede, "Lutte contre la polygamie," Libenge, 14 November 1923, A.I. (1416), A.A., Brussels; Requier, "Note sur la polygamie dans le territoire de Budjala," Itoko, 10 September 1921, A.A., Brussels; E. Hertveld, "Lutte contre la polygamie," District de l'Ubangi, Libenge, 14 November 1923, A.I. (1416), A.A., Brussels.

27. Hertveld, "Lutte contre la polygamie."

28. "Secteur Bwere, Gurba Dungu."

29. Vansina, *Paths*, 79.

30. J. Fabian, *Language and Colonial Power* (Berkeley: University of California Press, 1986).

31. T. Reefe, "The Societies of the Eastern Savanna," in *History of Central Africa*, ed. D. Birmingham and P. Martin (London: Longman, 1983), 1:185; J. Janzen, *The Quest for Therapy: Medical Pluralism in Lower Zaire* (Berkley: University of California Press, 1978), 39.

32. Interview with Lwaka Mukandja, Lubumbashi, 14 August 1986; interview with Lotika Lwa Botende, Kisangani, 16 March 2003.

33. G. Brausch, "Origine de la politique indigène belge en Afrique, 1879–1908," *Revue de l'Institut de Sociologie* 3 (1955): 469; Cattier, *Etude*, 33.

34. Likaka, "Rural Protest."

35. Depoorter, *Stanleyville*, 152; "Rapport d'enquête," 30 May 1925, A.T.O., Opala; A. Van Zandycke, "La révolte de Luluabourg (4 juillet 1895)," *Zaire* 11 (1950): 937.

36. Verbeke, "Etude sur la peuplade des Bombesa," 1927, A.I. (1412), A.A., Brussels.

37. Ibid.

38. Likaka, "Rural Protest."

39. J. Magotte, *Circonscriptions indigènes* (La Louvière: Imprimerie Louvièroise, 1938); "Organisation judiciaire."

40. Bakua Lufu Badibanga, "Note sur l'évolution de la politique colonial belge à l'égard des chefs traditionnels," *Mbegu: Revue pédagogique et culturelle* 3 (1977): 39.

41. L. Yaskold-Gabszewicz, "Rapport annuel sur la culture cotonnière 1937/1938," Stanleyville, 7 May 1938, A.P.O., Kisangani; "Dossier politique," A.P.O., Kisangani; "Dossier Z. 265, no. 29001, 1957," A.P.O., Kisangani.

42. Interview with Lwaka Mukandja, Lubumbashi, 14 August 1986.

43. Interview with Lotika Lwa Botende, Kisangani, 16 March 2003.

44. Van Zandycke, "La révolte de Luluabourg," 931; Lambrecht, *In The Shade*, 148.

45. Van Zandycke, "La révolte de Luluabourg," 931; "Rapport relatif au projet de création."

46. "Papiers E. Janssens," D. (1367), A.A., Brussels.

47. Interviews with the following: Kashi, Lubumbashi, 19 March 1988; Katayi Tende, Lubumbashi, 24 August 1986; Katumbo, Lubumbashi, 30 July 1986; Kidumu, Kisangani, 17 July 1988.

48. Dallons and Cornet, "Evolution de poste de Kasongo."

49. Ibid.

50. R. Philippart, "Rapport de la prise de contact entre monsieur Joset chargé de la mission du Ministère des colonies et l'Administrateur PPAL Philippart a Stanleyville le 4-5-1956," A.I. (4736), A.A., Brussels. Green was the color of Islam that has been indigenized as a symbol of peace in Province Orientale and Maniema District where Islam was practiced.

51. Likaka, *Rural Society*, 61–63; Ravet, "La fête du coton," *Bulletin du comité cotonnier congolais* 10 (1938): 56.

52. R. Anstey, *King Leopold's Legacy: The Congo under Belgian Rule, 1908–1960* (London: Oxford University Press, 1966), 47, 63, 78–80.

53. Nkulu Kalala, "Les réactions africaines aux impositions des cultures: Cas du Territoire de Kamina, 1935–1959" (MA thesis, Université de Lubumbashi, 1983), 86;

O. Likaka, "The Mbole conseil des chefs et notables and the Politics of Negotiations," *Anthropos* 92 (1997): 471–483; "Rapport relatif au projet de création"; "Rapport d'enquête," 30 March 1925, A.T.O., Opala; Depoorter, *Stanleyville*, 152–153.

54. Maniema remained a district of Orientale Province until 1933, when it became a district of Constermansville Province, later named Kivu Province.

55. "Organisation judiciaire et procédure du tribunal coutumier de Kimese," A.I. (1618), A.A., Brussels.

56. Likaka, "Colonialisme et clichés sociaux," 1–27.

Chapter 7. Confronting African Voices

1. Colonial officials point out this difficulty in *Conseil de Province Orientale* (1955), 1.

2. O. Likaka, "The Mbole conseil des chefs et notables and the Politics of Negotiations, 1910–1960," *Anthropos* 92 (1997); Pakasa Nayipere, "La politique indigène dans la vallée du Haut-Lubilashi, 1900–1940" (MA thesis, Unaza, Lubumbashi, 1974).

3. Cultural expressions remained the major concerns for the colonial government officials as they were interpreted as the sites of resistance. See, for example, A. Ryckmans, "Etude sur les signaux de 'mondo' (– nbour-téléphone) chez les Bayaka du Territoire de Popokabaka," *Zaire* (1956); "Tam-tam," 28 November 1945, A.I. (1414), A.A., Brussels; "Questions sociales," 1936, A.I. (1397), A. A, Brussels.

4. Likaka, "Mbole conseil," 475.

5. Interview with Mugaza wa Beya, Lubumbashi, 16 August 1986; interview with Masudi Shabani, Kisangani, 11 January 2003.

6. Resistance, protests, day-to-day resistance, and rebellions were forms of Congolese responses to colonialism. G. Nzongola-Ntalaza, *The Congo, from Leopold to Kabila: A People's History* (London: Zed Books, 2002), 41–54; Sikitele Gize, "Les racines de la révolte pende de 1931," *Etudes d'histoire africaine*, 5 (1973); M. Lovens, "La révolte de Masisi-Lubutu (Congo belge, Janvier–Mai, 1944)," *Cahiers du CEDAF* 3–4 (1974).

7. Likaka, "Mbole conseil."

8. J. Pirson, "Le territoire de Ligasa," 1923, A.I. (1407), A.A., Brussels.

9. Likaka, " Mbole conseil."

10. "A propos des problèmes du milieu rural congolais," *Problèmes sociaux congolais* 36 (1957): 152; E. Leplae, "L'agriculture coloniale dans la discussion du budget du Congo belge pour 1914," *Bulletin agricole du Congo belge* (1914): 17; F. Van der Linden, "Paysans et prolétaires noirs," *Revue de la société belge d'études et d'expansion* 47, no. 31 (1948): 371. See also F. Cattier, *Etude sur la situation du Congo* (Brussels, 1905), and A. Bertrand, *Le problème de la main-d'oeuvre au Congo* (Brussels, 1955).

11. "Organisation judiciaire et procédure du tribunal coutumier de Kimese," A.I. (1618), A.A., Brussels; A. Dallons and V. Cornet, "Evolution de poste de Kasongo à travers le temps, 1865–1931," A.I. (1407), A.A., Brussels.

12. Pirson, "Le territoire de Ligasa."

13. R. Philippart, "Rapport de la prise de contact entre monsieur Joset chargé de la mission du Ministère des colonies et l'Administrateur PPAL Philippart à Stanleyville le 4-5-1956," A.I. (4736), A.A., Brussels.

14. Van de Lanoitte, *Sur les rivières glauques*," 36–37; P. Salmon, *La carrière africaine de Harry Bombeeck, agent commercial (1896–1899)* (Brusselss: Institut de sociologie, Université libre de Bruxelles, 1990), 93.

15. M. Querton, "Rapport trimestriel," Lusambo, 16 July 1926, A.P.O., Kisangani; "Dossier Z. 265, no. 29001, 1957," A.P.O., Kisangani.

16. Likaka, *Rural Society*, 57-70; A. Ravet, "La fête du coton," *Bulletin du comité cotonnier congolais* 10 (1938): 56; A. Ravet, "L'exposition agricole de Buta (Uele) 4 et 5 Novembre 1939," *Bulletin du comité cotonnier congolais* 16 (1940); Jérôme, "Cultivons du coton," *Bulletin du comité cotonnier congolais* 7 (1937); "Propagande cotonnière," 1939, A.P.O., Kisangani; "Rapport annuel sur la culture et le commerce du coton, modèle C, District du Congo-Ubangi," 1938, A.P.O., Kisangani.

17. "Rapport sur l'attitude des Noirs en général," 1911, A.A., Brussels; Ravet, "La fête du coton," 56; Ravet, "L'exposition agricole de Buta," 3-4.

18. This propaganda was a complete reversal of ideas of laziness propagated through the stereotyping of Congolese.

19. O. Likaka, "Forced Cotton Cultivation and Social Control in the Belgian Congo," in *Cotton, Colonialism, and Social History in Sub-Sahara Africa*, ed. A. Isaacman and R. Roberts (Portsmouth, N.H.: Heinemann, 1995).

20. Françoise-Marie, "Lettre," *Bulletin du comité cotonnier congolais* 15 (1939).

21. Rapport sur l'inongo," 1911, A.I. (1397), A.A., Brussels.

22. J. Fabian, "Popular Culture in Africa: Findings and Conjectures," in *Readings in African Popular Culture*, ed. K. Barber (Bloomington: University of Indiana Press, 1997).

23. R. Depoorter, *Stanleyville où le Lualaba devenait Congo* (Brussels: Didier Hatier, 1992), 152; Georges Schepers, "Mon père, le commissaire de district Tshitoko," 25 July 1998, personal e-mail (22 July 1998); interview with Kumingi Yuma, Kisangani, 12 February 2003.

24. A. Cauvin, *Bwana Kitoko: Un livre réalisé au cours du voyage du roi des Belges au Congo et dans le Ruanda-Urundi* (Paris: Elsevier, 1956). These languages were spoken in Kinshasa, the capital city, Equateur Province, Katanga, Kivu, Leopoldville Province, and Orientale Province.

25. Interview with Asomo Wenga, Letutu Yakuma, 12 July 1980; interview with Ofunga, Yanga, 24 July 1980; interview with Lomata, Yaokoko, 24 July 1980.

26. Van de Lanoitte, *Sur les rivières glauques*, 92-93; interview with Ndjadi Vincent, Kisangani, 27 April, 2003; interview with Lunyasi Tanganyika, Kisangani, 22 March 2003; interview with Mugaza wa Beya, Lubumbashi, 16 August 1986.

27. R. Pecheur, "Observations sur la mentalité des populations du Congo," A.I. (1412), A.A., Brussels,

28. Cattier, *Etude*, 353-354.

29. O. Likaka, "Colonialisme et clichés sociaux au Congo belge," *Africa* (Rome) 52, no. 1 (1997).

30. E. M'Bokolo, Introduction to *Naître et mourir au Zaïre: Un demi-siècle d'histoire au quotidien*, ed. B. Jewieswicki (Paris: Karthala, 1993), 28.

31. A. Dallons and V. Cornet, "Evolution de poste de Kasongo à travers le temps, 1865-1931," A.I. (1407), A.A., Brussels.

32. Ibid.

33. Ibid.

34. Interview with Risasi, Lubumbashi, 6 September 1988; interview with Mugaza wa Beya, Lubumbashi, 16 August 1986.

35. Cattier, *Etude*, 350-351.

36. Delanghe, "Principaux événements concernant l'histoire du district du Lac

Léopold II depuis la pénétration européenne (Stanley) (1877–1930)," 1958, A.I. (1407), A.A., Brussels.

37. O. Likaka, "L'impact de l'organisation politique et administrative dans le Territoire d'Opala" (MA thesis, Unaza, Lubumbashi, 1981), 55.

38. Van de Lanoitte, *Sur les rivières glauques*, 128.

39. Ibid.

40. Depoorter, *Stanleyville*, 152; interview with Mungeni Mateso, Kisangani, 23 June 1989.

41. J. Vansina, *Paths in the Rainforests* (Madison: University of Wisconsin Press, 1994), 75.

42. Van de Lanoitte, *Sur les rivières glauques*, 128.

43. Interview with Yolande Lamerat, Brussels, August 1987.

44. "Dossier politique" and "Dossier Z 265, no. 29001, 1957," Kisangani, A.P.O.

45. J. Pirson, "Le territoire de Ligasa," 1923, A.I. (1407), A.A., Brussels.

46. "Questions sociales."

Conclusions

1. O. Likaka, "The Mbole conseil des chefs et notables and the Politics of Negotiations, 1910–1960) *Anthropos* 92 (1997); O. Likaka, *Rural Society and Cotton in Colonial Zaire* (Madison: University of Wisconsin Press, 1997); B. Jewsiewicki, "African Peasants in the Totalitarian Colonial Society of the Belgian Congo," in *Peasants in Africa: Historical and Contemporary Perspectives*, ed. M. Klein (Beverly Hills, Calif.: Sage, 1980).

2. Likaka, *Rural Society;* J. Vansina, personal communication.

3. B. Lincoln, *Discourse and the Construction of Society* (New York: Oxford University Press, 1989); B. Lincoln, *Authority: Construction and Corrosion* (Chicago: University of Chicago Press, 1994); J. Scott, *Domination and the Arts of Resistance: Hidden Transcripts* (New Haven, Conn.: Yale University Press, 1990).

4. M. Merlier, *Le Congo de la colonisation belge à l'indépendance* (Paris: Maspero, 1962); Sikitele Gize, "Les racines de la révolte Pende de 1931," *Etudes d'histoire africaine*, 5 (1973); M. Lovens, "La révolte de Masisi-Lubutu (Congo belge, Janvier–Mai, 1944)," *Cahiers du CEDAF* 3–4 (1974); Likaka, *Rural Society*, 108–134.

5. J. Scott, *Weapons of the Weak: Day-to-Day Forms of Resistance* (New Haven, Conn.: Yale University Press, 1985); Scott, *Domination;* L. Vail and L. White, "Forms of Resistance: Songs and Perceptions of Power in Colonial Mozambique," in *Banditry, Rebellion and Social Protest in Africa*, ed. D. Crummey (Portsmouth N.H.: Heinemann, 1986); A. Isaacman, *Cotton Is the Mother of Poverty, 1938–1961* (Portsmouth, N.H.: Heinemann, 1996); J. Fabian, *Remembering the Present: Painting and Popular History in Zaire* (Berkeley: University of California Press, 1993); B. Jewsiewicki, ed., *Naître et mourir au Zaire: Un demi-siècle d'histoire au quotidien* (Paris: Karthala, 1993).

6. Isaacman, *Cotton Is the Mother;* Scott, *Domination*, 140; Likaka, *Rural Society*, 108–134.

7. R. Palmer and N. Parsons, eds., *The Roots of Rural Poverty in Central and Southern Africa* (Berkeley: University of California Press, 1977); W. Rodney, *How Europe Underdeveloped Africa* (London: Bogle-l'Ouverture: 1972); B. Jewsiewicki, "African Peasants in the Totalitarian Colonial Society of the Belgian Congo," in *Peasants in Africa: Historical and Contemporary Perspectives*, ed. M. Klein (Beverly Hills, Calif.: Sage, 1983).

8. For concepts such as "Vent-for-surplus," "Rational Peasants," and "Moral Economy of the Peasants," see J. Scott, *The Moral Economy of the Peasant: Rebellion and Subsistence in Southeast Asia* (New Haven, Conn.: Yale University Press, 1976); S. Popkin, *The Rational Peasant: The Political Economy of Peasants in Vietnam* (Berkeley: University of California Press, 1979).

9. O. Likaka, "Colonialisme et clichés sociaux au Congo belge," *Africa* (Rome) 52, no. 1 (1997).

10. L. Vail and L. White, "Forms of Resistance: Songs and Perceptions of Power in Colonial Mozambique," in *Banditry, Rebellion and Social Protest in Africa*, ed. D. Crummey (Portsmouth N.H.: Heinemann, 1986); Isaacman, *Cotton Is the Mother;* Likaka, *Rural Society*, 108–134.

11. C. Laye, *The Dark Child. The Autobiography of an African Boy*, translated from the French by James Kirkup and Ernest Jones (Paris: Farrar, Straus, and Giroux, 1954); R. Grinker, *Houses in the Rainforest: Ethnicity and Inequality among Farmers and Foragers in Central Africa* (Berkeley: University of California Press, 1994).

12. Interview with Atsidri Nyelegodi, Kisangani, 16 February 2003; interview with Ujanga, Kisangani, August and September 1989.

13. "Rapport sur l'attitude des Noirs en général," 1911, A.A., Brussels.

WORKS CITED

Archives Africaines (A.A.) and Archives de la Province Orientale (A.P.O.)

Achten. "Rapport." Léopoldville, 15 October 1912. A.A., Brussels.
Agri (385). "Prix de vente moyen." A.A. Brussels.
Agri (378). "H Coton." A.A. Brussels.
Aimo/14 B. Boma, 26 May 1926. A.A., Brussels.
Bertrand, A. "Lettre au G.G. à Boma." 18 June 1917. A.A., Brussels.
Brandt, A. "Etude sur les peuplades Mongelima." 1928. A.I. (1407), A.A., Brussels.
Brausch, G. "Polyandrie et mariage clanique au Kasai." 1947. A.I. (1411), A.A., Brussels.
Brenez, A. "Pourquoi je ne ferai pas parti du corps des volontaires." *Avenir colonial Belge*, 8 December 1932. A.A., Brussels.
Campill, J. "Monsieur l'officier de police judiciaire de et à Kilo." Irumu, 17 July 1924. A.I. (1416), A.A., Brussels.
Colinet. "Le Sura: Etude sommaire d'une nouvelle secte secrète se développant dans le Territoire de Doruma." 1931. A.I. (1397), A.A., Brussels.
Commissaire Général. "Recrutement: Appui à accorder aux entreprises industrielles." June 1917. A.P.O., Kisangani.
Dallons, A., and V. Cornet. "Evolution de poste de Kasongo à travers le temps, 1865–1931." A.I. (1407), A.A., Brussels.
Decoster, L. "Etude sur les populations Babua." 1933. A.I. (1408), A.A., Brussels.
Delanghe. "Principaux événements concernant l'histoire du district du Lac Léopold II depuis la pénétration européenne (Stanley) (1877–1930)." 1958. A.I. (1407), A.A., Brussels.
de Meulemeester, A. "Rapport, mines de Moto." Stanleyville, 16 April 1925. A.P.O., Kisangani.
"Dénonciation Siffer par Leplae: Dossier Siffer." Stanleyville, 7 March 1917. A.A., Brussels.
"Déplacement de villages." 29 April 1938. A.I. (1403), A.A., Brussels.
"Dossier politique." A.P.O., Kisangani.
"Dossier Z 265, no. 29001, 1957." A.P.O., Kisangani.
"Emploi des contraints aux mines." Stanleyville, July 1917. A.I. (1416), A.A., Brussels.
Engels, A. "Polygamie: dot." Conquilathville, 15 September 1919. A.I. (1416), A.A., Brussels.

Farber, J. "Enquête sur les Bazela, district de Tanganyika, territoire des Kibara." 1932, A.I. (1367), A.A., Brussels.

Heinzmann. "Les Bagbe." 1913. A.A., Brussels.

Hertveld, E. "Lutte contre la polygamie." District de l'Ubangi, Libenge, 14 November 1923. A.I. (1416), A.A., Brussels.

"Historique de Luluabourg." A.I. (1407), A.A., Brussels.

"Historique des Bambole." A.T.O., Opala.

"Hygiène des travailleurs occupés à la construction de routes." Boma, 26 May 1926. A.A., Brussels.

"Ind. no 121 RIM no. 4457." Irumu, 17 July 1924. A.A., Brussels.

"Inspection du Kwango et Bashilele." Léopoldville, 30 September 1933. A.A., Brussels.

Keyaser, H. L. "Notes synthétiques complétant la documentation des Rapports annuels AIMO 1933 des A. T. du Tanganyika." A.A., Brussels.

"Kultur Schande." *Danziger Zeitung.* A.I. (1407), A.A., Brussels.

Lauwers. "Notes sur la peuplade des Bambole." 1932. A.I. (1410), A.A., Brussels.

"Mines-Moto." Arebi, 26 September 1913. A.I. (1416), A.A., Brussels.

Mscart, M. "Village Monia." 2 December 1921. A.A., Brussels.

"Note pour Monsieur le Gouverneur Ger.· -al." [1917]. A.A., Brussels.

"Notes sur les Gwaka." A.I. (1411), A.A., Brussels.

"Organisation judiciaire et procédure du tribunal coutumier de Kimese." A.I. (1618), A.A., Brussels.

"Papiers E. Janssens." D (1367), A.A., Brussels.

Pecheur, R. H. "Observations sur la mentalité des populations du Congo." A.I. (1412), A.A, Brussels.

Philippart, R. "Rapport de la prise de contact entre monsieur Joset chargé de la mission du Ministère des Colonies et l'Administrateur PPAL Philippart a Stanleyville le 4-5-1956." A.I. (4736), A.A., Brussels.

Pirson, J. "Le territoire de Ligasa." 1923. A.I. (1407), A.A., Brussels.

"Portage route Andulu-Mongbalu." Bula, 6 January 1925. A.A., Brussels.

"Propagande cotonnière." 1939. A.P.O., Kisangani.

"Quelques notes sur l'inongo recueillies par le sous-lieutenant Grégoire à l'occasion d'une opération de police exécutée dans la région des Lokonge (poste de Mompono)." 1912. A.I. (1397), A.A., Brussels.

Querton, M. "Rapport trimestriel." Lusambo, 16 July 1926. A.P.O., Kisangani.

"Questions sociales." 1936. A.I. (1397), A.A., Brussels.

"Rapport annuel AIMO." Territoire d'Albertville, 1933. A.A., Brussels.

"Rapport annuel AIMO." Territoire de Paulis, 1957. A.P.O., Kisangani.

"Rapport annuel sur la campagne cotonnière." 1937/38. A.P.O., Kisangani.

"Rapport annuel sur la culture et le commerce du coton, modèle C, District du Congo-Ubangi." 1938. A.P.O., Kisangani.

"Rapport annuel sur l'administration du Congo." 1917. A.P.O., Kisangani.

"Rapport annuel sur l'agriculture." 1910–32. A.A., Brussels.

"Rapport annuel sur la situation générale du district de l'Uele, Zone de Bomokandi." 1910. A.I. (1372), A.A., Brussels.

"Rapport d'enquête." 30 March 1925. A.T.O., Opala.

"Rapport d'enquête." 30 May 1925. A.T.O., Opala.

"Rapport de la Commission de la main-d'oeuvre au Congo." 1924–25. A.A., Brussels.

"Rapport de la Commission de la main-d'oeuvre indigène." 1928, 1930–31. A.A., Brussels.

"Rapport d'inspection au Kwango." A.I. (1383), A.A., Brussels.

"Rapport d'inspection du Teritoire d'Ango." 1933, 1938. A.P.O., Kisangani.

"Rapport d'inspection du Territoire d'Angu." 1945. A.P.O., Kisangani.

"Rapport d'inspection du Territoire de Buta." 1954. A.P.O., Kisangani.

"Rapport d'inspection du Territoire de Dungu." 1952. A.P.O., Kisangani.

"Rapport d'inspection judiciaire du premier trimestre de Niangara." 1949. A.P.O., Kisangani.

"Rapport politique sur la situation politique: Rapport mensuel sur la situation générale du district de l'Uele, zone de Bomokandi, 1910." 1910. A.I. (1372), A.A., Brussels.

"Rapport relatif au projet de création du secteur Kazu-Zimba-Kindunga." A.I. (1409), A.A., Brussels.

"Rapport sur l'administration du Congo belge." 1919, 1932, 1935, 1938, 1951. A.P.O., Kisangani.

"Rapport sur l'agriculture." District du Haut-Uele, 1917, 1938, 1951. A.P.O., Kisangani.

"Rapport sur l'agriculture." District du Maniema, 1928, 1930. A.P.O., Kisangani.

"Rapport sur l'attitude des Noirs en général." 1911. A.A., Brussels.

"Rapport sur l'inongo." 1911. A.I. (1397), A.A., Brussels.

"Rapports d'enquêtes." A.I. (1388), A.A., Brussels.

"Rapports politiques." A.I. (1385), A.A., Brussels.

"Recrutement: Appui à accorder aux entreprises industrielles." June 1917. A.A., Brussels.

Recueil usuel pour les fonctionnaires et agents du service territorial. 1935. A.P.O., Kisangani.

"Relegations et police pour chefs." A.I. (1385), A.A., Brussels.

"Relevement moral des indigenes, service de la justice." Coquilathville, 14 April 1920. A.A., Brussels.

"Reppression de l'adultère." A.I. (1395), A.A., Brussels.

Requier. "Note sur la polygamie dans le territoire de Budjala." Itoko, 10 September 1921. A.A., Brussels.

Ruwet. "Panorama industriel du Congo: Le coton (II)." 22 February 1945, A.A., Brussels.

"Secteur Bwere, Gurba Dungu." Sili, 4 September 1908. A.A., Brussels.

Stocker. "Rapport sur la campagne cotonnière 1923/1924." Niangara, 30 April 1924. A.A., Brussels.

"Tam-Tam." 28 November 1945. A.I. (1414), A.A., Brussels.

Vanden Broeck. "Abus aux mines de Moto." Léopoldville, 30 October 1925. A.I. (1416), A.A., Brussels.

Van den Eede. "Lutte contre la polygamie." Libenge, 14 November 1923. A.I. (1416), A.A., Brussels.

———. "Etude sur la tribu des Bobango." A.I. (1407), A.A., Brussels.

Verbeke, L. "Etude sur la peuplade des Bombesa." 1927. A.I. (1412), A.A., Brussels.

Yaskold-Gabszewicz, L. "Rapport annuel sur la campagne cotonnière 1937–1938." Stanleyville, 7 May 1938. A.P.O., Kisangani.

Government Documents and Newspapers

Bulletin Administratif. 1917.

Bulletin Officiel. 1910.

Chrononique du Katanga. Elisabethville, 7 October 1921.
Conseil de Province de l'Equateur. 1959.
Conseil de Province de Lusambo. 1940–42.
Conseil de Province Orientale. 1947–58.
Manuel pour le fonctionnaire s'intéressant au coton. 1922.
"Record for Handing and Taking Over." Tanganyika District Books and Rufiji and Mafia Districts Books.
Recueil mensuel. 1914–18.

Published Materials and Theses

Abrams, P. *Historical Sociology*. Ithaca, N.Y.: Cornell University Press, 1982.
Achebe, Chinua. *Things Fall Apart*. New York: Anchor Books, 1994.
Adas, M. "From Foot-dragging to Flight: The Evasive History of Peasant Avoidance Strategies in South and South Asia." *Journal of Peasant Studies* 13, no. 2 (1986): 64–86.
Agomatanakahn, R. *Introduction à l'anthroponymie zairoise*. Lubumbashi: Celta, 1974.
Akyeampong, E. *Drink, Power, and Cultural Change*. Portsmouth, N.H.: Heinemann, 1996.
Alpers, E. "'To Seek a Better Life': The I...plications of Migrations from Mozambique to Tanganyika for the Class Formation and Political Behavior." *Canadian Journal of African Studies* 18, no. 2 (1984): 367–388.
Anstey, R. *King Leopold's Legacy: The Congo under Belgian Rule, 1908–1960*. London: Oxford University Press, 1966.
"A propos des problèmes du milieu rural congolais." *Problèmes sociaux congolais* 36 (1957).
Asad, T. *Anthropology and the Colonial Encounter*. New York: Humanities Press, 1973.
Asiwaju, A. "Migration as Revolt: The Example of the Ivory Coast and the Upper Volta before 1945." *Journal of African History* 17 (1976): 577–594.
Ayi Kwei Armah. *The Beautyful Ones Are Not Yet Born*. London: Heinemann, 1968.
Bâ, M. *So Long a Letter*. Trans. Modupé Bodé-Thomas. Portsmouth: Heinemann, 1981.
Bakonzi Agoyo. "The Gold Mines of Kilo-Moto in Northeastern Zaire, 1905–1960." PhD diss., University of Wisconsin–Madison, 1982.
Bakua Lufu Badibanga. "Note sur l'évolution de la politique colonial belge à l'égard des chefs traditionnels." *Mbegu: Revue pédagogique et culturelle* 3 (1977): 32–42.
Balandier, G. *Daily Life in the Kingdom of the Kongo: From the Sixteenth to the Eighteenth Century*. Trans. from the French by Helen Weaver. New York: Pantheon Books, 1968.
Bauer, R., and A. Bauer. "Day to Day Resistance in Slavery." *Journal of Negro History* 27 (1942): 388–419.
Beinart, W. "Introduction: The Politics of Colonial Conservation." *Journal of Southern Congolese Studies* 15 (1989): 145–162.
Beinart, W., and C. Bundy. *Hidden Struggles in Rural South Africa: Politics and Popular Movements in the Transkei and Eastern Cape, 1890–1930*. Berkeley: University of California Press, 1987.
Berger, J. *Pig Earth*. New York: Pantheon, 1979.
Bernal, V. *Cultivating Workers: Peasants and Capitalism in a Sudanese Village*. New York: Columbia University Press, 1991.
Bernstein, H. "African Peasantries: A Theoretical Framework." *Journal of Peasant Studies* 6 (1979): 420–443.

Berry, S. *No Condition Is Permanent: The Social Dynamics of Agrarian Change in Sub-Saharan Africa*. Madison: University of Wisconsin Press, 1993.

Bertrand, A. *Le problème de la main-d'oeuvre au Congo*. Brussels, 1955.

Biaya, T. "Ethnopsychologie de quelques anthroponymes africains des missionnaires catholiques du Kasai colonial." *Annales Aequatoria* 16 (1995): 183–227.

Biebuyck, D. *Hero and Chief: Epic Literature from the Banyanga, Zaire Republic*. Berkeley: University of California Press, 1978.

Birmingham, D. *Empire in Africa: Angola and Its Neighbors*. Athens: Ohio University Press, 2006.

Birmingham, D., and P. Martin, eds. *History of Central Africa*. 2 vols. London: Longman, 1983.

Blassingame, J. *The Slave Community: Plantation Life in the Antebellum South*. New York: Oxford University Press, 1972.

Boelaert, E., H. Vinck, and C. Lonkama. "Addenda et Corrigenda: Annales Aequatoria 1980–1999." *Annales Aequatoria* 21 (2000): 362–488.

———. "Arrivée des Blancs sur les bords des rivières equatorials (Part II et fin)." *Annales Aequatoria* 17 (1996): 7–415.

Bontinck, F. "Les deux Bula Matari." *Etudes congolaises* 13, no. 3 (1969): 83–97.

Bozzoli, B., with the assistance of Mmantho Nkotsoe. *Women of Phokeng: Consciousness, Life Strategy, and Migrancy in South Africa, 1900–1983*. Portsmouth, N.H.: Heinemann, 1991.

Bradford, H. *A Taste of Freedom: The ICU in Rural South Africa, 1924–1930*. New Haven, Conn.: Yale University Press, 1987.

Brausch, G. "Origine de la politique indigène belge en Afrique, 1879–1908." *Revue de l'Institut de Sociologie* 3 (1955): 455–478.

Cattier, F. *Etude sur la situation du Congo*. Brussels: F. Larcier, 1905.

Cauvin, A. *Bwana Kitoko: Un livre réalisé au cours du voyage du roi des Belges au Congo et dans le Ruanda-Urundi*. Paris: Elsevier, 1956.

Césaire, A. *Discourse on Colonialism*. Trans. Joan Pinkham. New York: Monthly Review, 1972.

Ceulemans, P. *La question arabe et le Congo (1883–1892)*. Brussels: ARSOM, 1959.

Chechu Dyilo. "Recrutement de la main-d'oeuvre aux mines de Kilo-Moto." MA thesis, Unaza, Lubumbashi, 1981.

Clanchy, M. T. *From Memory to Written Record*. London: Edward Arnold Edward, 1979.

Cohen, R. *Men Own the Fields, Women Own the Crops*. Madison: University of Wisconsin Press, 1996.

Cooper, F. *Decolonization and African Society: The Labor Question in French and British Africa*. New York: Cambridge University Press, 1996.

Cooper, F., and A. L. Stoler, eds. *Tensions of Empire: Colonial Cultures in a Bourgeois World*. Berkeley: University of California Press, 1997.

Coquery-Vidrovitch, C. *Le Congo au temps des compagnies concessionnaires, 1893–1930*. Paris, 1972.

Cordell, D. "The Savanna Belt of North-Central Africa." In *History of Central Africa*, ed. D. Birmingham and P. Martin, 1:30–74. London: Longman, 1983.

Cornet, R.-J. *Bwana Muganga: Hommes en blanc en Afrique noire*. Brussels: Académie royale des sciences d'Outre-Mer, 1960.

Crine, B. *La structure sociale des Foma.* Brussels: CEDAF 4, 1972.

Crokaert, J. *Boula Matari.* Brussels: Librairie Albert Dewit, 1929.

Crummey, D., ed. *Banditry, Rebellion and Social Protest in Africa.* Portsmouth, N.H.: Heinemann, 1986.

Cyrier, J. *"Anioto:* 'Putting a Paw on Power?': Leopard Men of the Belgian Congo, 1911–1936." MA thesis, University of London, 1998.

De Lannoy, D., Mabiala Seda Diangwala, and Bongeli Yeikelo Ya Ato. *Tango ya ba Noko. Le temps des oncles: Recueil des témoignages zairois.* Brussels: CEDAF 5–6, 1986.

Delcommune, A. *Vingt années de vie africaine.* Brussels: Ferdinand Larcier, 1922.

Denis, P. *Histoire des Mangbetu et Matsaga jusqu'à l'arrivée des Belges.* Tervuren: MRAC, 1961.

Depi, G. "La Caisse de réserve cotonnière." *Bulletin de la Banque Centrale du Congo belge et du Ruanda-Urundi* (1957).

Depoorter, R. *Stanleyville où le Lualaba devenait Congo.* Brussels: Didier Hatier, 1992.

De Sousberghe, L. "Noms donnés aux Pygmées et souvenirs laissés par eux chez les Pende et Lunda de la Loange." *Congo-Tervuren* 6, no. 3 (1960): 86.

Dibwe dia Mwembu, D. *Faire de l'histoire orale dans une ville africaine: La methode de Jan Vansina appliquée à Lubumbashi (R-D Congo).* Paris: L'Harmattan, 2008.

———. "Popular Memories of Patrice Lumumba." In *A Congo Chronicle: Patrice Lumumba in Urban Art,* ed. B. Jewsiewicki, 59–72. New York: Museum for African Art, 1999.

Doyle, A. *The Crime of the Congo.* New York: Doubleday, Page and Company, 1909.

Ela, J. *L'Afrique des villages.* Paris: Karthala, 1983.

Fabian, J. *Language and Colonial Power.* Berkeley: University of California Press, 1985.

———. "Popular Culture in Africa: Findings and Conjectures." In *Readings in African Popular Culture,* ed. K. Barber, 18–28. Bloomington: University of Indiana Press, 1997.

———. *Out of Our Minds: Reasons and Madness in the Exploration of Central Africa.* Berkeley: University of California Press, 2000.

———. *Remembering the Present: Painting and Popular History in Zaire.* Berkeley: University of California Press, 1993.

Fanon, F. *The Wretched of the Earth.* Trans. Constance Farrington. New York: Grove Press, 1963.

Fetter, B. "The Mines of Southern and Central Africa: An Ecological Framework." *Health Transition Review* 2, supplementary issue (1992): 125–135.

———. "Pitfalls in the Application of Demographic Insights to African History." *History in Africa* 19 (1992): 299–308.

———. "Relocating Central Africa's Biological Reproduction, 1923–1963." *International Journal of African Historical Studies* 19, no. 3 (1986): 463–478.

———. "The Union Minière and Its Hinterland: A Demographic Reconstruction." *African Economic History* 12 (1983): 67–81.

Françoise-Marie. "Lettre." *Bulletin du comité cotonnier congolais* 15 (1939): 77.

Fredrickson, G. *Black Liberation: A Comparative History of Black Ideologies in the United States and South Africa.* New York: Oxford University Press, 1995.

———. *The Comparative Imagination: On the History of Racism, Nationalism, and Social Movements.* Berkeley: University of California Press, 1997.

Freire, P. *The Pedagogy of the Oppressed.* Trans. Myra Berqman Ramos. New York: Continuum, 2006.

Gaston-Joseph. *Koffi: Roman vrai d'un noir*. Paris: Editions du monde nouveau, 1923.

Gramisci, A. *Letters from Prison*. New York: Harper and Row, 1973.

Grevisse, F. *La grande pitié des jurisdictions indigènes*. Brussels: IRCB, 1949.

Grinker, R. *Houses in the Rainforest: Ethnicity and Inequality among Farmers and Foragers in Central Africa*. Berkeley: University of California Press, 1994.

Hamidou Kane, C. *Ambiguous Adventure*. Portsmouth, N.H.: Heinemann, 1972.

Hamilton, C. "Ideology and Oral Tradition: Listening to the Voices 'From Below.'" *History in Africa* 14 (1987): 67–86.

Harms, R. "The End of the Red Rubber: A Reassessment." *Journal of African History* 16, no. 1 (1975): 73–88.

———. *Games against Nature: An Eco-cultural History of the Nunu of Equatorial Africa*. Cambridge: Cambridge University Press, 1987.

Haynes, D., and G. Prakash, eds. *Contesting Power: Resistance and Everyday Social Relations in South Asia*. Berkeley: University of California Press, 1991.

Headrick, R. *Colonialism, Health and Illness in French Equatorial Africa, 1885–1935*. Atlanta: African Studies Association, 1994.

Higginson, J. *A Working Class in the Making: Belgian Colonial Labor Policy, Private Enterprise, and the African Mineworker, 1907–1951*. Madison: University of Wisconsin Press, 1989.

Hochschild, A. *King Leopold's Ghost: A Story of Greed, Terror, and Heroism in Colonial Africa*. Boston: Houghton Mifflin, 1998.

Hodge, N. *To Kill a Man's Pride*. Johannesburg: Ravan Press, 1982.

Hofmeyr. *We Spend Our Years as a Tale That Is Told: Oral Historical Narrative in a South African Chiefdom*. Portsmouth, N.H.: Heinemann, 1993.

Howard-Malvelde, R., ed. *Creating Context in Andean Cultures*. New York: Oxford University Press, 1997.

Hudson, R. A. *Sociolinguistics*. 2nd ed. Cambridge: Cambridge University Press, 1996.

Hulstaert, G. "Noms de personnes chez les Nkundo." *Aequatoria* 19 (1956): 91–102.

Hunt, N. *A Colonial Lexicon of Birth Ritual, Medicalization, and Mobility in the Congo*. Durham, N.C.: Duke University Press, 1999.

Isaacman, A. *Cotton Is the Mother of Poverty, 1938–1961*. Portsmouth, N.H.: Heinemann, 1996.

Jackson, M. *Allegories of the Wilderness: Ethics and Ambiguity in Kuranko Narratives*. Bloomington: Indiana University Press.

Janssens, P., et al. *Médicine et hygiène en Afrique centrale de 1885 à nos jours*. Brussels: Bibliothèque Royale Albert I, 1992.

Janzen, J. *The Quest for Therapy: Medical Pluralism in Lower Zaire*. Berkeley: University of California Press, 1978.

Jérôme. "Cultivons du coton." *Bulletin du comité cotonnier congolais* 7 (1937): 72–73.

Jewsiewicki, B. "African Peasants in the Totalitarian Colonial Society of the Belgian Congo." In *Peasants in Africa: Historical and Contemporary Perspectives*, ed. M. Klein, 45–75. Beverly Hills, Calif.: Sage, 1983.

———. *A Congo Chronicle: Patrice Lumumba in Urban Art*. New York: Museum for African Art, 1999.

———. *Mami Wata: La peinture urbaine au Congo*. Le Temps des Images. Paris: Gallimard, 2003.

———. *Musique urbaine au Katanga: De Malaika à Santu Kimbangu*. Mémoires Lieux de Savoir. Archive Congolaise. Paris: L'Harmattan, 2003.

————. *Naître et mourrir au Zaire: Un demi-siècle d'histoire au quotidien.* Paris: Karthala, 1993.

Johnston, H. *George Grenfell and the Congo.* Vol. 1. New York, 1890.

Joyce, P., and R. Lewin. *Les trusts au Congo.* Brussels: Société belge d'Editions, 1961.

Kaniki, M. H. Y., ed. *Tanzania under Colonial Rule.* London: Longman, 1980.

Kasendwe Kibonge. "Les cultures obligatoires dans le Tanganyika." MA thesis, Unaza, Lubumbashi, 1981.

Ki-Zerbo, J. *Histoire générale de l'Afrique.* Paris: Hatier, 1972.

Klein, M., ed. *Peasants in Africa: Historical and Contemporary Perspectives.* Beverly Hills, Calif.: Sage, 1980.

Lambrecht, F. *In the Shade of an Acacia Tree: Memoirs of a Health Officer in Africa, 1945–1959.* Philadelphia: American Philosophical Society, 1991.

Landeghem, A. "1921–1936: Quinze années de culture de coton au Congo belge." *Bulletin du comité cotonnier congolais* 4 (1936): 3–4.

Laude, J. *The Arts of Black Africa.* Trans. from the French by Jean Decock. Berkeley: University of California Press, 1971.

Laya, D., ed. *La tradition orale: Problématique et méthodologie des sources de l'histoire africaine.* Abbeville: P. Paillart, 1972.

Laye, C. *The Dark Child: The Autobiography of an African Boy.* Trans. from the French by James Kirkup and Ernest Jones. New York: Farrar, Straus, and Giroux, 1954.

Lejeune-choquet, A. *Histoire militaire du Congo.* Brussels: Edition Alfred Castaigne, 1906.

Leplae, E. "Comment les Bantous du Congo s'acheminent vers le paysannat." *Bulletin agricole du Congo belge* 4 (1931): 574.

————. "Comment les indigènes du Congo belge sont arrivés à produire annuellement 20.000 tonnes de coton-fibre." *Coton et culture cotonnière* 3 (1935): 181.

————. "L'agriculture coloniale dans la discussion du budget du Congo belge pour 1914." *Bulletin agricole du Congo belge* (1914): 17.

Lestringant, F. *Cannibals: The Discovery and Representations of the Cannibal from Columbus to Jules Verne.* Trans. R. Morris. Berkeley: University of California Press, 1997.

Liénart, G. "La signification du nom chez les peoples Bantu." *Le langage et l'homme* 5 (1968): 43–54.

Likaka, O. "Colonialisme et clichés sociaux au Congo belge." *Africa* (Rome) 52, no. 1 (1997): 1–27.

————. "Colonisation et construction d'identités: L'administration belge et l'identité Mbole, 1910–1960." *Revue Française d'Histoire d'Outre-mer* 85, no. 321 (1998): 27–41.

————. "Forced Cotton Cultivation and Social Control in the Belgian Congo." In *Cotton, Colonialism, and Social History in Sub-Saharan Africa,* ed. A. Isaacman and R. Roberts, 200–220. Portsmouth, N.H.: Heinemann, 1995.

————. "Le commerce dans l'Uele au 19ième siècle." Graduate thesis, Unaza, Lubumbashi, 1977.

————. "L'impact de l'organisation politique et administrative dans le Territoire d'Opala." MA thesis, Unaza, Lubumbashi, 1981.

————. "The Mbole conseil des chefs et notables and the Politics of Negotiations, 1910–1960." *Anthropos* 92 (1997): 471–483.

————. "Rural Protest: The Mbole against the Belgian Colonial Rule, 1893–1959." *International Journal of African Historical Studies* 27, no. 3 (1994): 589–617.

————. *Rural Society and Cotton in the Belgian Congo.* Madison: University of Wisconsin Press, 1997.

————. "Working for the Taxman Makes People Thinner: Economy and Demography in the Congo." Unpublished manuscript.

Lincoln, B. *Authority: Construction and Corrosion.* Chicago: University of Chicago Press, 1994.

————. *Discourse and the Construction of Society.* New York: Oxford University Press, 1989.

Lotar, L. "Souveniers de l'Uele." *Congo* 4, no. 2 (1931): 493–514.

————. "Souveniers de l'Uele." *Congo* 2, no. 2 (1930): 607–11.

Lovens, M. "La révolte de Masisi-Lubutu (Congo belge, Janvier–Mai, 1944)." *Cahiers du CEDAF* 3–4 (1974): 4–136.

Lwamba, B. "Histoire du mouvement ouvrier au Congo belge (1914–1960): Cas de la Province du Katanga." PhD diss., Université de Lubumbashi, 1985.

Lyons, M. *The Colonial Disease: A Social History of Sleeping Sickness in Northern Zaire, 1900–1940.* Cambridge: Cambridge University Press, 1992.

MacGaffey, W. "Dialogues of the Deaf: Europeans on the Atlantic Coast of Africa." In *Implicit Understandings: Observing, Reporting, and Reflecting on the Encounters between Europeans and Other Peoples in the Early Modern Era,* ed. S. Schwartz, 249–267. New York: Cambridge University Press, 1994.

Magotte, J. *Circonscriptions indigènes.* La Louvière: Imprimerie Louvièroise, 1938.

Malengreau, G. "Les lotissements agricoles au Congo beige." Special issue, *Bulletin agricole du Congo beige* 43 (1952).

Mandala, E. *The End of Chidyrano: A History of Food and Everyday Life in Malawi, 1860–2004.* Portsmouth, N.H.: Heinemann, 2005.

————. *Work and Control in a Peasant Economy.* Madison: University of Wisconsin Press, 1990.

Marchal, J. *L'état libre du Congo: Paradis perdu.* 2 vols. Brussels: Editions Paula Bellings, 1996.

Martin, P. "The Violence of Empire." In *History of Central Africa,* ed. D. Birmingham and P. Martin, 2:1–26. London: Longman, 1983.

Mbiti, J. *African Religions and Philosophy.* 2nd ed. Portsmouth, N.H.: Heinemann, 1989.

M'Bokolo, E. Introduction to *Naître et mourir au Zaire: Un demi-siècle d'histoire au quotidian,* ed. B. Jewsiewicki, 17–41. Paris: Karthala, 1993.

McDowell, J. "Toward a Semiotics of Naming: The Kamsá Example." *Journal of American Folklore* 92, no. 371 (1981): 1–17.

Memmi, A. *The Colonizer and the Colonized.* Trans. Howard Greenfield. Boston: Beacon Press, 1967.

Merlier, M. *Le Congo de la colonisation belge à l'indépendance.* Paris: Maspero, 1962.

Mieder, W. *The Politics of Proverbs.* Madison: University of Wisconsin Press, 1997.

Miller, J. *Ways of Death: Merchant Capitalism and the Angolan Slave Trade, 1730–1830.* Madison: University of Wisconsin Press, 1988.

"Monographie du coton congolais." *Bulletin trimestriel du comité cotonnier congolais* 6 (1937): 58.

Monteiro, J. *Angola and the River Congo.* 2 vols. London: Frank Cass, 1968.

Morel, E. *Red Rubber: The Story of the Rubber Slave Trade Flourishing on the Congo in the Year of Grace 1906.* New York: Haskell House, 1906.

Mudimbe, V. *The Idea of Africa.* Bloomington: Indiana University Press, 1994.

————. *The Invention of Africa: Gnosis, Philosophy, and the Order of Knowledge.* Bloomington: Indiana University Press, 1988.

————, ed. *The Surreptitious Speech: Présence Africaine and the Politics of Otherness, 1947–1987.* Chicago: University of Chicago Press, 1992.

Mulambu, F. "Cultures obligatoires et colonisation dans l'ex-Congo belge." *Cahiers du CEDAF* 6–7 (1974): 7–99.

Mutamba, M. *Makoko: Roi des Bateke (1880–1892).* Kinshasa: Edideps, 1987.

Ndinga-Mbo, A. *Onomastique et histoire au Congo-Brazzaville.* Paris: L'Harmattan, 2004.

Nelson, S. *Colonialism in the Congo Basin: 1880–1940.* Athens: Ohio University Center for International Studies, 1994.

Nkulu Kalala. "Les réactions africaines aux impositions des cultures: Cas du Territoire de Kamina, 1935–1959." MA thesis, Université de Lubumbashi, 1983.

Northrup, N. *Beyond the Bend in the River: Congolese Labor in Eastern Zaire, 1865–1940.* Athens: Ohio University Center for International Studies, 1988.

Nyunda ya Rubando. "Patrice Lumumba at the Crossroads of History and Myth." In *A Congo Chronicle: Patrice Lumumba in Urban Art,* ed. B. Jewsiewicki, 43–58. New York: Museum for African Art, 1999.

Nzongola-Ntalaza, G. *The Congo, from Leopold to Kabila: A People's History.* London: Zed Books, 2002.

Nzula, A., et al., eds. *Forced Labour in Colon:..' Africa.* London: Zed Press, 1979.

Oyono, F. *Une vie de boy.* Paris: Julliard, 1956.

Pakasa Nayipere. "La politique indigène dans la vallée du Haut-Lubilashi, 1900–1940." MA thesis, Unaza, Lubumbashi, 1974.

Palmer, N., and N. Parsons, eds. *The Roots of Rural Poverty in Central and Southern Africa.* Berkeley: University of California Press, 1977.

Parkhill, T. *Weaving Ourselves into the Land: Charles Godfrey Leland, "Indians," and the Study of Native American Religions.* Albany: State University of New York Press, 1997.

Peck, R. *Lumumba: La mort d'un prophète.* 1992, 69 min., video and 16mm film.

Peemans, J. *Diffusion du progrès et convergence des prix: Congo belge, 1900–1960.* Louvain: Nauwelaerts, 1970.

Popkin, S. *The Rational Peasant: The Political Economy of Peasants in Vietnam.* Berkeley: University of California Press, 1979.

Portelli, A. *The Battle of Valle Giulia: Oral History and the Art of Dialogue.* Madison: University of Wisconsin Press, 1997.

————. *The Death of Luigi Trastulli and Other Stories: Form and Meaning in Oral History.* Albany: State University of New York Press, 1991.

Ranger, T. "Connections between 'Primary Resistance' Movements and Modern Mass Nationalism in East and Central Africa." *Journal of African History* 9, no. 3 (1968): 437–453, 631–641.

————, ed. *Emerging Themes of Congolese History.* Nairobi: East Congolese Publishing House, 1968.

Ravet, A. "La fête du coton." *Bulletin du comité cotonnier congolais* 10 (1938): 55–56.

————. "L'exposition agricole de Buta (Uele) 4 et 5 Novembre 1939." *Bulletin du comité cotonnier congolais* 16 (1940): 3–4.

Reefe, T. "The Societies of the Eastern Savanna." In *History of Central Africa,* ed. D. Birmingham and P. Martin, 1:160–204. London: Longman, 1983.

Renault, F. *Lavigérie, l'esclavage africain et l'Europe.* Paris: Editions E. de Boccard, 1982.

Rodney, W. *How Europe Underdeveloped Africa.* London: Bogle-l'Ouverture, 1972.

Roelens, V. "Les abus du recrutement de la main-d'oeuvre au Congo: Une protestation des chefs religieux catholiques de la Colonies." *Le Flambeau* (1923): 129–130.

Ryckmans, A. "Etude sur les signaux de 'mondo' (tambour-téléphone) chez les Bayaka du Territoire de Popokabaka." *Zaire* 5 (1956): 493–515.

Salmon, P. *La carrière africaine de Harry Bombeeck, agent commercial (1896–1899).* Brussels: Institut de sociologie, Université libre de Bruxelles, 1990.

Sanchez Vazquez, A. *Art and Society: Essays in Marxist Aesthetics.* New York: Monthly Press Review Press, 1965.

Sautter, G. *De l'Atlantique au fleuve Congo: Une géographie de sous-peuplement.* 2 vols. Paris, 1966.

Schatzberg, M. *The Dialectics of Oppression in Zaire.* Bloomington: Indiana University Press, 1988.

Schwartz, S., ed. *Implicit Understandings: Observing, Reporting, and Reflecting on the Encounters between Europeans and Other Peoples in the Early Modern Era.* Cambridge: Cambridge University Press, 1994.

Schweinfurth, G. *Au Coeur de l'Afrique.* 2 vols. Paris: Hachette et cie, 1875.

———. *The Heart of Africa.* 2 vols. London, 1873.

Scott, J. *Domination and the Arts of Resistance: Hidden Transcripts.* New Haven, Conn.: Yale University Press, 1990.

———. *The Moral Economy of the Peasant: Rebellion and Subsistence in Southeast Asia.* New Haven, Conn.: Yale University Press, 1976.

———. *Weapons of the Weak: Day-to-Day Forms of Resistance.* New Haven, Conn.: Yale University Press, 1985.

Sembene Ousmane. *God's Bits of Wood.* London: Heinemann, 1970.

Shallington, K. *History of Africa.* New York: St. Martin's Press, 1989.

Sikitele Gize. "Les racines de la révolte pende de 1931." *Etudes d'histoire africaine* 5 (1973): 99–153.

Smith, R. "L'administration coloniale belge et les villageois, les Yansi du nord de Bulungu, 1920–1940 (Zaire)." *Cahiers du Cedaf* 3 (1976): 2–32.

Stanley, H. *Through the Dark Continent.* London, 1890.

Storme, M. "Het Onstaat van de Kasai Missie." *Bulletin d'ARSOM* 24, no. 3 (1961).

———. "Konflikt in de Kasai-Missie." *Bulletin d'ARSOM* 33, no. 1 (1965).

———. "La mutinerie militaire au Kasai en 1895." *Bulletin d'ARSOM* 38, no. 4 (1970).

Sunseri, T. *Vilimani: Labor Migration and Rural Change in Early Colonial Tanzania.* Portsmouth, N.H.: Heinemann, 2002.

Suret-Canale, J. *French Colonialism in Africa.* Paris, 1964.

Tanghe, B. *Le culte du serpent chez les Ngbandi.* Bruges: Les Presses Gruuthuuse, 1926.

Tempels, P. *Bantu Philosophy.* Paris: Présence africaine, 1959.

Thuriaux-Hennebert, A. "Les grands chefs Bandia et Zande de la région Uele-Bomu, 1860–1895." *Etudes d'histoire africaine* 3 (1972): 167–207.

Tshonga, O. "Les noms des jumeaux dans la région de l'Equateur (Zaire)." *Annales Aequatoria* 4 (1983): 57–62.

Turnbull, M. *The Lonely Africa.* New York: Simon and Schuster, 1962.

Turner, T. "Memory, Myth and Ethnicity: A Review of Recent Literature and Some Cases from Zaire." *History in Africa* 19 (1992): 387–400.

Vail, L., and L. White. "Forms of Resistance: Songs and Perceptions of Power in Colonial Mozambique." In *Banditry, Rebellion and Social Protest in Africa,* ed. D. Crummey, 193–227. Berkeley: University of California Press, 1976.

———. *Power and the Praise Poem: Southern African Voices in History.* Charlottesville: University Press of Virginia, 1991.

Vancraenbroeck, M. *Les médailles de la présence belge en Afrique centrale, 1876–1960.* Brussels: Bibliothèque Royale, 1996.

Van de Lanoitte, C. *Sur les rivières glauques de l'Equateur.* Paris: Editions de la revue Iris, 1938.

Vanden Bossche, J. *Sectes et associations indigènes au Congo belge.* Léopoldville: Editions du Bulletin militaire, 1954.

Van Der Kerken, G. *L'ethnie Mongo.* Brussels: IRCB, 1944.

Van der Linden, F. "Paysans et prolétaires noirs." *Revue de la société belge d'études et d'expansion* 47, no. 31 (1948): 371.

Vangroenweghe, D. *Du sang sur les lianes: Léopold II et son Congo.* Brussels: Didier Hatier, 1985.

Vansina, J. *The Children of Woot: A History of the Kuba Peoples.* Madison: University of Wisconsin Press, 1978.

———. *De la tradition orale: Essaie de méthode historique.* Kinshasa: Editions universitaires du Congo, 1961.

———. *How Societies Are Born: Governance in West Central Africa before 1600.* Charlottesville: University of Virginia Press, 2004.

———. *Kingdoms of the Savanna.* Madison: University of Wisconsin Press, 1965.

———. *Living with Africa.* Madison: University of Wisconsin Press, 1994.

———. "Noms personnels et structures socials chez les Tyo (Teke)." *Bulletin des scéances de l'Académie royale des sciences d'Outre-Mer,* n.s. 10 (1964): 794–804.

———. *Oral Tradition as History.* Madison: University of Wisconsin Press, 1985.

———. *Paths in the Rainforests.* Madison: University of Wisconsin Press, 1994.

———. "Probing the Past of the Lower Kwilu Peoples (Zaire)." *Paideuma* 19–20 (1974): 332–364.

———. "The Roots of Congolese Cultures." In *African History: From Earliest Times to Independence,* ed. P. Curtin et al., 1–28. 2nd ed. London: Longman, 1995.

Van Zandycke, A. "La révolte de Luluabourg (4 juillet 1895)." *Zaire* 11 (1950): 931–964.

Vellut, J.-L., ed. *Kisangani: Histoire d'une ville.* Kisangani: PUZ, 1976.

———. "La violence armée dans l'Etat Indépendant du Congo." *Culture et développement* 16, no. 3–4 (1984): 671–707.

———. "Matériaux pour une image du blanc dans la société coloniale du Congo belge." In *Stéréotypes nationaux et préjugés raciaux au XIXe et XXe siècles: Sources et méthods pour une approche historique,* ed. J. Pirotte, 91–116. Leuven: Editions Nauwelaerts, 1982.

———. "Mining in the Belgian Congo." In *History of Central Africa,* ed. D. Birmingham and P. Martin, 2:126–162. New York: Longman, 1983.

———. "Rapport Casement." *Enquêtes et documents d'histoire africaine* 6 (1985): 1–175.

———. "Rural Poverty in Western Shaba, ca. 1890–1930." In *The Roots of Rural Poverty in Central and Southern Africa,* ed. R. Palmer and N. Parsons, 303–310. Berkeley: University of California Press, 1977.

Verhaegen, B. *Introduction à l'histoire immediate.* Gembloux, 1974.

Ward, H. *Five Years with the Congo Cannibals.* London, 1890.

White, L. *The Comforts of Home: Prostitution in Colonial Nairobi.* Chicago: University of Chicago Press, 1990.

———. *Speaking with Vampires: Rumor and History in Colonial Africa.* Berkeley: University of California Press, 2000.

White L., and T. Couzens. *Literature and Society in South Africa.* New York: Longman, 1984.

Windschuttle, K. *The Killing of History: How Literary Critics and Social Theorists Are Murdering Our Past.* New York: Free Press, 1997.

Wolf, E. *Europe and the People without History.* Berkeley: University California Press, 1997.

Yelengi, N. "Building a Colonial Railroad and the Labor Crisis in the Belgian Congo: Case of the Port-Franqui-Bukama, 1923–1928." *Likundoli: Histoire et Devenir* 2 (1999–2000): 248–302.

———. "The Impact of the Construction and Development of the Port Francqui-Bukama Railroad on the Rural Population of Katanga, Belgian Congo." PhD diss., University of Minnesota, 1996.

———. "The PFB Railroad, Society and Culture in Rural Katanga (Colonial Zaire)." *Africa* (Rome) 52, no. 2 (1997): 182–211.

Yogolelo wa Kasimba. "Mission du recrutement de la main-d'oeuvre de l'Union Minière du Haut-Katanga au Maniema, 1928." MA thesis, Unaza, Lubumbashi, 1974.

Young, C. *The African Colonial State in Comparative Perspective.* New Haven, Conn.: Yale University Press, 1994.

Young, C., and T. Turner. *The Rise and Decline of the Zairian State.* Madison: University of Wisconsin Press, 1985.

Zagourski, C. *Lost Africa.* Milano: Skira Editore, 2001.

List of Interviews

Akandji Masudi. Kisangani. March 2003.

Akombe. Kisangani. September 1989.

Ali Musa. Kisangani. March 2003.

Ambele Asomba. Kisangani. April 2003.

Amisi. Kisangani. 28 May 2003.

Asangu, Victor. Kisangani. 26 July 1989.

Aserme Azibolia. Kisangani. 18 March 2003.

Aserme Azibolia Mango. Kisangani. 2 April 2003.

Asi Loosa. Kisangani. July 1989.

Asomba Letoko. Opala. 15 July 1980.

Asomo Wenga. Letutu Yakuma. 12 July 1980.

Atsidri Nyelegodi. Kisangani. 16 February 2003.

Avochi. Kisangani. March 1989.

Bakonzi Ngilinga. Kisangani. 25 February and 23 March 2003.

Base Banakabe. Kisangani. 23 May 2003.

Basikaba Tanabanu. Kisangani. 23 May 2003.

Bili. Kisangani. August 1989.

Bobwande. Lubumbashi. 12 and 16 July 1986.

Boloko. Kisangani. 16 April 1989.

Bwise. Kisangani. June 1989.

Denda. Kisangani. 25 June 1989.

Dibwe Dia Mwembu. Lubumbashi. 22 August 2003.

Dombo. Kisangani. March 1989.

Elila. Kisangani. February 1989.

Gesege. Kisangani. February 2003.

Ilunga Luboza. Kisangani. February and March 2003.

Kabuji Bualu. Kisangani. 12 January 2003.

Kasala. Lubumbashi. 14 and 25 June 1989.

Kashi. Lubumbashi. 19 March 1988.

Katayi Tende. Lubumbashi. 24 August 1986.

Katumbo. Lubumbashi. July 1986.

Kidumu. Kisangani. 17 July 1988.

Koko. Kisangani. 1989.

Kongolo, Ilunga, and Kinku. Lubumbashi. 28 May 1988.

Kumingi Yuma. Kisangani. 12 and 14 February 2003.

Lamerat, Yolandeï. Brussels. August 1987.

Litale. Lelema. 1970.

Lola. Lelema. 3 August 1977.

Lomata. Yaokoko. 24 July 1980.

Longange Elenga. Kisangani. 28 March 2003.

Lonyoyo Tamile, Louise. Kisangani. 25 and 28 March 2003.

Losembe wa Losembe. Kisangani. April 2003.

Lotika Lwa Botende. Kisangani. 16 March 2003.

Lufundja. Lubumbashi. 14 and 18 August 1986.

Lumbalumba Botokoyo. Kisangani. 11 April 2003.

Lunyasi Tanganyika. Kisangani. 22 March 2003.

Lwaka Mukandja. Lubumbashi. 14 August 1986.

Lwamba Bilonda. Lubumbashi. 16 August 1986.

Madi, David. Kisangani. April 2003.

Masudi Akandji. Kisangani. April 2003.

Masudi Shabani. Kisangani, 11 January 2003.

Matata Moelealongo. Kisangani. 18 and 19 February, 18 March 2003.

Mbala. Lubumbashi. 26 October 1989.

Mbali Nondolo. Kisangani. 24 April 2003.

Mbombo. Lubumbashi. September 1988.

Meya Katoto. Lubumbashi. 24 July 2003.

Midi Abuba. Kisangani. 18 and 22 February 2003.

Misite, Paul. Kisangani. 22 April 2003.

Mosolo. Kisangani. February 1989.

Mugaza wa Beya. Lubumbashi. 16 August 1986.

Mumba. Lubumbashi. March 1988.

Mungeni Mateso. Kisangani. 23 June 1989.

Ndjadi Vincent. Kisangani. 27 April 2003.

Ngandali Dabet. Minneapolis. July 1990.

Ngbabu. Kisangani. 11 February 2003.

Ngoyi Bukonda. DeKalb, Ill. 17 March 2002.

Ngoyi Bukonda. Minneapolis. March 1990.

Ngoziombo Ngbenzi. Kisangani. 9 February, 12 and 16 March 2003.

Nkasa T. Yelengi. Duluth, Minn. 13 February 2006.

Ntambwe Mukendi. Kisangani. 29 March 2003.

Ntumba. Likasi. October 1988.

Ofunga. Yanga. 24 July 1980.

Osodu, Joseph. Kisangani. April 2003.
Osoko Litale. Lelema. 21 July 1980.
Owe. Lekolisa. 1980.
Pene wa Pene. Kisangani. 24 April 2003.
Paluku, Jean. Kisangani. 11 February and March 2003.
Risasi. Lubumbashi. 6 and 23 September 1988.
Sombo. Kisangani. 18 September 2003.
Tebonge Dame. Kisangani. March 2003.
Tshibanda Nduba Musaka. Lubumbashi. 12 August 1986.
Tshishiku. Lubumbashi. October 1989.
Ucay Liberiwum. Kisangani. 22 April 2003.
Ujanga. Kisangani. August and September 1989.
Umba. Lubumbashi. April 1988.
Wenga Asomo. Letutu Yakuma. 12 July 1980.

INDEX

213

in names given, 56, 68–69, 96–97; names given specific individuals, 55–56; as voice of Congolese, 136–37. *See also* agronomists and crop supervisors; Congo Free State; taxation and tax collectors
strength, names referring to, 120–21, 131
suffixes, 60, 148; indicating "badness," 81
surveillance, names related to, 99

Tamile, Lonyoyo Louise, 118
Tange "He who can strangulate me" and "Lying face down," 153
Tata "Father," 154
taxation and tax collectors, 19; malnutrition linked to, 5, 90; names given tax collectors, 5, 81, 92, 94–95, 148–49, 154; precolonial tribute and, 51–52; road construction and, 37–38, 110–11; as shameful begging, 111. *See also* fines
teknonymy, 23–24
"Le territoire de Ligasa" (Pirson), 138–39
territorial administrators, names given, 92
theophores, 26
time: names referring to regulation of, 74–75; temporal instability of names as historical records, 14–15
titles, indicators of social status, 25–26
tobacco, smoking, 67–68, 182n64
Tobback, Nicolas, 67–68
traditional life ways. *See* village life
trees, names related to, 131
Tshoma-Tshoma "He who burns people," 149, 152–53, 154
Tuku-Tuku "Motorcycle," 13–14, 70
twins, naming of, 23, 27–28

Vail, Leroy, 17
Van Berghe, 144
Vancraenbroeck, Marc, 8
Van de Lanoitte, Charles, 3, 115–16, 148–52, 154
Van de Moere, Philibert-Joseph, 148
Van den Broeke, Leon, 65–66
Van Malderen, 119–20
Van Nimmen, Father F., 63
Van Uden, Father J., 63
Vellut, Jean-Luc, 17

village life: cash crop economy as assault on, 36, 75, 92; and collective observation of Europeans and colonialism, 3–4; colonialism as assault on, 14; colonial legal system as assault on, 45; disruption of traditional political structure, 97–98; generic names regarding the disruption of, 94; individual names and colonial assault on, 92; mandatory wild product collection as disruption of, 35, 66; mining and disruption of, 41, 45, 51; names as historical record of events in, 7, 8–11, 161–62; political agency in traditional, 137; political destabilization of, 133, 159; relocation and disruption of, 38–39, 43, 97, 101; roads as assault on, 110–12; rubber collection and disruption of, 87
Vinck, H., 17
violence, 19–20; ambiguous naming as defense against retaliation, 13, 75–76; amputations as punishment, 88–90, 94; avoidance of, 155–56; beatings as instrument of colonialism, 39–40, 69–70 (*See also* whipping); conflict linked to cash-crop economics, 33; discouraged by Belgian central administration, 145–46; individual beatings *vs.* punitive expeditions, 39–40, 94; individual names and colonial, 92; as instrument of social control, 94, 137–38; names as historical memory of, 54, 56–57, 66; names as instruments of terror or coercion, 20, 136, 145–56, 161; names related to, 13, 14, 54, 56–57, 66, 92, 94–95, 101–2 (*See also* verbal threats and expressions of violence in names *under this heading*); native courts and, 93; punishments administered to enforce domination and humiliation, 69–70; rationalizations and minimization of charges of, 13–14; rubber collection and atrocities, 66, 86, 88–90, 153–54; sexual abuse, 116; verbal assaults, 108–9; verbal threats and expressions of violence in names, 69–70, 105–7, 109–10, 146–51, 154–55; whippings, 107–8
vision, names related to, 99